More praise for *Pentecostal Republic*

'An authoritative work on the politics of Nigeria's Pentecostal revolution during the country's fourth attempt at constitutional democracy. An important text in African political studies.'
Olufemi Vaughan, Amherst College

'A must read. Clearly argued and highly informative, there is nothing quite like it on the market given its contemporary focus. Tackling questions beyond those focused on a single religious tradition, it will find an avid scholarly readership.'
Brandon Kendhammer, Ohio University

'An accessible yet astute analysis of the profound impact that popular forms of Christianity have on the political landscape in Nigeria. A key text for anyone with an interest in contemporary Christianity, democracy and politics in Nigeria, Africa and beyond.'
Adriaan van Klinken, University of Leeds

'What happens when the theological meets the political in a formally secular state? In this lucid account of Pentecostalism, Obadare offers perspectives on its phenomenal rise.'
Birgit Meyer, Utrecht University

T0347822

African Arguments

Written by experts with an unrivalled knowledge of the continent, *African Arguments* is a series of concise, engaging books that address the key issues currently facing Africa. Topical and thought-provoking, accessible but in-depth, they provide essential reading for anyone interested in getting to the heart of both why contemporary Africa is the way it is and how it is changing.

African Arguments Online

African Arguments Online is a pan-African platform for news, investigation and opinion, managed by the Royal African Society. www.africanarguments.org

Series editors

Adam Branch, University of Cambridge
Alex de Waal, World Peace Foundation
Richard Dowden, journalist and author
Alcinda Honwana, University of Cambridge

Managing editor

Stephanie Kitchen, International African Institute

Editorial board

Emmanuel Akyeampong, Harvard University
Tim Allen, London School of Economics and Political Science
Akwe Amosu, Open Society Institute
Breyten Breytenbach, Gorée Institute
Peter da Costa, journalist and development specialist
William Gumede, journalist and author
Abdul Mohammed, InterAfrica Group
Robert Molteno, editor and publisher

Published by Zed Books and the IAI with the support of the following organisations:

The principal aim of the **International African Institute** is to promote scholarly understanding of Africa, notably its changing societies, cultures and languages. Founded in 1926 and based in London, it supports a range of seminars and publications including the journal *Africa*.
www.internationalafricaninstitute.org

The **Royal African Society** is a membership organisation that provides opportunities for people to connect, celebrate and engage critically with a wide range of topics and ideas about Africa today. Through events, publications and digital channels it shares insight, instigates debate and facilitates mutual understanding between the UK and Africa. The society amplifies African voices and interests in academia, business, politics, the arts and education, reaching a network of more than one million people globally.
www.royalafricansociety.org

The **World Peace Foundation**, founded in 1910, is located at the Fletcher School, Tufts University. The Foundation's mission is to promote innovative research and teaching, believing that these are critical to the challenges of making peace around the world, and should go hand in hand with advocacy and practical engagement with the toughest issues. Its central theme is 'reinventing peace' for the twenty-first century.
www.worldpeacefoundation.org

About the author

Ebenezer Obadare is Professor of Sociology at the University of Kansas and Research Fellow at the Research Institute for Theology and Religion, University of South Africa. He is co-editor of *Journal of Modern African Studies*. He is the author of *Humor, Silence, and Civil Society in Nigeria* (2016), editor of *The Handbook of Civil Society in Africa* (2014), and co-editor of *Civic Agency in Africa: Arts of Resistance in the 21st Century* (2014) and four other books.

PENTECOSTAL REPUBLIC

RELIGION AND THE STRUGGLE FOR STATE POWER IN NIGERIA

EBENEZER OBADARE

In association with
International African Institute
Royal African Society
World Peace Foundation

ZED

Pentecostal Republic: Religion and the Struggle for State Power in Nigeria
was first published in 2018 by Zed Books Ltd, The Foundry, 17 Oval Way,
London SE11 5RR, UK.

www.zedbooks.net

Copyright © Ebenezer Obadare 2018

The right of Ebenezer Obadare to be identified as the author of this work has been
asserted by him in accordance with the Copyright, Designs and Patents Act 1988.

Typeset in Haarlemmer by seagulls.net
Index by Ed Emery
Cover design by Jonathan Pelham
Cover photo © Seamus Murphy/Panos

All rights reserved. No part of this publication may be reproduced, stored
in a retrieval system or transmitted in any form or by any means, electronic,
mechanical, photocopying or otherwise, without the prior permission of
Zed Books Ltd.

A catalogue record for this book is available from the British Library

ISBN 978-1-78699-238-3 hb
ISBN 978-1-78699-237-6 pb
ISBN 978-1-78699-239-0 epdf
ISBN 978-1-78699-240-6 epub
ISBN 978-1-78699-241-3 mobi

To my parents

and

to Dapo Olorunyomi and Odia Ofeimun – two journalistic
eminences – for a piercing apprenticeship in the Russian classics

In memory of Dr Gabriel Akindele Akinola (1934–2018)

The influence of the clergy, in an age of superstition, might be usefully employed to assert the rights of mankind; but so intimate is the connection between the throne and the altar, that the banner of the church has very seldom been seen on the side of the people.

Edward Gibbon,
The History of the Decline and Fall of the Roman Empire

CONTENTS

LIST OF ABBREVIATIONS

AC	Action Congress
ACF	Arewa Consultative Forum
AD	Alliance for Democracy
AICs	African Initiated Churches (AICs)
ANPP	All Nigeria People's Party
APC	All Progressives Congress
APP	All People's Party
CAN	Christian Association of Nigeria
CPC	Congress for Progressive Change
EEG	Eminent Elders Group
EFCC	Economic and Financial Crimes Commission
FCT	Federal Capital Territory
FEC	Federal Executive Council
ING	interim national government
MFM	Mountain of Fire and Miracles Ministries
NADECO	National Democratic Coalition
NPN	National Party of Nigeria
NRC	National Republican Convention
OIC	Organisation of Islamic Cooperation
PDP	People's Democratic Party
PFN	Pentecostal Fellowship of Nigeria
RCCG	Redeemed Christian Church of God
SDP	Social Democratic Party
SNG	Save Nigeria Group

ACKNOWLEDGEMENTS

I could not have completed this manuscript without the generous support of a network of friends and colleagues. My most profound gratitude goes to Abu Bakarr Bah, Carole Enahoro and Lynn Davidman, for reading and commenting on early drafts of the chapters. My colleagues in the Sociology Department at the University of Kansas have conspired to ensure a congenial environment for my work. I am indebted to Joane Nagel, David Smith, Bob Antonio and Bill Staples for their kindness, friendship and all-round collegiality.

On countless occasions – face to face, over the phone, via email, on Skype, at academic conferences, or, in the case of a particular individual, while adjudicating the fate of pyramids of French toast – I have discussed the ideas in this book with Wale Adebanwi, Akin Adesokan, Olufemi 'Malam' Taiwo, Wendy Willems, Kunle Ajibade, Babafemi Ojudu, Jide Wintoki and Tade Ipadeola. I thank them for the great gift of conversation, for their patience and indulgence, and for their sustained interest in this project.

This book draws on data from field research undertaken over the past several years in Nigeria. For generous financial support, I am grateful to the Social Science Research Council's (SSRC) New Directions in the Study of Prayer (NDSP) initiative, the Contending Modernities Program at the Kroc Institute for International Peace Studies, University of Notre Dame, the University of Kansas General Research Fund (GRF), and the Institute for Policy and Social Research (IPSR) at the University of Kansas. At the IPSR,

I was fortunate to receive logistical support from the brilliant trio of Nancy Myers, Whitney Onasch and Jena Gunther. I also thank the Watson Library at the University of Kansas for the use of the carrel that provided much-needed escape from the infernal clutter in my office, and privacy to concentrate on my writing. Against insuperable odds, Zuleica Gerardo delivered on a promise to help organise the bibliography. My debt to her is inestimable.

The rigour of my frequent trips to Nigeria was alleviated by the hospitality of my friend Babajide Aribaloye, his wife Funlola, and their two boys, Araoluwa and Oluwamitundara, aka 'Uncle Pof'. I thank them for making me a part of their family, and for their warmth and generosity.

For their criticisms, comments and instigations to clarity, I owe special thanks to the three anonymous reviewers. Judith Forshaw cleaned up the manuscript and purged it of numerous infelicities. I am genuinely in awe of her first-rate oversight. Finally, I wish to express my gratitude to both Ken Barlow and Stephanie Kitchen for their thoughtful comments on the manuscript, and for their assistance throughout the production process.

As always, my most important debt is to the dedicated staff of Obadare Homeland Security – Kemi, Justice and Ayotunde – for keeping me grounded and providing the platform from which I launch all my dreams.

I first sketched out the argument in Chapter 2 in my 2006 article 'Pentecostal presidency? The Lagos–Ibadan "theocratic class" and the Muslim "other"' (*Review of African Political Economy* 33 (110): 665–78). Although the original spirit tarries, Chapter 2 is a wholly different text, anchored to a larger body of data, and pressed into the service of a broader intellectual agenda.

Ebenezer Obadare, Lawrence, Kansas

June 2018

INTRODUCTION

This book is an account of the interplay of religion and politics in Nigeria since the country's celebrated return to civil rule in May 1999. It is the first instalment of an envisaged dyad (or a trilogy, if I am lucky) on the impact of religion on politics and society in contemporary Nigeria. Two complementary theses are advanced. The first is that the dawn of democratic rule in 1999 coincided with the triumph of Christianity over its historical rival, Islam, as a political force in Nigeria. At the same time – and secondly – the political triumph of Christianity came about just as Pentecostalism was muscling its way to the front of the line as the dominant expression of Christianity in the country and beyond. Hence the title of the book, *Pentecostal Republic*, which is my way of acknowledging the profound impact of Pentecostalism and Pentecostal forces on politics and the social imaginary in the Nigerian Fourth Republic (from 1999 onwards). In placing the Fourth Republic under the lodestar of Pentecostalism, I am making a categorical assertion: that the Nigerian democratic process since 1999 is ultimately inexplicable without recourse to the emergent power of Pentecostalism, whether as manifested in the rising political influence of Pentecostal pastors, or in a commensurate popular tendency to view socio-political problems in spiritual terms.

Nigerian readers, or scholars and students well acquainted with the contours of Nigeriana, will be familiar with the events and personalities described and analysed here. Yet, its historical and sociological particularities notwithstanding, the account is far from idiosyncratic. On the contrary, the book's story – of the deep imbrication of politics and spirituality and the contradictions that arise – is contemporaneous and global, and very much so. As such, the master template of continued accommodation and contestation between political and religious actors locked in a perennial struggle for power should resonate with close observers of religio-politics everywhere. I draw two examples from South Korea and the United States respectively as a way of de-exoticising the Nigerian situation.

In late 2016, the attention of the world was captured by events in South Korea, specifically the (ultimately futile) efforts of President Park Geun-hye to hold on to power amid a deepening political scandal. The scandal that consumed President Park (in December 2016, South Korean lawmakers voted to impeach her, a decision later ratified in March 2017 by the country's Constitutional Court) had an interesting aspect: it concerned the president's relationship with Choi Soon-sil, daughter of Choi Tae-min, founder of a para-Christian sect called the Church of Eternal Life. Although President Park and Choi Soon-sil were friends before the former ascended to the Korean presidency in 2013, their friendship strengthened once Park took office, as Choi rapidly transformed from close friend to spiritual confidant. Choi reportedly leveraged this ambiguous role to the hilt, using her unfettered access to President Park to curry financial and political favours, including securing unbridled access to confidential state documents.

Reports of what transpired between President Park and her confidant (apparently, these included private seances in the presidential residence, the Blue House) sent shock waves through Korean society, sending thousands of Koreans to the streets in protest. The disclosures dealt two specific blows to the Korean psyche. First, they destroyed public confidence in President Park, whom many had come to respect as an honest leader, the moral antithesis of the very acts contained in the revelations. Second, and directly relevant to my analysis, the fact that a morally ambiguous 'spiritual adviser' could so easily wiggle her way into the highest levels of power and insinuate herself into policymaking wounded Koreans' pride in their country as an emblem of Weberian rationality, raising new questions about who controls the levers of power in the country.

If South Korea's 'Shaman Scandal' offers a model of the mutual embrace of politics and religion in a state notionally predicated on the separation of the two, contemporary United States offers another. Here, a deep liberal commitment to the separation of church and state has historically been at odds with mobilisation by the Christian Right to return the country to its perceived 'Christian roots' and the kind of moral regimen presumed to be its logical appurtenance. Over the past three decades, this mobilisation has increasingly intensified, fuelled largely by fears that secularisation and its attendant moral relativism are eroding the ethical foundations of the American republic. Whether such fears are justified or not, they offer one plausible explanation for the flight of American evangelicals towards the Republican Party, and, subsequently, their unflagging support for incumbent president Donald Trump. Contra the Korean model, the American case offers us a set of (Christian conservative) religious agents who: (1) are not content to operate behind the scenes; and, in fact, (2) push a political agenda that seems to suggest that they are not entirely convinced that church and state should continue to remain separate.[1]

The Nigerian scenario as described in this book combines elements from the two models. For one thing, à la South Korea, Nigerian politicians consult freely with a wide range of 'spiritual advisers', and this tends not to be seen as a contradiction, nor is there reputational damage, in a society where all political power is assumed to rest on a spiritual warrant of some sort. And while, for many reasons, there is no direct equivalent of the Christian Right in Nigeria (for example, there is no obvious parallel to what is in effect an ideological merger between the bulk of American evangelicals and the Republican Party), a perennial Christian–Muslim struggle rages to claim state power and clothe it in religious symbols and regalia. In fact, and as I argue in this book, Christian determination to undo perceived Muslim 'colonisation' of state power was one reason for the establishment of the Christian Association of Nigeria (CAN) in 1976. Of the many paradoxes of Nigerian politics, the realisation that, wittingly or not, it is this inter-religious struggle for political supremacy that continues to guarantee the country's secular status must count among the most confounding.

To return to the broader point: sociological characteristics notwithstanding, the Nigerian case as described and analysed in this book is most fruitfully approached as one example of the different ways in which, in contrast to the certitudes of secularisation, religion and religious factors continue to shape politics globally. Across the global South, and incontrovertibly in most of sub-Saharan Africa and Latin America, this religious resilience is characterised by – or at least substantially enabled by – the efflorescence of Pentecostalism. Suffice it to say that this flowering has had many witnesses, as evidenced by the plethora of academic writings on Pentecostalism, and, to that extent, this book is a contribution to an ongoing scholarly dialogue.

The chief difference is in my focus, emphasis and overall argumentation. I focus primarily on the politics of the Nigerian Fourth Republic, hatched from elite compromise, headed at inception by a self-proclaimed 'born again' president, and 'claimed' and christened at birth by Pentecostals. In my telling, while the emergence of a Southern Christian president is arguably the culmination of a process that began with CAN's founding in 1976, Obasanjo's emergence was at best a pyrrhic victory for CAN, which ceded ground willy-nilly to the inexorable force of Pentecostalism and its train of politically influential pastors. As such, one of the driving tensions of Christian politics in the Fourth Republic is the disagreement between CAN and Pentecostal/charismatic churches loosely coalesced under the aegis of the Pentecostal Fellowship of Nigeria (PFN). The basis of their disagreement is mainline Christian denominations' perfectly admissible charge that Pentecostals are doctrinally reckless, favouring the spectacular (for example, the emphasis on miracles) to the detriment of basic Christian teaching. Further, Pentecostal leaders have been accused of betraying the original mission of political Christianity by, among other things, aggressively cultivating politicians, hence effectively blurring the line between critical engagement and political assimilation.

Because my focus is explicitly political, I pay scant attention to Pentecostalism as a theological project, as is the practice of a section of the literature. Theorist Nimi Wariboko's oeuvre is an exemplar of this kind of approach.[2] On the contrary, as far as I am interested in any of Pentecostalism's dogmas, it is to the extent that they can be said to carry a political significance. My temporal remit being the Fourth Republic, my aim is to explicate the struggle for state power among agents mobilising religious reason. With respect to the general political impact of Pentecostalism, I contend, against the laudatory grain, that while it has *affected* the socio-political order in Nigeria, Pentecostalism, being more apologetic than critical, has largely shied away from *challenging* it. Does Nigerian Pentecostalism harbour a reactionary gene?

A dominant trope in social theorising on religion insists that religion is something that the elite manipulate for the acquisition of power. No doubt there is considerable evidence in the Nigerian context to justify this perspective. At the very least, one must acknowledge: (1) the nascent power of the theocratic class concentrated in the Lagos–Ibadan axis; and (2) the intriguing perspective that Pentecostalism itself is ultimately a strategic political instrument deployed by the south-western political elite. Yet, to focus on this alone would be to deny the obvious appeal of Pentecostalism as a mass religion, one that, if only in theory, opens up radically new agential vistas.

I have maintained that, within the specific context of the historical Christian–Muslim struggle for supremacy in Nigeria, Christianity, *in its Pentecostal mode*, moved into pole position with the inception of the Fourth Republic, and has been more or less hegemonic ever since. The outline of the chapters in this book is in accord with this conviction: the 'Pentecostal presidencies' of Olusegun Obasanjo (1999–2007) and Goodluck Jonathan (2010–15) are respectively narrated as being punctuated by a 'Muslim interregnum' – the ill-starred tenure of Umaru Musa Yar'Adua (2007–10). The Muslim incumbent, President Muhammadu Buhari (2015–) is assisted (some would say watched over) by Vice President Yemi Osinbajo, legal scholar and bona fide Pentecostal pastor. Clearly, Pentecostal domination of politics speaks for itself, and, as I have demonstrated elsewhere, the perfect acknowledgement of its successful monopolisation of the religious economy is the wholesale appropriation of its evangelistic strategies and methodologies by the Muslim competition.[3]

Because the outline of the chapters in the book corresponds to the core idea that democratic rule in the Nigerian Fourth Republic has evolved in the far-reaching shadow of Pentecostalism, the analysis unfolds chronologically over the lifespan of successive administrations, with analytic privilege given to whichever milestones help ground the book's main ideas. Hence, it would seem that the most rewarding way to read the book is sequentially from the first chapter through to the last. Chapter 6 is a bit of an exception, a shift in register that may be read either as part of the series or as a standalone analysis. The reason is simple. I conceived of it as an extended illustration of one of the driving arguments of the book concerning the influence of Pentecostal ideas, specifically ideas about spiritual warfare and ubiquitous evil. As a result, the chapter's approach is more theoretical, and there is a deliberate attempt: (1) to make the analysis speak to the relevant literature on violence and the state in Africa; and (2) to show how the analysis matters to ongoing transnational conversations. For the same reason, the tone is more abstract and the language is pitched at a slightly higher – though I would hope not necessarily forbidding – elevation. In any event, whether it is read separately or following the preceding chapters, my hope is that the reader will recognise an opportunity to take a deep dive into the social process through which the legitimation of a narrative (in this case about ubiquitous evil) becomes a means of bolstering the social power of an elite – the Pentecostal elite, that is.

While Pentecostalism has greatly influenced the struggle for state power, this book argues that it has had little effect on the state itself, whether in terms of its governing philosophy or its animating spirit. On the contrary, and not just because of the proven cohabitation between the Pentecostal elite and the political class, it has been a legitimating force, nestled, albeit contingently, between state and civil society.

Chapter 1

PENTECOSTAL REPUBLIC, ENCHANTED DEMOCRACY

Introduction: demons in the villa

On Friday 14 October 2016, Reuben Abati, one-time spokesperson for the administration of President Goodluck Jonathan (2010–15), published an article in his weekly newspaper column titled 'The spiritual side of Aso Villa'.[1] Prior to his appointment in July 2011 as replacement for former *TELL* magazine associate editor Ima Niboro, Abati had established a long-standing reputation as one of Nigeria's most forthright newspaper columnists, a model of pugnacious integrity in a notoriously venal media landscape. However, by October 2016, things had turned sour between Abati and his avid followers, the greater part of whom struggled to reconcile themselves with his decision to serve the same administration he once pilloried in his writings. Others took exception to what they decried as the petulant manner in which he discharged his duties as Special Adviser on Media and Publicity, launching peevish attacks on perceived enemies of his boss. Therefore, by the time Abati started writing for *The* [Lagos] *Guardian* again following his controversial stint in Aso Villa, few bothered to pay him any heed. The columnist who had once told everyone what they needed to think had become a social undesirable many would rather not think about.

Despite this, the article in question was widely circulated and vigorously debated across the vast spectrum of Nigeria's boisterous social media. Presumably, this was due to the subject of the essay – spirituality and power. But another reason the article generated such intense interest was because of Abati's core claim, that Aso Villa, the seat of the Nigerian presidency, was under siege by demonic forces, and is a place where 'most people … always bathed in the morning with blood. Goat blood. Ram blood. Whatever animal blood.'

Abati's essay invoked and consecrated four related narratives about power and spirituality in Nigeria.

First, for many people, it validated the popular belief that there is something sinister about Aso Villa, the physical seat of executive power in the country. When the administrative capital was moved from Lagos to Abuja in December 1991, there were wild rumours of the move having been sanctioned only after a cautious President Ibrahim Babangida had made the place safe through 'spiritual cleansing' facilitated by sundry 'mallams' and conclaves of Muslim marabouts recruited from across the West African sub-region and beyond.[2] Abati's testimony about 'colleagues who lost daughters and sons, brothers and uncles, mothers and fathers, and the many obituaries that we issued' reinforced the image of Aso Villa as a space associated with mortal danger.

The following excerpt from an article by *Vanguard* Abuja reporter Ben Agande, written in response to the Abati article, captures the popular belief about the 'strangeness' of Aso Villa and the spiritual precautions successive presidents are rumoured to have taken:

> As a correspondent of the *Vanguard* newspaper who covered presidents Olusegeun [sic] Obasanjo, Umaru Yar'Adua and Goodluck Jonathan, I can relate well with some of the stranger than fiction scenario painted by Dr. Abati. But beyond the strange incidence, the foundation of the construction of the villa itself was laid in strange circumstances. According to a staff of Julius Berger, the construction company that built the Villa, from the very day that the excavation for what is now known as the presidential Villa was made, it was mired

in strange incidences. The staff who has [worked] for the construction company for over thirty years and claimed he was there when the very first excavation began narrated the strange occurrences that marked the first few months. 'When we moved in here, it was as if we were in a war zone. There were multiple incidences of equipment failure, workers developing strange illnesses and in one particularly poignant case, a very senior officer of the company who was brought in from Germany to supervise the construction collapsed and died on site while supervising the uprooting of a particular tree that defied all attempts to remove. Strangely, his death brought an end to the many equipment failures that we had witnessed over many weeks,' he said.[3]

Agande continued:

Whether the strange incidences that have been noticed in the Villa are products of striking coincidences or handiwork of higher, inexplicable spiritual powers is hard to decipher. But since President Ibrahim Babangida, the first occupant of the presidential Villa left office, subsequent occupants of the sprawling edifice have brought spirituality to bear on their stay in the edifice. From General Sani Abacha to Abdulsalami Abubakar to Olusegun Obasanjo to Umaru Yar'Adua down to the present occupant, Muhammadu Buhari, these occupants have had to carry out spiritual cleansing of the place before moving in with their families and hordes of aides.[4]

Second, Abati poured fuel on the fire of the common belief that political success is neither secured nor maintained without the 'donation' of blood, often other people's, but, if necessary, the blood of a close relative or kin of the individual either seeking office or desperate to keep it.[5] For most people, therefore, incidents such as the shocking discovery by the Nigerian police in August 2004 of dozens of corpses at a shrine in Okija, Anambra State and the subsequent revelations that senior political figures had attended the shrine and sworn oaths there merely confirmed a reality that they always took for granted.[6] It was in that spirit, presumably, that Abati wrote about 'days when convoys ran into ditches and lives were lost', and other occasions when the plane in which then President Jonathan and his team were travelling 'had to be recalled' because it was 'acting like it would crash', or other times when the aircraft either 'refused to start' or 'just went dead'. There is an obvious logical contradiction here: if Aso Villa is such a place of danger, why have successive Nigerian heads of state shown such desperation in their attempts to cling on to power? Nigerians' unique resolution of this contradiction is that the mechanisms of the same dark forces create the leaders' fatal attraction to power.

Third, with his allusion to 'all those colleagues who used to come to work to complain about a certain death beneath their waists and who relied on videos and other instruments to entertain their wives' quite suddenly experiencing 'a reawakening' after vacating Aso Villa, Abati was, for many, merely affirming the connection between power and masculinity, between sex and power, and the general impression of the (politically) powerful man as one who is also invariably sexually potent. In Nigeria, no discussion of the powerful is complete without salacious gossip about their sex lives. For political theorist Achille Mbembe, such talk about the orifices and genitalia of the powerful must be seen as 'powerful referents or critical metaphors in the production of the political in the postcolony'.[7]

In fact, it is widely assumed that the highest echelons of power in the country are guaranteed only to those willing to participate in any named variety of unconventional sexual acts, including same-sex acts and sex with animals.[8] In this account, Aso Villa itself is little more than a political bordello, a place of sexual licentiousness where famous residents frequently indulge in infamous orgies. Even today, rumours persist that former military ruler General Sani

Abacha (who was in power from 1993 to 1998) did not expire from food poisoning, as the grapevine has it, but in a tryst involving two Dubai-imported Indian prostitutes.

Fourth, and most significantly from the standpoint of the underlying sentiment of this book, Abati's essay strengthened the by no means unpopular narrative that Nigeria, Nigerians and most definitely Nigerian politicians have been under a demonic spell (since political independence in 1960 according to some accounts, or since the ill-advised hosting of the Second World Black and African Festival of Arts and Culture [Festac '77] in others);[9] and that liberation from this malign energy is unattainable in the absence of collective contrition and the necessary spiritual amelioration. Here is Abati reprising this particular sentiment:

> When Presidents make mistakes, they are probably victims of a force higher than what we can imagine. *Every student of Aso Villa politics would readily admit that when people get in there, they actually become something else. They act like they are under a spell.* When you issue a well-crafted statement, the public accepts it wrongly. When the President makes a speech and he truly means well, the speech is interpreted wrongly by the public. When a policy is introduced, somehow, something just goes wrong. In our days, a lot of people used to complain that the APC [All Progressives Congress] people were fighting us spiritually and that there was a witchcraft dimension to the governance process in Nigeria. *But the APC folks now in power are dealing with the same demons.* Since Buhari government assumed office, it has been one mistake after another. Those mistakes don't look normal, the same way they didn't look normal under President Jonathan. I am therefore convinced that there is an evil spell enveloping this country. We need to rescue Nigeria from the forces of darkness. Aso Villa should be converted into a spiritual museum, and abandoned.[10]

On 24 October 2016, ten days after the publication of his essay, Abati was picked up in Abuja, Nigeria's Federal Capital Territory (FCT), by operatives of the Economic and Financial Crimes Commission (EFCC) investigating his and others' alleged involvement in a 50 million naira bribery scandal.

Did Abati publish his essay in the hope of pre-empting the massive outcry that he was certain media reports of his involvement in a bribery scandal and his eventual arrest would provoke? In saying of Aso Villa that 'when people get in there, they actually become something else', and that President Buhari's 'mistakes' since assuming office 'don't look normal, the same way they didn't look normal under President Jonathan', was he in fact admitting guilt while at the same time providing grounds for exculpation?

Considering Abati's pedigree, such assumptions are not far-fetched. Following his appointment in 2011 by President Jonathan, he had morphed quite rapidly from celebrity into pariah. In his heyday, such was his fame and popularity that Abati could afford to write a twice-weekly column – on Fridays and Sundays – and still count on the attention and admiration of the reading public. As a government spokesperson, however, Abati quickly unravelled. Not only did he fail to rise to anything remotely approaching the level of the soaring moral rhetoric that had characterised his column, but in a unique spectacle of self-immolation he took every opportunity to contradict everything he had previously articulated and apparently stood for as a progressive journalist. His transformation came as a shock to his followers, many of whom had fallen for his flowing prose and had taken his every word as gospel. It is quite possible, then, that 'The spiritual side of Aso Villa' was, if not a desperate attempt to recapture the ardour of his disappointed followers, at least an effort to explain away his gauche comportment as a presidential spokesperson.

State of siege

Whatever his intentions, Abati's essay – and the reaction to it – offers a didactic moment for understanding the mentality that has animated the Nigerian Fourth Republic since its inception in 1999. The mentality in question is evident in a reported encounter between Abati and a colleague, recalled in the essay's closing paragraph as follows:

> A colleague called me one day and told me a story about *how a decision had been taken in the spiritual realm about the Nigerian government.* He talked about *the spirit of error* and how every step taken by the administration would appear to the public like an error. He didn't resign on that basis but his words proved prophetic. I see the same story being re-enacted. *Aso Villa is in urgent need of redemption.* I never slept in the apartment they gave me in that villa for an hour.[11]

The key question for me is not whether this encounter actually took place, but what Abati had successfully communicated: within an explanatory paradigm, he implicitly accepts that decisions are regularly taken in 'the spiritual realm' concerning the fortunes (or misfortunes) of the Nigerian state, and that a 'cloud of evil' veils all the key decisions taken by those in office.

This book is about the ascendancy of this paradigm, one of enchantment, and its impact on the politics and the democratic process in the Nigerian Fourth Republic. It is because this ascendance coincides with the birth of the Fourth Republic that I describe it – the republic – as a Pentecostal republic, and Nigerian democracy as an enchanted democracy. While Paul Gifford, from whom I have borrowed the term, speaks of an 'enchanted Christianity',[12] I have applied it, for reasons that I elaborate, to democratic politics in the Nigerian Fourth Republic.

That the paradigm is widely shared (not just by a section of the public, but, crucially, by those who have either worked in the villa or occupied political office) can be deduced from the overall flavour of responses to the Abati piece. For example, for Femi Adesina, the Special Adviser on Media and Publicity to President Muhammadu Buhari, the problem with Abati's essay is not that it brings everyday politics and life in Aso Villa under the aegis of 'demonic infestation and manifestation',[13] but that it does so 'in a way that stoked and kindled the kiln of fear, rather than of faith'. For Adesina, the issue is not just that Aso Villa is enveloped in evil, but that evil is ubiquitous and can be countered only through strict adherence to biblical principles. Thus:

> To believe and teach otherwise is to carry superstition to ridiculous level, and venerate the Devil, granting him omnipotence, an attribute that belongs to God only. For the Devil, doing evil is full-time business, and whether you had anything to do with Aso Villa or not, he continued with his pernicious acts … If you are under the pavilion of God, sleep, wake and operate daily in Aso Villa, you are covered, no matter *the evil that lurks around*, if any. There is a better covenant established on greater promises, and that is the canopy under which you should function. God can spare you from all evils, and if He permits any other thing, it is 'such as is common to man,' and not because of Aso Villa.[14]

Not only did former Ogun State Commissioner for Information Sina Kawonise agree with Abati and Adesina that the country is besieged by 'Satan, demons and their human agents in high places',[15] he commended Abati for:

> pointing our attention to a serious aspect of our national life: there is *gross spiritual evil going on in the seat of power* more than anywhere else. We do well to transcend empiricism and living in denial and cry unto God to deliver us from men and women who use *evil powers* to keep us down as a country. God admonishes us in the Holy Bible that we should pray especially for those in

authority so that we may live a peaceful (and good) life. Why? Because they are more susceptible to *dark spiritual forces*.[16]

Femi Fani-Kayode, Special Assistant (Public Affairs) to President Olusegun Obasanjo from July 2003 until June 2006, also threw his weight behind Abati's claim that 'strange things' happen in Aso Villa because 'something evil' is at work there.[17] Although he concedes that 'leaders all over the world' 'suffer loss and tragedy', he insists that 'in Nigeria it is far more pronounced and common than anywhere else' because:

> Here the angel of death, misfortune and sorrow seem to stalk those that find power, and, like an ugly old crow plucks out the pink feathers and precious eyes of a beautiful flamingo, she cuts short and plucks away their lives or the lives of their loved ones. Like a light bulb attracts a moth and leads it to a sudden end, so power attracts those who seek it with equally tragic consequences.

Arguing that 'virtually every single one of our national leaders and those that have ever ruled this country has suffered immeasurably at some point or the other in their lives, whether it be before, during or after they came to power', Fani-Kayode went on to provide a random list of Nigerian leaders and the personal losses they all suffered, presumably on account of having had connections with office.

To be sure, not everyone found Abati's claims regarding roaming demons and 'persons in the Villa walking upside down, head to the ground' convincing. For *Punch* columnist Abimbola Adelakun, the article amounted to nothing more than an attempt on Abati's part to 'pass off incompetence (his and his former boss's) as metaphysically induced "mistakes"'.[18] And to Abati's claim that 'when presidents make mistakes, they are probably victims of a force higher than what we can imagine', Adelakun responded with a blizzard of questions:

What unimaginable higher forces could have been responsible for the massive looting carried out by human – superhuman – agents right under President Goodluck Jonathan's nose? To what extent were evil spirits responsible for the profligacy of the very corrupt government Abati worked with? Did those evil spirits also join their company to indulge in the bacchanal feasts through which they frittered valuable public resources? What supernatural power could account for Jonathan's lethargy that caused the security issues that plagued the country under his watch to greatly deteriorate?

While obviously not fully convinced by what he describes as 'the demon thesis', Segun Adeniyi, former spokesman for President Umaru Musa Yar'Adua (2007–10) and chair of the editorial board of *This Day* newspaper, nonetheless embraces it as a heuristic for illuminating the 'diabolical means' employed '[w]hen people seek power in Nigeria, whether in the political or spiritual realms'.[19] In the two examples he goes on to cite, we see a confirmation of this:

For instance, in January this year [2016], some shallow graves were unearthed under the foundation of a popular church in Enugu. Following the shock find, it was discovered that the three deceased persons were members of the Tricycle Riders Association in the state, who had earlier been declared missing. What was the pastor looking for? Power, money and fame! Two years ago in Ilorin, an Islamic cleric was arrested by the police after being caught while performing rituals with the placenta of a baby whose naming rite he had conducted a few days earlier. On searching the house, they found several human parts and a boy who confessed that the cleric asked him to exhume the placenta to prepare charms. What could the Imam possibly be looking for? Power, money and fame!

It seems probable, as suggested earlier, that the main purpose of Abati's fatalistic melodrama was to elicit sympathy for a Jonathan administration that was very unpopular, as well as to massage the public mood in anticipation of a damaging EFCC arrest that he, Abati, may well have known was in the offing. This, after all, was a different Abati, desperate for public rehabilitation following a period in Aso Villa during which his erstwhile professional reputation had plummeted. Yet, this probable use of spirituality as a ruse is only partially interesting, being, after all, a tactic as old as politics itself. The greater challenge, in my opinion, is to develop an explanatory paradigm, one that not only takes the existence of powerful demons and other nefarious invisible agents for granted, but also assumes that such 'principalities and powers', having the ability to overwrite human agency, are to be blamed for Nigeria's (and any number of African countries') socio-economic and political struggles. The following is an excerpt from a private communication with a colleague who teaches at the University of Ibadan, on the day when Abati's essay was published:

We have always suspected that Nigeria, including its presidency and universities and churches and mosques etc., is in the clutches of the devil and its minions. You feel it, especially so if you are in any sphere of power, no matter how low, as I was in UI [University of Ibadan], not to talk about in the heights of Aso Rock. I think Abati should be thanked for broaching this issue in the way he has done. I will send a note to him in that regard.[20]

Where does this socio-political demonology come from? How has it shaped politics and the political imagination in the Nigerian Fourth Republic since its inception in 1999? What is the significance of its salience for civic engagement and the development of a critical public sphere, which is required for the evolution of a democratic culture? Anchored within both the broader sociological literature on politics and religion and specifically the literature on African

Pentecostalism, the analysis in this book wrestles with these three crucially important questions.

A Pentecostal republic

I suggest that the Abati essay and the response to it constitute a didactic miniature of the particular mentality that has largely shaped and invigorated Nigerian society, and hence its politics, for the duration of the Fourth Republic. Nor is the conviction that the country is 'targeted for evil' merely the sentiment of the unlettered.[21] In his inaugural lecture, presented at the University of Ibadan on 20 February 2014 and titled 'Is Physical Security Alone Enough for the Survival, Progress and Happiness of Man?', political science professor Osisioma B. C. Nwolise gives us the closest to an academic articulation of this demonology. The (Nigerian) universe that Nwolise describes, the existence and power that he assumes, is every bit as operatic as the one in Abati's essay. It is 'a world of **"familiar, roving and static spirits"** that constitute threats to human survival, progress, and happiness'.[22] Hence:

> When we want to watch our television, we switch it on with our remote control by pressing a button. Then we can stay in Ibadan and watch a football match being played live in Athens, London, Sydney or Paris. In the same way, a witch stays in her house in Lokoja or any other town, stirs water in a pot, or conjurs [sic] a mirror, and can monitor any targeted person or object in London, Athens, or Sydney. In these two instances, one (the former) is seen as science, and the other (latter) is seen as magic. A witch can also stay in South Africa or the United Kingdom, and break the leg of an effigy spiritually programmed to represent a person domiciled in the United States, and the person's leg will break mysteriously there. The scientist or intellectualist may not see or accept these as real based on his training, *but they happen daily and are factual.*[23]

Or:

> There are **static spirits** attached to walls, plants, leaves, found in bushes, on people's clothes, etc.; and there are **roving spirits** that move about especially between 12 noon and 2.00pm, and at night. Some of these spirits are benevolent, while others are malevolent. It is the malevolent spirits that constitute threats to humans. *They can project sickness into people's bodies, change people's star or destiny, or change the sex of a baby in the womb, remove the baby completely or turn it into a stone, tortoise, snail, horse, snake, or a disabled [person].*[24]

And finally:

> if it were possible to carve out a block of the air for spiritual analysis, we can find several arrows, and many other dangerous pollutants, spiritual weapons of mass destruction flying in various directions 24 hours of the day.[25]

Nwolise's solution to this world of inexorable, always imminent, 'spiritual attacks', remote 'spiritual programming' and 'spiritual warfare' is taking 'spiritual security' and 'Strategic Spiritual Intelligence' seriously, and countering adversity with 'Divine Security Insurance'. In matters of politics in particular:

> In an election opportunity for an organization, institution or nation, the electorate should seek out and elect into [a] leadership position only people who in addition to possessing excellent leadership qualities, also have *spiritual credibility*, and belonging [sic] to the first eleven category. This is because only such people can obtain abundant favours from God, nature, and humanity, and also use these favours for the good of all.[26]

The copious literature on Pentecostalism in Africa[27] has captured the religion's subtle, yet powerful, deflection of theological emphasis from holiness to prosperity. Yet, what endures, the shift in emphasis notwithstanding, is African Pentecostalism's obsession with evil and occultist forces, invariably and vigorously remonstrated against as the ubiquitous impediment to the individual believer's attainment of holiness or prosperity. As I have noted elsewhere, this obsession makes radical and ever-present evil forces the 'other' with which Pentecostalism appears inextricably twinned.[28] On the one hand, this is nothing more than common evidence of Pentecostalism's continuity with the past or 'tradition' in Africa.[29] Not only does the Pentecostal world view draw directly from indigenous traditions of witchcraft, Pentecostalism presents a unique blend of more traditional and modern perspectives on politics that does not fit most previous moulds. The way in which its conviction – of a palpable and actively malevolent metaphysical realm – bleeds into and inundates the arena of politics demands sociological scrutiny.

In Nigeria, such an analysis is particularly pertinent for two important reasons. The first is the fact that Nigeria is arguably the epicentre of the Pentecostal revolution in Africa, the source from which many of the doctrines, forms and rituals largely associated with African Pentecostalism appear to have originated, and without doubt the place where they have found their most muscular expression. Both within and outside the continent, and invariably tracking the transnational migration patterns of the Nigerian diaspora, the creativity, brashness and entrepreneurship of Nigerians have propelled the Pentecostal gospel across places and spaces as disparate as South Africa, Canada, the Ukraine and China, to name but a few.

The second reason is that the political ascendance of Pentecostalism in Nigeria is bound up with the inception of the Nigerian Fourth Republic to such an extent that it almost seems impossible to narrate the evolution of one without examining the other. That is my point of departure in this book. While Pentecostalism definitely predates the inception of the Fourth Republic in 1999, its emergence as a political force and as a theology directly focused on the appropriation of state power in Nigeria occurred with the ascension to the presidency of former army general Olusegun Obasanjo in 1999. The story of this realisation, understandable only within the rubric of Christian–Muslim struggle for supremacy in the country, a struggle that is not without its global ramifications and reverberations, is told in greater detail in Chapter 2.[30]

First, I argue that the inception of the republic coincided with the period in Nigeria's political history when Christians, formally organised under the aegis of CAN, appeared to gain a decisive political advantage over their Muslim counterparts. It was also during this period that Pentecostalism became the dominant mode of Christianity in the country. The way I see it – and the way in which I trace the narrative in this book – is that General Olusegun Obasanjo (1999–2007) was Nigeria's first openly Pentecostal president; he interpreted his accession to power in divine terms, and his tenure was widely seen by many Christians, especially Pentecostal Christians in the geopolitical South of the country, as an answer to their earnest supplications to God for a 'power shift' – both religious and geopolitical.

Second, I categorise the Fourth Republic as a Pentecostal republic because of the way in which the arc of its development neatly maps onto the evolutionary arc of the social visibility and political influence of a Pentecostal 'theocratic class'. Drawing in part on the work of Jeff Haynes,[31] the theocratic class is used throughout this book to refer to the core Pentecostal leaders who have burst into prominence over the past 25 years, and whose social visibility has increased over the course of the Nigerian Fourth Republic. For Nigerian scholar Toyin Falola:

> The power of this class comes from the power to preach, teach, dogmatize, and lead congregations. They depend on perceptions of moral uprightness and justness, opposing themselves

to the corruption of those in political power. They also rely on their charisma, their ability to arouse, inspire, and stimulate a crowd.[32]

Led by a cohort of wealthy Pentecostal pastors, the theocratic class has taken it upon itself to provide a cogent narrative about the fate of the Fourth Republic, if not Nigerian democracy itself. On the whole, leading lights among the theocratic class (the enhanced status of whom logically corresponds to the diminished influence of secular poles of authority such as universities and trade unions) have managed to redraw the boundary between the pulpit and state power, often in ways that seem to suggest concern for their own corporate existence and continued preservation as a class. Accordingly, and as an acknowledgment of the growing influence of this class, two chapters are dedicated to an exploration of aspects of pastoral power in the Fourth Republic. In Chapter 5, I use the politics of the March 2015 presidential election to illuminate the reach and limits of Pentecostal pastors' influence. Chapter 6 amplifies the theme of demonic excess through an examination of the writings of Pastor D. K. Olukoya, General Overseer of the Mountain of Fire and Miracles Ministries (MFM).

Third, the Fourth Republic has seen the rise and consolidation of the Pentecostal imaginary in Nigeria. By Pentecostal imaginary, I refer, *pace* sociologist Charles Taylor,[33] to the Pentecostal understanding of society, culture, politics and historicity in Nigeria, and the values and normative commitments that result from that understanding. The notion of Nigeria as a country shackled by satanic bondage and held hostage by sundry demonic forces and 'principalities' – a notion evident in Abati's essay and on full display in Nwolise's inaugural lecture – is both testimony to and spillover from this imaginary. To reiterate: the point is not whether such a notion has any rational solidity. Rather, it is to pursue its sociological implications, in particular the ways it figures as political leverage in Nigeria's unending Christian–Muslim rivalry.

An African test case

Over the past three decades, the worldwide resurgence of religiosity has effectively retired – at least for the time being – previous assumptions regarding the inevitability of secularisation and the privatisation of piety. In Africa, the pietistic turn has taken place in the wake of state retreat and its attendant mass precarisation. In general, not only have religious organisations of various affiliations stepped into the hiatus created by state withdrawal, religious leaders, often invoking divine authority, have also taken advantage of what Harvard leadership scholar Barbara Kellerman has described as the global 'diminishment of the expert', a phenomenon that, she argues, 'is in evidence in nearly every area of twenty-first century life'.[34]

While the upsurge of faith is a social given – as evidenced in Africa by Pentecostalism and reformist Islamic movements respectively – its long-term impact on democratic practice in the continent's transitioning societies remains contested. Yet, the question is fundamental (in Nigeria as well as in other African countries), not just because an overwhelming majority of people ardently profess a religious belief, as attested to by several students of the subject, but also because religious conviction continues to provide a foundation not so much for moral behaviour (which is another topic entirely) as for commissions and omissions in the political marketplace.

This kind of disposition is a politician's dream, and, as we have seen in numerous examples the world over, the ability to 'make political capital out of displays of religious allegiance or respect'[35] is not always positively correlated to the spiritual fidelity of the politician. But the African scenario seems different in at least one respect. According to Stephen Ellis and Gerrie ter Haar:

> In Africa ... unlike in Europe or North America, there is reason to believe that political elites do not use religion solely as a means of increasing their base of popular support but that

in many cases they also believe that access to the spiritual world is a vital resource in the constant struggle to secure advantage over their rivals in political in-fighting. This can be done by conventional techniques of communication with the spirit world, including the use of sacrifices and protective objects or through divination.[36]

The persistence of the belief in the necessity and power of access to the spiritual world explains in part the resort to 'diabolical means' that Segun Adeniyi referenced in his response to Reuben Abati's article.

This leads me to three important caveats. The first is that, while I classify the Fourth Republic as a Pentecostal republic and for that reason define its democracy as an enchanted democracy, and while I argue that what I call a Pentecostal imaginary is its defining leit-motif, this by no means implies a lessening of fervour within other faiths, or their irreversible socio-political relegation. Quite the contrary. For one thing, and to emphasise a point noted earlier, the ascendance of Pentecostalism has in fact resulted in a new obses-sion with the world of 'traditional' religion. Second, as I have shown in previous work on new developments in the dynamics of religious interaction in western Nigeria,[37] Christian resurgence, epitomised by Pentecostalism, has provided an impetus for Muslim revivalism and charismatisation.

A third caveat is that, despite the undoubted vigour and influ-ence of Pentecostalism as an ideological force, its precise effects on politics can be difficult to judge. For example, it stands to reason that in a political environment dominated, as I claim, by Pentecos-talism, the political process ought to produce only outcomes that Pentecostals favour or are willing to tolerate. Without doubt, the upsurge of Pentecostalism, marking the reinvigoration of Christi-anity as a social force in Nigeria, has transformed the parameters of political manoeuvring among Christians and Muslims, and it continues to structure political action, especially the formation of power alliances.

Although political competition during the Fourth Republic has unfolded in Pentecostalism's looming shadow, the coalitions and electoral outcomes produced have forced a reckoning with other social elements with which religion necessarily has to interact. In Nigeria, the structural dynamic is such that 'purely' religious calculations must contend with ethno-regional and sectional preferences; this brings to mind Ken Post and Michael Vickers' description of Nigeria as a 'conglomerate society' in which citizens struggle to balance various 'social identifications'.[38] We see the tenacity of these constraints at several moments during the course of the Fourth Republic, and most notably in the politics of the election of Muhammadu Buhari as president in 2015, discussed in Chapter 5.

All this makes the Nigerian experiment with democracy a provocative test case. There is the element of a struggle to establish the basic precepts of a constitutional democracy, a struggle in which the country has failed repeatedly. While Christian–Muslim rivalry has been a constant driver of this quest for liberal constitutionalism, or indeed for politics and policymaking at federal, state and local levels, the interposition of Pentecostalism in the Fourth Republic complicates the nascent democratic culture, exposing it to new tensions and pressures, but also to new possibilities. As such, the usual travails of democratic stability must be negotiated, even as dynamic religious competition shapes and conditions political opportunities and challenges.

Furthermore, and as a result, Nigeria is also a fascinating test case for studying the challenges of inaugurating a secular political order. As noted above, recent intensification of religious fervour in different regions of the world has laid to rest premature celebrations regarding the triumph of secularisation. The irony, however, is that in many countries with vibrant religious communities that are attached to regional groups with competing claims to power and resources, secularity becomes a necessary modality to discipline the excesses to which religious claim making seems prone by its very nature. This, it has always seemed to me, is the way in which religiously motivated agents in Nigeria have typically approached the issue of the country's secular status: something to be tolerated in lieu of an alternative that is guaranteed to be messy, and an instrument to be embraced pending such time in the historical future when the favoured group will become triumphant. Political scientist Brandon Kendhammer's analysis[39] of debates among ordinary Muslims in Northern Nigeria to reconcile 'Islamic values' and democratic norms indicates that, if anything, conflicts over secularity do not happen only between adherents of different faiths. On the contrary, such debates must be seen as an extension of a new wave of vigorous interrogation of the assumptions and conceits of secularism.[40]

A study of religion and politics in Nigeria, of the kind undertaken here within the context of a still unfolding Fourth Republic, must take account of a nagging sense of religious grievance, mercifully neutered by a shaky consensus on the necessity of secularity.

Intellectual context and outline of chapters

This book follows and departs from a crop of recent studies of religion and politics in Nigeria.[41] As a corpus, these studies illuminate various aspects of the religion–politics conundrum in the country, and, in this broad sense, mine merely complements them. But, crucially, I depart from them in the following ways. First, my specific focus is on the Nigerian Fourth Republic, and on transformations in the state, state power and the democratic process in the shadow of religious contestation and Pentecostalist supremacy. Hence, whereas the aforementioned studies focus on different aspects of the Pentecostal explosion (a specific church, the Redeemed Christian Church of God (RCCG), in the case of Ukah; the origins and social drivers of Pentecostalism in the case of Ojo; and meaning and politico-philosophical context in the case of Marshall), this book postulates Pentecostalism as the ideational fulcrum of the Fourth Republic, one that has given a different shape and a new level of urgency to Christian political engagement, especially in relation to the Islamic 'other'. The approach adopted here is simultaneously chronological and analytical: that is, I am attentive to the twists and contours of the Christian–Muslim struggle for political hegemony from the dawn of the Fourth Republic and through the lives of the four successive administrations. I examine the ways in which religious forces seek to influence and dominate the state, and at the same time how state agents seek to extend state power into the realm of civil society through the manipulation of religious agents, symbols and metaphors.

I also depart from the bulk of the studies referred to above – and, indeed, from an influential strand of the global literature – especially in regard to their mostly positive appraisal of the socio-economic and political effects of Pentecostalism. For instance, echoing a popular trope relating to Pentecostalism's assumed capacity to provide a vehicle for economic transformation and social justice, sociologist Peter Berger highlights the good that Pentecostals do, 'especially among poor and marginalized people'.[42] In the same vein, urban theorist Mike Davis suggests that one of the great sources of Pentecostalism's appeal:

> is that it's a kind of para-medicine. One of the chief factors in the life of the poor today is a constant, chronic crisis of health and medicine. This is partially a result of the World Bank's Structural Adjustment Programs in the 1980s, which devastated public health and access to medicine in so many countries. But Pentecostalism offers *faith healing*, which is a major attraction – and it's not entirely bogus. When it comes to things like addictive behavior, Pentecostalism probably has as good a track record curing alcoholism, neuroses, and obsessions as anything else. That's a huge part of its appeal. Pentecostalism is a kind of spiritual health delivery system.[43]

That Pentecostalism has profoundly changed the landscape of religious practice in Africa and globally over the past quarter of a century can hardly be disputed. For example, mainline churches have effusively embraced Pentecostalism's 'modern worship styles, speaking in tongues, and emphasizing healing/deliverance'.[44] Theologian Jesse Zink uses the term 'Anglocostalism' to describe (and partly to deplore) the influence of 'new generation' churches on modes of worship within Anglican and other mainline churches.[45]

Nor can it be denied, as Davis seems to imply, that Pentecostalism has been a real source of solidarity for communities torn apart by economic crisis and political instability. Nevertheless, in this book I distance myself from these pro-social assessments and (on the basis of the evidence currently available) take a darker view of the impact of Nigerian (or African) Pentecostalism on social life, politics and the political process. In the sceptical mode of Paul Gifford and Femi Kolapo,[46] I argue that Pentecostalism, as the dominant form of Christianity, has a tremendous potential to be a reactionary force with a demobilising effect on civil society in Nigeria. I attempt to show how, in this possible reactionary incarnation, Pentecostalism might contradict the social progressivism that was once characteristic of Nigerian Christianity, as illustrated by its role in the historic coalition that stood up to the military in the 1980s and 1990s, leading to the inauguration of a new democratic era in the country.[47] Following Ruth Marshall, and to a large extent Nimi Wariboko and Asonzeh Ukah,[48] I take the point about the intrinsic politicality of Nigerian Pentecostalism. What I emphasise is its effect and instrumentalisation and, in doing so, I find myself more in agreement with the tentative tone of scholars such as Jeff Haynes,[49] Lydia Boyd,[50] or Roger Southall in a South African context,[51] than the relative bullishness of Wariboko, Marshall, and, to some extent, Freeman.[52]

This book critically complements, updates and, where applicable, extends previous studies with a similar intellectual emphasis on the interplay of faith and politics.[53] This interplay is understood and analysed in three related aspects. One is the contestation between agents belonging to two opposing and politically sensitive faiths

(Christianity and Islam) for control of the state and the political destiny of Nigeria. The second is the transformation of confessional praxes as a result of political contestation; while the third is the ensuing redrawing of the boundaries separating the theological from the political in ways that challenge standard representations of the state, politics and religion. Because, as I argue, the return to civil rule in 1999 also coincided with the ascendance of Pentecostal Christianity as a socio-political force in Nigeria (a point most powerfully illustrated by the inauguration of Olusegun Obasanjo, a self-confessed born-again Christian, as president), the book is also an account of the struggle to 'Pentecostalise' power and governance – if not democracy itself – against the backdrop of perceived creeping Islamisation of politics by the Muslim 'other'.

Variations in historical contexts, ideologies and personalities notwithstanding, Pentecostal incursions into the political realm in Nigeria necessitate comparisons with observed patterns and outcomes in other African countries. In Côte d'Ivoire and Ghana respectively, Sasha Newell[54] and Paul Gifford[55] find a similar 'demonic discourse' that presents challenges with regard to political participation and civic mobilisation. In Liberia, journalist Helen Cooper's account[56] of a presidential mansion where '[s]pirits are said to roam the hallways, while the applause of ghosts can be heard late at night, as if clapping at the end of a speech' demonstrates that Nigerians' dystopia of a jinxed presidential lodge is not unique. In Zimbabwe, David Maxwell[57] observes a Pentecostalism that appears uniquely responsive to the changing hues of the political scene. Zambia, the first post-independence African country to be officially declared a 'Christian nation', in December 1991 by the late President Frederick Chiluba, offers a distinctive and far more complicated model of Christianity's relationship with other faiths within a democratic framework.[58] In the concluding chapter, I flag these regional patterns with a view to anchoring and illuminating transformations within Nigerian Christianity and the Christian–Muslim struggle for dominance.

To my knowledge, this is the first systematic account of the role of religion in societal ordering and political contestation in the Nigerian Fourth Republic. Using the lens of religion, several studies, mostly journal articles and book chapters, have addressed different administrations and historical moments in the Fourth Republic. Others have examined the relationship between the Nigerian state and religious organisations in different parts of the country. In recent times, quite understandably, there has been considerable interest in the Islamic fundamentalist group Boko Haram and its violent activities across the north-eastern part of the country. I, however, offer a synoptic and systematic appraisal of the overlap of religion with politics, from the inauguration of the Nigerian Fourth Republic to the present. Analytically, the book privileges the struggles of religious agents who are pressured to advance private religious agendas even as they continue to affirm a commitment to the secular status of the Nigerian state.

Chapter 2 begins with an assessment of the religio-political scene on the eve of the transition from military rule to formal democracy in 1999. The thrust of this chapter is that the civilian administration of Olusegun Obasanjo (his 'second coming' in more than a literal sense) coincided with a marked rise in the socio-economic and political power of Pentecostal Christianity in the country, and hence constituted a new milestone in Christian–Muslim rivalry for political control. The chapter contends that effectively, as an openly born-again Christian, Obasanjo was the first president in the country's history to 'Pentecostalise' power, drawing on Christian symbols in his everyday performance, and appointing in key positions individuals who envisioned their official roles within the matrix of the Pentecostal *Weltanschauung*.

In 1999, Obasanjo was elected president against the backdrop of strident clamour for a 'power shift' from the Northern/Muslim section of the country (which, in the view of many Southerners, had unfairly hoarded political power since independence) to a largely Christian Southern section. As a result, Yar'Adua's ascension to the presidency in 2007 was, according to this view, a political loss for the South and a net gain for the Muslim North. But Yar'Adua, who died in office in May 2010, did not stay in power long enough for the North to enjoy its own 'share', prompting accusations that Obasanjo had installed in power a Muslim successor whom he knew very well would not last the course. Yet, by all accounts, Yar'Adua himself was a middle-of-the-road Muslim who courted both Muslim clerics and Pentecostal pastors equally, thus inadvertently strengthening their social standing. As he lay dying in a Saudi hospital, and as the issue of his succession by a Southern Christian vice president took the country to the brink of a constitutional crisis, religion once again became the focal point of Nigerian politics. The story of this 'Islamic interlude' is the focus of Chapter 3.

The theme of Chapter 4 is the arguable return of Pentecostalism to the centre of political power in the Fourth Republic. Following the unexpected demise of President Yar'Adua, Christian leaders were quick to embroider the administration of his successor, Goodluck Jonathan, with religious symbolism. To an extent perhaps not imaginable under the first born-again president, Jonathan not only wore his Christian bona fides on his sleeve, he also enthusiastically embraced the widespread clerical and popular narrative that attributed his succession to power as supernatural. The Christian–Muslim struggle for power was intensified in the dying embers of the Jonathan administration as a beleaguered president desperately mobilised symbolic and financial resources in order to retain power. Drawing on examples of President Jonathan's political 'performance', I argue that being perceived as a Christian president was a central part of Jonathan's overall presentation, and that this was something that had to be done continually in order to achieve discursive legitimacy. Jonathan's subsequent failure to hold on to power may point to the limitations of this particular political strategy.

The analysis in Chapter 5 centres on the role of religion and sundry religious agents in the 2015 presidential election, eventually won by the APC candidate Muhammadu Buhari. In a giddy electoral moment deeply suffused with 'religion talk' and various kinds of religious imagery, Buhari's 'Muslimness' was deemed inadequate, if not politically risky, without the apparent ballast of the Christianity of his vice-presidential candidate, Yemi Osinbajo, a proud pastor of the RCCG, the foremost Pentecostal church in Nigeria. Although the selection of Osinbajo was a gesture aimed partly at assuaging fears of Islamisation under Buhari, concern about northernisation re-emerged as the country approached the middle part of the Buhari presidency.

A core claim of this book is that a cohort of Christian leaders – a theocratic class – has steadily gained influence over the course of the Nigerian Fourth Republic, due in large part to its astute construction and maintenance of a discourse whereby the country's economic and political problems are defined in spiritual terms. Such a definition is consistent with the Pentecostalist world view of ubiquitous and apparently inexhaustible evil, which is only (if at all) eliminable through aggressive prayer and other forms of 'spiritual warfare'. In Chapter 6, I pursue this theme by analysing a representative sample of the writings of Pastor D. K. Olukoya, General Overseer of the Lagos-based MFM. The chapter argues that the stress placed on the ubiquity of unseen enemies and invisible diabolical forces allows the theocratic class to seize the narrative, through which it is able to leverage tremendous social and political power. This power threatens the democratic project insofar as it is mobilised to enter into alliances with various state actors, and to advance the corporate interests of the theocratic class, much to the detriment of the citizenry.

In the concluding chapter, the role of religion in Nigerian politics as analysed in the preceding chapters is parlayed into an exploration of the broader place of religion in democratic consolidation. Keeping in view the literature on the subject, in both regional and other contexts, I consider the ways in which competition for power among religious agents can strengthen nascent democratic structures and institutions. At the same time – and, admittedly, with one eye on the Islamist Boko Haram insurgency – I analyse how religious mobilisation can produce social fragmentation. Not least because of its perceived threat to the territorial integrity and political stability of the country, the insurgency has generated interest among scholars and public policy specialists. Simultaneously consolidating and breaking away from these efforts, Boko Haram is treated here as a symbolic point of convergence among many 'discourses' on the interpenetration of religion and politics in Nigeria.[59] Perhaps the most popular among such discourses is that, when all is said and done, Boko Haram is the handiwork of politically ambitious Northern agents intent on using 'religious' conflict to leverage power. The objectivity or validity of this discourse becomes secondary to its analytical value as a reminder of the merging of the political and the religious in Nigeria. By anticipating the points at which the spiritual and the political intersect, the chapter affirms that religio-political contestation will continue to play a prime role in state making and the democratic process in Nigeria for the foreseeable future.

Conceptually, this matters for at least two reasons. As mentioned in the Introduction, the interplay of religious and political forces in Nigeria is merely one model. But it is a didactic model, if only because, 20 odd years into the Fourth Republic, Nigeria remains a fledgling democracy, susceptible to sudden stalls and reversals, as is clearly the case. The analysis here can help explain what happens to weak political institutions when they fall under the sway of powerful religious forces.

Over the past couple of decades, claims for taking religion (more) seriously have gained global currency. Across Europe and America, disillusionment with Enlightenment liberalism – its valorisation of reason and its emphasis on individualism have drawn the most ire – has reignited interest in faith-based communities as imagined repositories of 'meaning' and social cohesion.[60] In Africa, the much-documented vicissitudes of the postcolonial state, and the fact that extensive swathes of socio-economic life have fallen under the informal rule of sundry non-state actors, has revived policy and academic interest in religious leaders and organisations. As a cautionary tale against the rush to endow religious communities and actors with transhistorical attributes, my analysis here indicates the dangers to both religion and politics, especially when religion is so deeply politicised that the liberal desideratum of separation of church and state is honoured more in the breach than in the observance.

Chapter 2

1999–2007: PENTECOSTALISM ASCENDANT

Obasanjo builds a mosque

In March 2017, as part of a range of activities to commemorate his eightieth birthday, former Nigerian president Olusegun Obasanjo officially commissioned a mosque to be built next to the Olusegun Obasanjo Presidential Library, the presidential archive named after him in Abeokuta, Ogun State. Previously, the former military general had erected a 1,000-seat church, the Chapel of Christ the Glorious King, in the vicinity. The construction of a mosque by a statesman who, since his release from prison in 1998, has never been shy about flaunting his Christian born-again credentials (and who signed up for a graduate diploma in Christian theology shortly before he left office in 2009),[1] left many observers flummoxed. Unsurprisingly, the gesture was viewed in some quarters as a political sop aimed, inter alia, at pacifying Muslim residents of Ogun State.

The reaction of Afis Oladosu, Islamic studies scholar at the University of Ibadan and columnist for *The Guardian* newspaper in Lagos, was typical of this suspicion. For him, this was a perfect example of 'a political mosque, a mosque built to "settle"[2] the Moslem segments of Ogun State, to solace them to forget the injustice being visited on them by Ogun politicians, who appear to have the notion that no Moslem is worthy of being a governor of the state as yet'.[3] Placing the mosque squarely within the orbit of politically motivated charity, he then asked: 'Is this mosque not a metaphor for the money usually given to the electorates by politicians in order to corner their conscience, corrupt their vision and appropriate their votes?'[4]

Given the sceptical reaction from a section of the public, the onus was on Obasanjo to explain his decision. Addressing the media after the commissioning, he explained that he had been motivated primarily by memories of his formative years in a Yoruba community where peaceful Christian–Muslim coexistence was the norm. In addition, Obasanjo was quick to remind those who doubted his sincerity that, as president of the country, he had fasted consistently during both Ramadan and Lent.[5] All in all, he said, his overall intention was to send out a powerful message to all Nigerians on the need to avoid using religion as a political wedge.

There is an unmistakable irony in the fact that it fell upon Obasanjo to offer a physical token of religious reconciliation to a country almost perennially seething with religious discontent. Part of the irony lies in the fact that the politics of Obasanjo's 'second coming' as president in 1999 had been so religiously freighted as to trigger a religio-political backlash whose iconic project was the embrace of sharia law by several Northern Nigerian states, or so the argument goes. There is no suggestion here that this was Obasanjo's personal fault, or that there are steps that he could have taken to prevent the backlash. On the contrary, given the history of political contention between a predominantly Muslim North and a largely Christian Southern part of the country, it seems perfectly logical that a 'power shift' from North to South would generate a reaction from the part of the country that had had to relinquish power.

This chapter places the Obasanjo presidency (1999–2007) within the context of Christian–Muslim conflict in Nigeria. In this light, it should be noted that his 'second coming' (in more than one sense)[6] coincided with a marked rise in the socio-economic and political power of Pentecostal Christianity in the country, and hence a new milestone in Christian–Muslim rivalry for political control. Effectively, the chapter contends, an openly born-again Obasanjo was the first president in the country's history to 'Pentecostalise' power, drawing on Christian symbolism in his political perfor-mance and rhetoric, and appointing into key positions personalities who, while not necessarily handpicked for public office on account of their born-again credentials, nevertheless interpreted their official roles as key moments in their Pentecostal discipleship. It is precisely for this reason – and for others discussed below – that the Obasanjo presidency is characterised in this book as Nigeria's first Pentecostal presidency. The second was the presidency of Goodluck Jonathan, discussed in Chapter 4.

Two elements are important for a proper contextualisation of the analysis in this chapter. The first is the palpable shift in Nigerian Christians' attitude towards political power, a process described by Christianity scholar Afe Adogame as the 'Christian scramble for a role in national public life'.[7] As part of this process, Chris-tians, perhaps envious of the perceived imbrication of state power with Islamic symbols, shifted from a long-standing insistence on the basic secularity of the Nigerian state to an affirmation of the imperative to Christianise it. A second element is the emergence of Pentecostalism as the dominant form of Christianity in the country. Accordingly, I discuss in some detail both elements: Christians' changed attitude towards political power and the secular status of the Nigerian state; and the emergence of Pentecostalism as a spiritual, and even cultural, juggernaut.

From chaos to order

The decade preceding the return to civil rule in 1999 and the instal-lation of Olusegun Obasanjo as civilian president of a newly minted Fourth Republic still remains among the most turbulent in Nige-ria's political history. The period was characterised by widespread civil unrest and bitter political, religious and ethnic feuding, which, for a brief while, put the very survival of the country as an independent entity in serious doubt. Nothing captures the sense of imminent mortality that was prevalent at the time better than the sudden popularity of such clichés and irresistible titles as 'political impasse', 'brink of the precipice', 'End game in Nigeria', 'Nigeria: inside the dismal tunnel', 'This house has fallen: midnight in Nigeria' and 'Nigeria: rivers of blood'.[8]

The origins of this life-threatening crisis lay in the annulment of the 12 June 1993 election by the military regime of General Ibrahim Badamasi Babangida (which lasted from 1985 to 1993). Babangida had pulled the rug from under the election just as it was about to produce a clear winner – his close friend and business associate, millionaire businessman M. K. O. Abiola – and there is no shortage of theories as to why he made the move. These vary from protecting the corporate interest of the military and assuaging Northerners' worries about the consequences of putting the levers of power in the hands of a Southerner to prolonging Babangida's stay in power. For Babangida himself, the annulment of the election was an unfortunate course of action forced upon his administration by, among other things, 'the tremendous negative use of money during the party primaries and presidential election', 'bad signals pertaining to the enormous breach of the rules and regulations' guiding the election, and, last but not least, 'a huge array of electoral malpractices in all the states of the federation before the actual voting began', including 'authenticated reports of the electoral malpractices against party agents, officials of the National Electoral Commission and also some members of the electorate'.[9]

If Babangida's justification sounds vague and appears hurriedly cobbled together, it is partly because Abiola's victory at the polls had seemed improbable at first. Because of the outpouring of support for his candidacy – a support strengthened by the perception that he had been unfairly treated by the military – it tends to be forgotten that, initially, Abiola's candidacy had been widely written off. Although respected for his philanthropy, he remained deeply unpopular, particularly among his Yoruba ethnic kin, because of his closeness to the Muslim Northern power bloc. During the Second Republic (1979–83), Abiola was a member of the Northern-oriented National Party of Nigeria (NPN), a platform he proudly championed through his newspaper, the *National Concord*. Furthermore, in heading a Muslim–Muslim ticket (both Abiola and his running mate, Borno-born Baba Gana Kingibe, were Muslims), thus clearly violating one of the sacred, if unwritten, rules of ethno-religious balance in Nigerian politics, Abiola seemed to have driven the final nail in the coffin of his own impending electoral defeat.[10]

As we now know, things turned out differently. Abiola, presidential candidate for the Social Democratic Party (SDP), leveraged his personal charisma and political connections and the political naiveté of his National Republican Convention (NRC) opponent, Kano-born Bashir Othman Tofa, into a stunning victory in what has since been considered the freest and fairest election in the country's political annals.

But if Abiola's victory at the polls was a singular testimony to the apparent capacity of the Nigerian electorate to see beyond ethno-religious divisions (although it has to be said that we still do not know how the same electorate might react to a Christian–Christian ticket), the aftermath of the annulment is a reminder of how easily those differences can rise to the surface. Sociologist Abu Bakarr Bah thinks that the unusual outcome of the 12 June 1993 presidential election can be accounted for by the fact that 'the election was conducted under a two-party system, which effectively forced Nigerians to vote for people that were not strongly affiliated with their ethnic group'.[11] Perhaps, but that does not explain why Northern voters preferred Abiola to Bashir Tofa, a Muslim from Kano State, or indeed why the latter lost to Abiola even in his own ward. In any case, it seems reasonable to speculate that Babangida probably counted on an annulment, knowing, as an astute student of Nigerian history, how easily ethnic suspicion could be aroused.

If that was Babangida's real intention, his calculations were accurate, as the country was immediately convulsed by widespread protests aimed at making the military president reverse his decision to abrogate the election and swear in the presumed winner. As the protesters dug in, bringing economic life across the country to a virtual standstill, the ethno-regional fault lines that have always haunted the country became increasingly pronounced. No one could have appreciated the potency of ethno-religious divide in Nigeria better than Babangida, whose gambit for pacifying an especially irate western part of the country was to announce the composition of an interim national government (ING) under the leadership of Ernest Oladeinde Shonekan, a successful Yoruba technocrat.

The installation of Shonekan at the head of the ING did little to subdue the mutinous fury of the Yoruba, who felt that Abiola had been thwarted mostly on account of his Yoruba ethnicity, and that, instructively, not even his Muslimness was enough to save him from the rough justice meted out by a Northern political elite hiding behind the mask of the military. In the end, Yoruba political indignation was to outlast Shonekan, who was removed in a military coup by General Sani Abacha in November 1993. It survived Abacha, who committed state resources on an unprecedented scale to the vilification of the democratic opposition until his sudden death on 8 June 1998. Nor was it laid to rest following the death of Abiola himself a month later on 7 July 1998.

When General Abdulsalami Abubakar took over as head of state following Abacha's passing, he faced two important challenges. One was to emotionally stabilise the country after the intense trauma of the Abacha years. Desperate to consolidate his hold on power, the infantry general had literally set the dogs on the opposition, which was organised under the aegis of the National Democratic Coalition (NADECO),[12] with Abacha himself reported to have personally ordered the killing of many key opposition figures, including Kudirat Abiola, wife of Chief M. K. O. Abiola.[13] The second was that Abubakar had to put the country back on the path to reconciliation, a path that had eluded it since the 1993 annulment.

The immediate steps taken by Abubakar showed that he understood the enormity of the crisis confronting the country and what needed to be done in order to put things back on an even keel. For example, in his second (and first major) address to the country on 20 July 1998,[14] he wasted little time in addressing the nagging question of the cancellation of the 12 June 1993 results as follows:

> The June 12 presidential election and the controversial events preceding it were unfortunate in our political history. We cannot pretend that they did not happen. Yet we must accept that elections had similarly been cancelled in earlier situations. Equally more important, fully elected governments have been toppled. A call to return to the past is not helpful as it will be neither just nor fair, nor even practicable.[15]

Nevertheless, and although he admitted that '[n]either the annulment of the last presidential elections, nor toppled elected governments can be brought back', he was quick to offer an olive branch to the aggrieved by ordering the release of all political detainees, withdrawing all charges against political offenders, and extending a blanket invitation to political exiles to 'return and join efforts to build a greater nation'. In the same vein, General Abubakar commuted to various terms of imprisonment the death sentences previously passed on those accused of plotting to overthrow Abacha in 1995. Finally, Abubakar announced that the Provisional Ruling Council had pardoned General Olusegun Obasanjo (imprisoned in connection with the same alleged coup) and Major-General Shehu Musa Yar'Adua, the latter posthumously.

Power shifts: the (second) coming of Obasanjo

Although Abubakar had made clear in his address that a return to the past was 'neither just, nor fair, nor practicable', it was obvious that something still had to be done to defuse the simmering resentment among the Yoruba and the larger community of 'June Twelvers' who felt that the country could not progress without righting such a fundamental wrong. Hence the unspoken consensus among the political elite that, because of the huge toll the campaign for the validation of the 12 June 1993 election had exacted on the country, and given the mysterious death in detention of Chief M. K. O. Abiola, the ethical, if not the pragmatic, thing to do was 'rotate' the presidency to the south-western region of the country. Since this was the region from which the unfortunate Abiola hailed, this would placate the political elite, if not the people more generally, in the south-west; at the same time, it would signal an end to the protracted political gridlock caused by the annulment.

Obasanjo clearly was the beneficiary of a gentleman's agreement among the country's elite, and there is no better proof that the presidency was 'awarded' to the south-west than the fact that the presidential elections held on 27 February 1999 were a straightforward contest between two Yoruba Christian candidates: Obasanjo, representing the People's Democratic Party (PDP), and Akure-born Chief Samuel Oluyemisi (Olu) Falae, a one-time Secretary to the Federal Government and Finance Minister, who ran on the combined Alliance for Democracy (AD)/All People's Party (APP) ticket. Unlike in 1993, when the majority of the electorate voted, unexpectedly, for a Muslim–Muslim ticket, in February 1999 the parties were headed by two Southern Christians (Obasanjo and Falae) but with two Northern Muslim running mates – Adamawa-born Atiku Abubakar and Sokoto-born Umaru Shinkafi respectively.

As presidential candidates, both Obasanjo and Falae had their problems, but these were mostly of an ethno-political rather than religious hue. For his part, Obasanjo faced tremendous opposition from the dominant Yoruba political establishment, which had always held him in suspicion, if not contempt. This was due, firstly, to his perceived hostility towards Obafemi Awolowo, the revered leader of the Yoruba people, and the core of social democratic ideas (Awoism) that Awolowo stood for; and, secondly, to his alleged kowtowing to the Northern political establishment, whose conservative ideas were believed to be in sharp contrast to the essential principles of Awoism. In fact, for this Yoruba elite, Obasanjo was not a 'proper' Yoruba, but an *omo ale* (a bastard) who could not be trusted to represent the Yoruba agenda on the national stage. It should be remembered that this was not the first time that Obasanjo had run into a political headwind because of being seen as a 'bad Yoruba', among other grievances. In 1991, when Obasanjo mounted a bid to become the first African Secretary General of the United Nations, his most aggressive opponents were his fellow Yoruba, notably Nobel laureate Wole Soyinka (like Obasanjo, an Egbaman from Ogun State) and prominent human rights lawyers Femi Falana and Gani Fawehinmi.[16]

Apart from being an 'alien' Yoruba man, Obasanjo's candidacy also attracted opposition because, as many saw it, he had stood to benefit from Abiola's death, despite failing to speak in favour of the latter after he was detained by the military. In fact, he seemed to have directly undermined Abiola and the 12 June cause with his comment that Abiola was not the political messiah that his supporters believed him to be.

If Falae's Yorubaness was not in doubt, his placing among the Yoruba elite in the overall genealogy of Yoruba politics was. Falae's challenger for the presidential ticket of AD was Chief Bola Ige, Second Republic governor of Oyo State and famous orator, who saw himself as being ordained – by fate, if not by Awolowo himself – as the inheritor of Awolowo's mantle of leadership, and hence the bearer of the Yoruba political standard. For Ige and his supporters, Falae was a political arriviste who had shouldered his way to the front of the line, and they were adamant that, for that reason, he was the wrong person to head the ticket.[17] Although AD eventually managed to put its house in some sort of order, winning all six Yoruba states in the 1999 election – Ekiti, Lagos, Ogun, Ondo, Osun and Oyo – it was not enough to clinch the presidency for Falae.

That Obasanjo coasted to victory without the support of the Yoruba political establishment made his success at the polls all the more spectacular. No doubt he benefited from the support of the Northern political establishment, who backed his candidacy, seeing in him a steady and experienced 'uniter' who could be trusted to rise above sectional interests. Furthermore, he profited handsomely from the fractures within the Yoruba political establishment, fractures he would skilfully exploit to his own advantage as president.

The rise of 'political Christianity'

What Obasanjo lost initially in ethnic support, he soon recovered through the backdoor of religion. In order to understand the backdrop to this support, and especially how Obasanjo came to be seen as the icon of a politically bullish Christianity, a brief outline of its emergence is necessary.

Until the mid-1980s, Christian political mobilisation in Nigeria appears to have been concentrated on holding the Nigerian state to its founding conceit as a secular formation. If Christians felt marginalised by Muslims in the historical struggle for power, the solution to that perceived marginality did not seem to include dressing the state itself in the symbolic garb of Christianity. Writing in 1986, Henry Bienen accurately observed: 'So far, the impact of Christianity in Nigeria has been less directly consequential for the struggle for political legitimacy and control of authoritative roles at central and state levels than has been the impact of Islam.'[18]

In retrospect, the mid-1980s was a turning point, one that coincided with deeper transformations on the global level. The world witnessed, in a clear sequence, 'an increase in concern on the part of ostensibly religious collectivities with governmental issues' and 'an inflation of interest among those with declared religious commitments in coordinating the latter with secular-ideological perspectives and programmes'.[19] Closer to home, 'the rather sudden and radical political changes in Africa in the 1990s encouraged the irruption of spiritual movements into political space as people sought alternative sources of authority and at the same time were freed from institutional constraints previously imposed by single party governments'.[20]

Nigerian Christian leaders' embrace of a 'theology of engagement' unfolded within this changing global and regional milieu, marking the beginning of a phenomenon that would eventually take shape across the African continent as a 'charismatic revolution'.[21] Early on, this transformation was indexed by two broad attitudinal shifts: the first was from a basic insistence on the secularity of the Nigerian state to what seemed like a determination to Christianise it. At first glance, the secular status of the state is an established fact (the 1999 constitution is clear that 'The Government of the Federation or of a State shall not adopt any religion as State Religion'), but this remains a perennial flashpoint between Muslims and Christians in Nigeria.[22] At least prior to the shift in question, Christians generally took secularity to mean freedom to practise one's religion without state interference, and, according to Lamin Sanneh, typically defended secularity on 'pragmatic grounds of equality under the law, national stability and participation in public life, rather than for theological reasons'.[23] However, for many Muslims, the problem (beside the fact that a clean separation of the political and the religious is almost an impossibility in Islam) lay in the way in which secularism was practised in Nigeria: that is, 'as an extension of the church concept of government'.[24] In this reading – or precisely, if pursued to its logical conclusion – secularism, connoting the privatisation of piety, runs counter to Islamic beliefs. In his study of the 'Izala' Islamic reform movement in Northern Nigeria, Ousmane Kane quotes one Aliyu Dawda, a scholar and Muslim activist, who summarises this disposition towards secularism thus:

> Any attempt to impose secularism on Nigeria or on any other country having a predominantly Muslim population is nothing short of injustice. This is because it is a Christian dogma, a Christian concept and a Christian worldview, which is parochial in nature, that is being superimposed on them.

The principle of secularism, wherever it is practiced, is nothing
short of the practicalization of the Biblical statement which says:
'Give unto Caesar what is Caesar's and unto God what is God's
... Therefore, right from the onset, secularism is not religiously
neutral. It is a Christian concept, a Biblical dogma, reflecting the
parochial nature of the Christian worldview. The principle and
practice of secularism, in other words, is Islamically obnoxious,
seriously revolting, and totally unacceptable because it is fundamentally based on what our Creator and Lord, Allah (may he
be glorified) considers as the greatest crime which He never
forgives once he dies committing it.[25]

In sum: while Christians embraced secularism as furnishing a
minimum guarantee of church–state separation, Muslims often saw
it, as set out by Dawda above, as a Christian dogma. It goes without
saying that the stringency implied by Dawda's statement is by no
means definitive of Islam, not even in Northern Nigeria, where
Islamic discourses and praxes are neither unipolar nor theologically
stable. In this regard, John Paden has identified, quite instructively,
seven cross-cutting tendencies within Northern Nigerian Islam:
traditional non-sectarian mainstream Muslim groups; Sufi broth-
erhoods; anti-innovation legalists, especially the Izala; intellectual
reformers; anti-establishment syncretists; Shi'ites; and unemployed
urban youth and Qur'anic student movements.[26] For politics scholar
Olufemi Vaughan, the debate itself – and its tenor – is a reminder of
the difficulty of conceptually pinning down 'Islam' and 'secularity',
particularly in a country such as Nigeria 'where the vestiges of
Western governance were steeped in Christian influences'.[27]

A second politically important shift on the part of Christians
related to the jettisoning (or at least a substantial relaxing) of the old
position on the Christian's involvement in public life. The question
of whether Christians should be involved in politics, on what terms
and under what directive principles has long been a sticking point
among Nigerian Christians. At the heart of the question is the

ethical and theological conflict over whether to 'moralize the state' or 'moralize society', as Terence Ranger once described it.[28] Part of this concern also related to anxiety over the presumably corrosive effect of realpolitik on the faith of those who enter public life. That these were serious issues over which there was considerable agitation can be seen in the following statement by CAN, a statement that, for all practical purposes, represented a change of strategy, if not direction, for Christians:

> Truly politics may be a dirty game – but who will make it clean? If Christians distance themselves from politics that leads to leadership, then demons will have a field day as had been the case with Nigeria up till today. If demons govern and rule us and burn our churches and marginalize and treat us like second class citizens in our country of posting, then why should the Christian complain? ... When will the righteous be in authority? Is it only when Christ comes? We do not think so ... *The righteous cannot rule if he is taught not to be interested in governance. Christians ought to be interested in politics which is the vehicle used in reaching the position of leadership in this country. Genuine, properly born-again Christians, filled with the Holy Spirit should come and contest elections.*[29]

Established in August 1976 to defend and pursue the interests of Nigerian Christians, CAN initially seemed to take a conservative approach to its overall mandate. But the formation of the Christian Students' Social Movement of Nigeria in 1977 and the establishment of PFN in 1986 steadily upped the ante of Christian agitation, as routine complaints about poor treatment of Christians slowly gave way to more assertive protestations. Following this, it was only a matter of time before leading Christian figures threw their hats into the ring of partisan politics. As General Secretary of the Nigerian Baptist Convention, for instance, Dr S. T. Ola Akande famously ran for president under the banner of the NRC.[30] Increasingly, incidents of religious violence in which Christians were believed to be unfairly treated met with more vigorous condemnation, which was consciously used to invoke fundamental grievances about the status of Christians in Nigeria.

Driving the Christian advocacy of a 'theology of engagement' and a more stringent political agenda, therefore, was a general suspicion of Muslim ambitions – and, indeed, a certain envy of what was seen as Muslim success in achieving them.[31] For many Christians, the decision in 1986 by the Babangida government (significantly, without any prior consultation) to upgrade the country's status from observer to full member of the Organisation of Islamic Cooperation (OIC) was a case in point.[32]

It is into this radicalising environment that the crisis following the abrogation of the 12 June 1993 election must be inserted. The crisis further energised nascent Christian political radicalism, while at the same time revealing CAN's pragmatic approach to politics. Abiola's selection of Kingibe as his running mate had been greeted with reservation by many Christians, while a section of the CAN hierarchy had openly expressed fears about its implications for Christian interests in the country. With the annulment, Christians, the majority of whom had voted for Abiola, now united in Abiola's defence. In the event, the annulment opened up channels for several Christian clerics, notably Bishop Alaba Job, Archbishop Anthony Olubunmi Okogie, Archbishop Sunday Mbang, Right Reverend Emmanuel Gbonigi and Reverend Ayo Ladigbolu, to have a greater say in political matters.[33] As an ecumenical cohort, they viewed the annulment as a symptom of the rotten ethical foundation of the Nigerian polity, and, in a virtual Christianisation of the pro-democracy struggle, used the pulpit as a platform for socio-political intervention focused on resistance to military tyranny.[34] As time went on, and as 'the status of PFN and CAN as important political voices became apparent',[35] Christianity increasingly became a religious, cultural and political vehicle in the ethnic, regional and national struggles for power and primacy in Nigeria.[36]

A prayer answered: the making of a 'born-again' president

On the eve of the inauguration of the Fourth Republic in 1999, the imbrication of religion with politics in Nigeria was palpable. For one thing, the rise of Islamism and Pentecostalism, which had begun in the 1980s, was an established fact of social praxis. For another, and as outlined above, the 12 June crisis had strengthened Southern resolve for a 'power shift'. Abiola's humiliation and eventual death in detention had a lot to do with this. For many, the fact that not even Abiola's Muslimness sufficed to save him was a bitter lesson in ethnic identity politics. For others, Abiola's tragic fate was proof positive of the belief that the presidency was 'reserved' for only a section of the country. In these circumstances, the transfer of power on 29 May 1999 was as much ethno-regional as religious.

Obasanjo's victory at the polls and his ascent to the presidency were heavily steeped in Christian Pentecostalist symbolism. To Christians, his 'second coming' was a powerful spiritual metaphor, one that transcended the ordinary fact of his fortuitous emergence as the beneficiary of an elite pact. In reality, the Northern power elite had acquiesced to the 'power shift' as part of an attempt to inter the ghost of the annulment and lower the overall political temperature in the country. For Christians, however, it was a fulfilment of God's promise to liberate his children (Southern Christians especially) from the yoke of Northern (Muslim) leadership.[37] This formulation of a new type of religious-political narrative brings to mind the late J. D. Y. Peel's work on the Ijesha and the Yoruba more widely, especially with respect to the way in which the recrafting of a narrative for national and political purposes was part and parcel of the Christian mission from the beginning.[38]

If a politically exigent 'second coming' could be invested with a spiritual halo, it is hardly surprising that, almost overnight, Obasanjo himself was quickly transformed into a 'messiah'. For instance, it was pointed out that, because no Christian had occupied the highest office in the land between 1979, when Obasanjo's 'first coming' ended, and May 1999 – with the exception of the 84 days of the Ernest Shonekan-led ING – Obasanjo's 'second coming' had to be part of a 'divine plan' to redress the imbalance.[39]

Messiah or not, Obasanjo's Christian credentials had been burnished by his personal travails. Tried and jailed in 1995 on bogus charges of plotting to overthrow the regime of Sani Abacha, Obasanjo eventually spent a little over three years in both Jos (Plateau State) and Yola (Adamawa State) prisons before his release shortly after Abacha's death in June 1998. At the beginning of his ordeals, Obasanjo had been a 'regular' Christian. But his prison experience had a transformative effect on him, significantly deepening his spirituality. The following excerpts from his autobiography testify to this transformation from 'common' Christian to 'prayer warrior':

> The prison experience is normally overpowering. It was, for me, sobering, sedating, reflective, meditative, challenging, and spiritually uplifting. The impulsiveness, hustle and bustle, and *garagara* [exertions] of life was quietly moderated, and suddenly, I was slowed down. It gave me a realization that, with or without me, things would go on and nobody should ascribe indispensability to himself or herself. It also heightened my belief and desire that while I am still breathing the free air of God and I remain healthy, I must not leave undone what needs to be done for the good of humankind and in the service of God.[40]

Furthermore:

> One other aspect of my life, particularly in the Yola prison, that is worth dwelling on was the Christian worship and fellowship, including prayer and fasting. I came to experience the spiritual chastening of fasting and prayer and their toning effect on the

body. I could pray for hours unending, particularly while I was also fasting. I normally had two days, three days, five days, and seven days fasting with prayers. During my fasts, I totally abstained from food and water. The more I fasted and prayed, the stronger I seemed to feel and the more spiritual I became.[41]

And finally:

When I was at Inter-Centre,[42] my mode of prayer was adversarial, acrimonious, and somewhat bitter, as I looked for Psalms where David showered near-curses on his enemies. As I grew in fasting, I became sober, forgiving and started to pray like Stephen, the first martyr in the New Testament, who prayed for forgiveness for his killers because they knew not what they were doing. I prayed for forgiveness for my tormentors, whether or not they knew what they were doing. There was a definite change in my prayer points as I became a greater prayer warrior, growing from bitterness to love, from hardness to softness of heart, from inadequate knowledge to more knowledge, from doom and dreariness to hope and greater hope, and from melancholy to joy ... During the periods of my intensive fasting and prayer in Yola, I used to feel as if I had developed a sixth sense. My intuitions were sharper; my inspirations at higher levels, and my dreams more vivid and poignant. I became an instant expert in the ACTS of prayer, in being in the mood of prayer, and in concentrating in prayer.[43]

Following his release, Obasanjo was not shy about going public about his spiritual rebirth, and, judging by at least some of his early post-prison statements, he seemed to have embraced what had happened to him as a necessary step towards a closer personal relationship with God. As he said on 20 June 1998 during the thanksgiving service at the Owu Baptist church following his release:

Much water has passed under the bridge over the past months and years. For some, not much has changed, but for me, something significant has changed. The officer-in-charge of one of the prisons in which I stayed remarked that prison is next to hell on earth. That is his perception and attitude. *But for me, God made the prison next to heaven because He used the hardship, deprivation, and the tribulation to draw me closer to Him in faith, obedience, worship, prayers, fasting, study of the Word of God, praises, and thanksgiving.* For me, it was all a humbling and chastening experience with God in charge and in control. He granted me His peace and joy out of His love and grace. He gave me satisfaction and contentment and kept my spirit high, my conscience free and clear, and my hands clean.[44]

And also:

But let me state categorically here and now and assure you that I harbour no bitterness or animosity against those who unlawfully and unjustly contrived to put me in prison. *For me, it is the fulfilment of John's prophecy in Revelation 2:10 in my life*: 'Do not be afraid of what you are about to suffer, I tell you, the devil will put some of you in prison to test you and you will suffer persecution for ten days. Be faithful even to the point of death, and I will give you the crown of life.' I have sympathy for the wicked because when they have exhausted the limit of their worst, God will commence to do His best and the wicked have the fear of retribution, judgement, and justice of God, which normally starts in this world and continues unto the other side of eternity.[45]

In making public his conversion to the 'New Christianity'[46] in this way, Obasanjo was reprising a move made by a succession of Nigerian leaders, most famously Chief Akin Omoboriowo, Professor Ishaya Audu and Chief Solomon Lar. However, his status as a former military ruler and, notoriously, one-time advocate of African juju[47] meant that his conversion was of greater moment. For many Christians, his survival of the terrible living conditions in Nigeria's jails was an indication that God had preserved his life in order for him to 'accomplish great things'. For others, being jailed by Sani Abacha was itself part of God's 'master plan' for both Obasanjo and the country. The following statement by Oby Ezekwezili, Minister of Solid Minerals (later Minister of Education) under Obasanjo, is an excellent illustration of this belief:

> And so God took that person, took him away into jail and the enemies thought they were the one doing it: they took him into jail and when he was there, he had an encounter. *The President had an encounter; he had an encounter all in the agenda of God to resurrect the nation.* He brought him out after the encounter and then orchestrated a lot of things. God himself orchestrated a lot of things and took a person, who now had understood what total submission to the Almighty is: that no matter your height or position, there is none greater than the Almighty God. At that place of revelation, he could use him. *He now set up events and got him back into the covenant of the nation. What do you think it was about? It was for the re-building to start.*[48]

Ms Ezekwezili was not alone in seeing Obasanjo's prison experience as part of an inescapably painful preparation for the 'new beginning' that God had apparently 'established' for the country. In an interview granted to the *Nigerian Tribune* to commemorate his sixtieth birthday in August 2016, Bishop Francis Wale Oke, Presiding Bishop of Sword of the Spirit Ministries, Ibadan, and a close ally of Obasanjo, spoke at length about what he saw as his personal role in 'anointing' Obasanjo as president in 1999. Parts of the interview are revealing in that they confirm that Obasanjo had been 'adopted' by the Christian elite right from the moment he stepped out of prison. The following excerpts illustrate this:

A day after he came out of prison, I saw his photograph on the front page of a newspaper, looking so haggard, skinny and I said 'how can a nation do this to its former president?' and I found myself praying for him for the next 45 minutes. The Holy Spirit then directed me to anoint him as the next president of Nigeria in 1999. That evening, about 400 pastors were present at a meeting with me and I asked if any of them knew how I could connect with General Obasanjo. Nobody knew. However, I knew that God's word would come to pass. Two days later, Apostolic Lawrence Achudume, who is based in Abeokuta, called me to come and preach for him. I asked him if there was some way I could connect to Obasanjo, and he said his late wife, Stella, attended his church. He arranged a meeting with Obasanjo. After the service at Abeokuta, we went to Obasanjo's place. For the first one and half hours after we met, we were talking about his experience in prison, how he fasted, read the Bible about three times; how he wrote five books while in prison, and he said he had promised God to serve him if God took him out of prison.[49]

He continued:

When he finished, I told him that God sent me to pray for him that he would be the next president of the Federal Republic of Nigeria. The response was instant. He said he was not interested. To quote him verbatim, he stated that he had been a very important person in Nigeria and a very important prisoner. I just want to rehabilitate my life. I told him God sent me and he still said he wasn't interested. I then asked to pray with him. We were four at that meeting: myself, General Obasanjo, Apostle Achudume and a personal assistant. He removed his cap and I prayed for him and anointed him and proclaimed him executive president of the Federal Republic of Nigeria by the word of God and I left. It was not two weeks after that IBB [Ibrahim

Badamasi Babangida] visited him to draft him into politics, and the rest is history.[50]

Obasanjo did this perception no harm by gradually releasing for publication several Christian-themed books that he had been working on while in confinement.[51] From the point of view of his new spiritual identity, perhaps the most consequential was *This Animal Called Man*, an 'attempt to examine man's existence on earth and the purpose and ways to achieving that purpose in this world and in the world to come'.[52] For Obasanjo, *This Animal Called Man* was an opportunity to articulate his views on faith and the centrality of the Bible to the discovery of moral truth as he saw it. For example, he writes on faith: 'A personal philosophy not deeply rooted in faith will be shallow-rooted and may not be able to withstand a windy situation turning into a gale and finally into a great storm. For me, faith is the anchor of my personal philosophy and it holds firm and steady in windy, gale or stormy weather.'[53] And, on the Bible:

> I find the Bible the best and the most comprehensive and author-itative book on the subject of life and living. It stands above all other books put together on the subject. It speaks clearly and accurately about the human condition but it is also an inspira-tion of the One who created us and knows us more than anyone else. It is God's gift of His word to humankind. When it talks on marriage, it is right on target. When it talks about inter-human relationships, it is more helpful than all the books on psychology, sociology and all the social sciences put together. But most importantly, when it talks about the purpose of life, it is the only source of truth.[54]

Marketed as a testament to his personal conversion and a codifica-tion of his socio-moral philosophy, *This Animal Called Man* went a long way in establishing Obasanjo's credentials among the Nigerian 'born-again' community, the cream of which would rally round to defend him against his political enemies, perceived or real. In doing so, they helped define the very identity of his presidency as Christian Pentecostalist.

Christians in power

Because many Christians saw Obasanjo's election in providential terms,[55] the Christian elite was quick to claim him as a response to their prayers and prophecies for the country. Many of them had visited him while he was in prison[56] and continued to do so throughout his presidency.[57] As Matthews Ojo describes it, Christian leaders 'adopted Olusegun Obasanjo as a symbol of the Christian control of the political sphere, believing that he was an answer to prayers about the ending of oppression and misgovernance and the ending of a Muslim political dominance'.[58] Such, indeed, was their elation that they converged in Abuja on the eve of the inauguration for an all-night prayer to usher in the new (spiritual) dispensation.[59]

Not every leading Pentecostal pastor was convinced that Obasanjo was the 'Special One'. Among the notable exceptions were Chris Okotie of the Household of God Church,[60] Felix Oluyemi (aka Baba Olomi Now Now!) of the Kingdom of Love Church of Christ, and Tunde Bakare, founder and leader of the Latter Rain Assembly church, Lagos, who, going against the evangelical grain, declared that 'Obasanjo is not your Messiah, he is King Agag and the prophetic axe will come upon his head before May 29, 1999'.[61] Although Bakare did not say explicitly that Obasanjo would be killed before his swearing-in on 29 May 1999, that was precisely how the 'prophecy' was understood by the general public and the media, a not unreasonable interpretation given that, in the Bible, Agag, King of the Amalekites, was initially spared by Saul only to be 'hacked in pieces' by Samuel.[62]

At any rate, denunciation of Bakare[63] by other Christian leaders (and, indeed, by a Yoruba public eager to see 'one of their own' succeed) was swift, and such was the seriousness with which the subject of Bakare's prophecy was taken that Obasanjo immediately convened a congress of sympathetic pastors at his farmhouse in Ota, Ogun State, to pray for him and nullify the prophecy, mostly through counter-prophecies.[64] Crucially, the key insights from this incident go beyond mere jousting over a pastor's prophecy. They concern, first, the use of prophecy itself to create a climate of opinion as well as a narrative about an administration or the country as a whole. I revisit this theme in Chapters 5 and 6. A second key issue is the attention increasingly given to prophecy by political agents as part of what Jean Comaroff calls 'the growing salience of revelation as a legitimate basis for knowledge, action, and the definition of worldly space and time'.[65]

Apart from this particular incident, the éminences grises of the Pentecostal pastorate were irrevocably committed to Obasanjo, who could not have made it any clearer that he understood the symbolism of his ascent to the presidency. Thus, in his address to the country on the occasion of his inauguration, he started by giving 'praise and honour to God for this day' and acknowledging that '[the] very thing created by God has its destiny and it is the destiny of all of us to see this day'.[66] Describing himself as 'a man who had walked through the valley of the shadow of death', he attributed his election to 'what God Almighty has ordained for me and for my beloved country Nigeria and its people'.[67]

A mix of denominational, ethnic and other institutionalist calculations combined to make Obasanjo the object of affection for leading Christian figures, and one idea pursued throughout this book is that, over the course of the Fourth Republic, these figures have tended to see their influence grow steadily. At this juncture, it helps to situate the relationship between these Christian leaders and the Obasanjo presidency within a conceptual matrix. A good place to start is Jeff Haynes' observation that leading religious figures are very often class actors who partner with political elites to seek mutually advantageous goals.[68] Such goals include, but are not necessarily limited to, what Stephen Ellis and Gerrie ter Haar have called 'the tendency for politicians to seek spiritual power, and for spiritual leaders to develop substantial material power'.[69] This is the overall economy in which, as Asamoah-Gyadu also demonstrates in a Ghanaian context, Pentecostal pastors have become socio-politically significant as 'purveyors of powerful prayers, potent medicines, and amulets for protection against evil'.[70] Nor is this merely a contemporary phenomenon: for instance, studies of the patterns of insertion of Christianity into Yoruba land[71] in the colonial period confirm that the emergent Christian clergy soon formed what Wale Adebanwi calls 'an important component of the super-elite'.[72]

If that is the case, what, if anything, makes the alliance between the theocratic class and the Obasanjo presidency of particular sociological interest? For me, the answer is the attempt on the part of this elite (as part of a project of 'winning Nigeria for Jesus') to embed the New Christianity into the heart of the state. This attempt, as anthropologists Brian Larkin and Birgit Meyer have pointed out, makes Pentecostalism the ideological kin of Islamism, as far as attitudes to state power are concerned. In Islam – or, more precisely, for Islamists – Larkin and Meyer argue that 'religion has never been something outside of state structures, but is profoundly intertwined with them'.[73] It is because of this, suggests Ogbu Kalu, that state power in the Nigerian context is perceived 'as central in promoting religion; thus, control of the centre of the federal government remained a cardinal goal' for Muslims.[74]

While this is largely true, it would be inaccurate to assume that, in the Nigerian context, only Muslims have entertained or pursued the fantasy of using state power to advance sectarian goals. There is tremendous evidence to show that, across the country, state power is perennially used to advance the competing interests of Christians and Muslims, a development that 'traditional worshippers' and secular humanists of various hues have frequently lamented. In any case, given the ideological congruence under discussion, it seems reasonable to surmise that, with respect to the use of federal power, Christians have a long-held 'Islam envy'. The realisation of this 'envy' – which, in principle, is what the 1999 Obasanjo presidency represented – crystallises Ellis and ter Haar's projections of the likelihood of 'unprecedented configurations of power' linking African politicians and charismatic religious leaders, and how 'the search for spiritual power, so prominent in Africa's new religious movements, must find institutional channels if it is to endure'.[75]

Once installed, this new power nexus sought expression and openly indulged in the deployment and manipulation of religious symbols, in particular the performance of religious rituals in public offices, institutions and functions;[76] the use of religious (Christian) criteria as a basis for appointment to public office; a particularly grating mode of moral triumphalism that seemed to draw its oxygen from the demonisation of Islam and traditional forms of belief; and, last but not least, the inundation of public debate with Christian rhetoric. Both the faith-based recruitment of public officials and the demonisation of Islam should be seen against the backdrop of Christians' long-standing complaint that, when the Muslim Northern elite wielded power, the distribution of social largesse tended to be based on the singular criterion of religion.

In this perspective, the height of this practice was seen during the Buhari–Idiagbon era (1983–85), when the then Supreme Military Council included 11 Northern Muslims (and one non-Muslim Northerner) out of a total of 19 members. As political scientist Umar M. Birai has shown, marginalisation is often in the eye of the beholder, determined more often than not by who is doing the counting, what is being counted, and where. Hence, under Buhari, the National Council of Ministers 'had twenty-one members: eleven Muslims and ten Christians. The National Council of States, made up of the military governors of the then nineteen states, had seven Muslims and twelve Christians.'[77]

During the same period, anxieties about Islamic/Northern domination were sharpened by reports of the construction of three separate mosques by successive military rulers in Aso Villa, the seat of federal power. (I should add in parenthesis that the siting of a mosque within the estate of the seat of power has been a point of contention between Christians and Muslims since President Babangida's decision to build one, following the relocation of the Nigerian capital to Abuja from Lagos. Similarly, there is sporadic tension over the presence of Arabic inscriptions on the Nigerian currency, the naira, and on the Nigerian army's crest. Other flash-points are the dome of the National Assembly complex in Abuja, which some Christians believe to be 'Islamic' and therefore in viola-tion of its very principle as a trans-religious symbol of unity;[78] the religio-geographic distribution of the population;[79] and the political status of Abuja, the federal capital – in this case the perception that the portfolio of Minister of the Federal Capital Territory appears to be permanently reserved for Northern Muslims.[80])

With this in mind, Christians saw Obasanjo's residency in the villa as an opportunity to 'retaliate' as well as to recover some lost ground. It is interesting, therefore, that one of the very first things that the new president did in Aso Villa was to organise regular Christian services to pray for Nigeria. This was soon followed by the conversion of the squash court in the villa into a Christian chapel, and the appointment of a Baptist chaplain, Reverend Aliyu Yusuf Obaje. Although Obasanjo later attributed the decision to build the chapel in the villa to the need to avoid the inconvenience caused to the public each time he worshipped at the First Baptist church in Garki, Abuja, it is also clear from the same statement that he was not totally insensible to its political meaning.

This is Obasanjo's justification in full:

When I came to Abuja, I thought that why should I establish a church in the seat of government? I should rather worship in a place of worship just like everybody else. And my intention was to come here [First Baptist church, Garki, Abuja] every Sunday … But, then, I found that every Sunday, when I was coming, the security will come with me and I believe everybody was put under pressure and I felt that why should my worship be a source of discomfort to other people? ... So I began to use the squash court. During the week, I will play squash there and on Sunday, I turned it into a place of worship. *Then by deciding to worship there, God did something wonderful. God made it possible to actually build a permanent place of worship within the highest seat of government in Nigeria.*[81]

For Christians, having a Christian chapel within the physical space of power was deeply symbolic, and, once it was in place, many key government dignitaries continued to turn up for the daily morning service.[82] After decades of perceived Northern Islamic domination, liberating and reconstructing the presidency and the presidential villa as a Christian bastion against both 'satanic' and invading 'jihadist' (caliphate) forces was seen as a spiritual imperative. Oby Ezekwezili's account (cited earlier) illustrates this thinking vividly:

So, every day at the Villa, it was like, the two-edged swords being in my hands: one to work, doing my policy thing and everything: the other one, to pray. It has to be a blend of both because *Satan had been sitting pretty before. Now, God has dislodged Satan but we needed to clear all the debris that Satan had put in what was his former territory.*[83]

In light of this world view, it is hardly surprising that, at least in a significant number of cases, individuals' denominational affiliation became a factor in their appointment to public office. Again, the testimony of Oby Ezekwezili (who, with her husband,[84] had apparently tried to convert Obasanjo before the latter found God in jail) is telling:

Look at somebody like the Minister of Finance. She is a sister. She is a member of the Everlasting-Arm Parish of the Redeemed Christian Church of God. The parish my husband pastors. She is a sister in Zion. She understands that without God she cannot do anything. She knows that … You think people don't know? They know that what we are it is God that is using the President. The president is a powerful instrument in the hand of God. If it were not for Olusegun Obasanjo, you think the likes of me and … the rest of us[85] … of this world would come anywhere near this government?[86]

Evident from this is a vision of a presidency established by God in order to execute a divine agenda. In this vision, government appointees and their close network of friends, relatives, husbands, wives and sundry spiritual supervisors were, *pace* Ezekwezili above, more divine 'missionaries' than secular office holders. Pentecostal pastors, courted consistently by Obasanjo, were critical to the sustenance of this vision.

Courting the theocratic class

The alliance between religious elites and holders of state power can be beneficial for both sides. On the one hand, 'being a de facto member of the state framework gives senior religious leaders opportunity to amass personal wealth, in just the same way as other leaders of important societal groups … may do'.[87] On the other hand, 'politicians try to associate themselves with charismatic religious leaders, in the hope that spiritual power will be reflected on themselves'.[88] This is a useful template for understanding the close relationship between Obasanjo and members of the theocratic class. For instance, and as we saw earlier with the example of Bishop Francis Wale Oke, Obasanjo entertained several leading Christian figures in Aso Villa multiple times. He also had a direct line to the most influential Pentecostal pastors, including Chris Oyakhilome of Christ Embassy, Matthews Ashimolowo of Kingsway International Christian Centre, Mike Okonkwo of the Redeemed Evangelical Mission, David Oyedepo of the Living

Faith Ministries (aka Winners Chapel), and Taiwo Odukoya of the Fountain of Life Church.

Their relationship had two decisive features. First, members of the theocratic class, acting as public defenders of the Obasanjo presidency, generally assisted in 'dusting off the image of the government as God-fearing and righteous'.[89] Second, and because of their conviction that Obasanjo was installed to break free of the 'Islamic yoke' under which the country (or at least the Southern part of it) had chafed for so long, they saw it as their spiritual responsibility to defend the regime against the perceived antics of Northern politicians. For instance, when Jamaat Nasril al-Islam (Group for the Victory of Islam), an umbrella group for the Nigerian Muslim community, spoke out against what it saw as the bias in federal appointments against Muslims, Christian leaders under the aegis of CAN were quick to dismiss the group's claims as unfounded.

Obasanjo did not fail to reciprocate their support, often turning personal milestones involving the theocratic class into occasions for celebration by the government. To take just one example, when David Oyedepo celebrated his fiftieth birthday in 2004, part of the president's congratulatory message read:

> you have touched millions educationally, you have crowned it with the establishment of Covenant University,[90] economically, you have provided jobs, morally God has used you to recreate moral integrity among millions. Physically, the grace of God has enabled you to provide infrastructure for a ministry related environment. In all these and many more, we give thanks to God for your life.[91]

Obasanjo then implored Oyedepo to:

> Continue to pray for religious tolerance and avoidance of any religious conflicts which might contribute to the delay or derailment of our effort to build a greater Nigeria. Continue to pray

for all three arms of government for divine wisdom to continue
to work together as a team towards Nigeria's greatness.[92]

While Obasanjo was generally close to the Pentecostal elite, his
relationship with Pastor Enoch Adejare Adeboye, General Overseer
of the RCCG, was arguably the most politically consequential.
Both Adeboye and the RCCG have attracted considerable scholarly
attention,[93] and I say more about them in Chapter 5. However, at
this juncture in our analysis, I wish to call attention to two important points. The first is that, inasmuch as the return to democracy
in Nigeria in 1999 also coincided with the inception of a nascent
Christian muscle flexing in politics and public policy, this was due
in large part to the rise of the RCCG under the leadership of Pastor
Adeboye. Sociologically speaking, there was a happy coincidence in
that, just as Nigeria became a more open society in a democratic
era, the RCCG, borne on the wings of a trinity of 'driven leadership, loose global oversight and staggering cash flow',[94] was on
the cusp of a phenomenal transformation that has seen it become
inarguably Nigeria's most economically and politically important
religious institution. To the extent that Pentecostalism has become
the dominant mode of Christian praxis in the country, Adeboye's
RCCG has become the Pentecostal church par excellence, the institutional icon of what Paul Gifford calls an 'enchanted religious
imagination'.[95] A second key point is that, by leveraging his rising
social profile and special relationship with Obasanjo and political
leaders across the country, Adeboye arguably did more than any
other individual to 'sacralise' Nigerian politics (without necessarily
extending its ethical compass), in the process pioneering a model
that, it seems reasonable to suggest, undermines the secular architecture of the Nigerian state.

For the Obasanjo presidency, Adeboye was an early stabilising
influence and source of socio-political strength. When Obasanjo
sought to rally the country in the bitter aftermath of a disputed
election, Adeboye's early support was absolutely crucial. It was

no less vital as the 2003 election loomed, with Obasanjo's public approval at its lowest level. In order to win the hearts of Adeboye's large congregation, Obasanjo did what has since become de rigueur for an increasing number of aspiring and serving office holders in the country, Christian and Muslim alike: he made a political pilgrimage, in this case to the Redemption Camp headquarters of the RCCG on the Lagos–Ibadan Expressway.

Obasanjo's alliance with the theocratic class was successful for most of his presidency; the exception was the tail end of his period in office, when, to the chagrin of the Nigerian public, including his Christian supporters, he sought – and desperately schemed – to stand for an unconstitutional third term of office. While Obasanjo had justified his quest in religious terms, saying that 'I ... believe that God is not a God of abandoned projects. If God has a project, He will not abandon it',[96] significantly, opponents of the 'third-term agenda' framed their opposition using the same register. The following rebuttal by Femi Adesina, a newspaper columnist, was typical of the opposition's language:

> Jesus came on a divine mission. You know how long it took him? Just three-and-a-half years. Was the job fully done by the time it became imperative for him to leave? Not by any means. But was the job abandoned? Not at all. Since he left over 2000 years ago, faithful disciples have continued with the job. Now if Jesus had said, oh, no one else can do the job, it is only me that can. Then it means he would not have gone to the cross, and the work of redemption would not have been accomplished. This is a vital lesson for Obasanjo, who is attempting to turn himself to Nigeria's God.[97]

Eventually, the scheme collapsed as Obasanjo found it difficult to unite the theocratic class, let alone the entire country, behind his third-term ambition.[98]

Sharia politics

Between 1999 and 2007, Nigeria experienced several incidents of religious violence. These included the May and February 2000 riots in Kaduna over the introduction of sharia law, and riots in Aba, Abia State, which were portrayed in the media as reprisals for the Kaduna riots in which an estimated 3,000 people were killed. Further outbreaks of violence, which may or may not have had anything to do with sharia, were also reported in the Northern states of Bauchi, Gombe, Niger, Sokoto, Kano, Borno, Jigawa and Plateau.[99] In November 2002, hundreds were killed in the violent protests that ensued after Isioma Daniel, a *This Day* newspaper columnist, made a joke that was viewed as denigrating the Prophet Muhammad and therefore insulting to Muslims. In 2004 and 2006, deadly religious conflicts broke out between Christians and Muslims in Adamawa and Borno States respectively. These crises were triggered by various local, regional or even transnational factors. However, and unsurprisingly, given the country's history, they tended to be viewed through an ethno-religious lens.

Neither the overall argument of this book nor the specific thrust of this chapter necessitates that these incidents be discussed in detail. Instead, I will focus briefly on what is now known as the 'sharia controversy' because of the light it throws on both the evolution of Islam in Northern Nigeria and the theme of Christian–Muslim rivalry in the country, particularly in the Obasanjo era. In practice, the sharia controversy centres on the mechanics of instituting an Islamic criminal code in religiously heterogeneous communities. Substantively, it refers to the perceived disharmony between the postulates and principles of Islam and those of democratic modernity.[100]

In an analysis that treats Muslim agents in Northern Nigeria with a degree of generosity and sensitivity greater than one normally encounters in the relevant literature, Brandon Kendhammer contends that the sharia project that began in Zamfara in

September 1999 hardly qualifies as 'the opening salvo of an organized political plot'.[101] Kendhammer makes this argument ostensibly in response to claims, especially from Southern supporters of Obasanjo, that the eruption of sharia politics so early in the life of the Obasanjo administration was part of a grand Northern political conspiracy to sabotage it.

I am sympathetic with Kendhammer on this point. Not only does the 'sharia as political blackmail' argument underplay the role of Northern support in making the Obasanjo presidency a reality, it fails to recognise how the project sparked by Sani Ahmed Yerima could be seen, not unreasonably, as the latest iteration in the complicated and contested history of Muslim reformism in Northern Nigeria. In his study of the reformist Izala movement, Ousmane Kane identifies three distinct moments in the evolution of reformist influence in Nigeria up until the early 1990s.[102] The point is not whether Kane's periodisation is valid, but that the reformist impulse is indeed historical, alternately propelled by 'long-simmering popular interest in religious revival, the intellectual appeal of the caliphate model, and the relative popularity of existing sharia institutions'.[103]

Despite the validity of Kendhammer's objection, the point nonetheless remains that the sharia movement did not have to signal a political plot in order to be politically potent or significant. For Southern Christians and other supporters of the new administration, the fact that it started barely four months into the administration, and that, in contrast to the reformist movements of earlier epochs, it was led by the elite (although theoretically in response to *Talakawa*[104] clamour) was enough to raise eyebrows. Second, unlike earlier reformist movements, which seemed to have accepted the restriction of the sharia appeals court to questions of Islamic personal law, the latest wave appeared animated by its intent on legislating 'the wholesale reintroduction of Sharia into the domains of criminal justice, thereby instituting ... a Shariacracy or Sharia-based governance'.[105] Third, it is no less interesting to speculate on the extent to which the success of Pentecostalism, as symbolised by the Obasanjo presidency, was a probable factor in triggering the sharia project, especially when one considers that Pentecostalism appeared to have unified Christians under a single sign, even if only momentarily. This was something that, until then, had seemed impossible despite the institutional umbrella of CAN, and was something that Muslims, for all the fantasy of a united *umma*, had thus far failed to accomplish.

Whatever might have motivated it, the sharia movement was an early critical charge in the early 2000s, and provided Northern Muslims with a political fulcrum throughout the Obasanjo presidency. It also galvanised Pentecostal leaders, many of whom, with the inception of the Fourth Republic, had 'increasingly connected their theological disposition to Nigerian nationalism, linking Obasanjo's national political project with God's divine plan for Nigeria's progress'.[106] From this perspective, the sharia movement was not just an attempt at undermining Obasanjo's reign; it was part of a systematic design by sundry 'spiritual enemies' to upstage 'a leader of destiny at the center of Nigeria's political narrative'.[107] The overall effect of the controversy was poignant – as 'Obasanjo's Christian supporters grew throughout the country, his core Northern Muslim supporters eroded during the sharia crisis'.[108]

Conclusion: Obasanjo, Pentecostal?

In his book, Obasanjo narrates an interesting encounter with one of the members of the Christian prison fellowship who used to visit and share lessons from the Bible during his incarceration in Jos prison. A 'fundamentalist Christian':

> would quote the passage from the Bible where it states, 'Do not be yoked with them.' For him, 'them' were Muslims. The fact that there were no Muslims in the days of Christ did not impress him, neither was the explanation that the passage was

referring to sinners. No Christian, according to him, should have anything to do with a Muslim politically, socially, or economically. My position, which I explained to him, that my only sister is a Muslim because she was married to a Muslim, did not seem to soften his fundamentalist posture. He advised me not to have anything to do with my sister for as long as she was a Muslim. The alternative was for my sister to divorce her husband and cease to be a Muslim. We only agreed to disagree. I have come to realise that there are fundamentalists in every religion, and, in fact, there are fundamental nationalists.[109]

In rejecting scriptural literalism in this way, Obasanjo was being true to the doctrinal pragmatism famously (notoriously?) characteristic of Yoruba spiritual praxis, the same pragmatism that may have been at work in his decision to build a mosque next to a Christian church within the environs of his presidential library.

There is no doubt that, by 1999, Nigerian Christianity was more or less subsumed under the label of Pentecostalism. While, for 'mainstream' Christians, it was deeply satisfying that a Christian Obasanjo was president of the country, for Pentecostals – or more precisely the rump of the Pentecostal elite – Obasanjo's significance partly lay in his symbolism as a vessel of 'liberation' from perceived Northern Muslim hegemony. This does not mean that Obasanjo did not see himself as born-again, or that he shunned public performances that could only possibly be seen in terms of his new Christian identity. Enough evidence has been adduced in this chapter to illustrate that, even when it could not be shown that certain appointments were dictated *exclusively* by religious reasons, the fact that several of his key appointees perceived their roles (and the administration in toto) *in such terms* is telling.

Nevertheless, although the Obasanjo presidency bore the imprint of Pentecostalism, such was his Yoruba cultural pragmatism (illustrated by the prison conversation above) and, more crucially, such are the difficulties and contradictions of grounding religion in politics generally, never mind the absolute imperative of cobbling together a pan-ethnic and pan-religious team in a country as fragmented as Nigeria, that Obasanjo could not afford to follow the path of essentialism. In fact, one doubts whether any Nigerian leader could do so. Hence, although his presidency was Pentecostalist, the state was never in danger of becoming a prototype of 'Christendom'. What could not be disputed was the growing power of the nascent theocratic class, a trend that would continue under Obasanjo's Muslim successor.

Chapter 3

2007–10: A MUSLIM INTERLUDE?

An Òrìṣà follower's stand

Early in April 2010, Nobel laureate Wole Soyinka gave a talk at the Civic Centre on Ozumba Mbadiwe Avenue, Victoria Island, Lagos. Organised by the Nigerian Economic Summit Group, the event took place amid the fog of uncertainty surrounding the health and whereabouts of President Umaru Musa Yar'Adua. However, what made the newspaper headlines the following day was not Soyinka's remarks on the subject of 'Leadership and Followership as Shared Responsibility'; rather, it was his demand, to an aghast audience, that he, in his capacity as an Òrìṣà worshipper (Soyinka has never hidden his admiration for Ogun, the Yoruba god of iron), be allowed to see the ailing president. Referring to media reports the previous week that Muslim and Christian clerics had been invited to Aso Villa to pray for the recovery of President Yar'Adua, Soyinka said: 'There is a kind of insolence going on around the precincts of Aso Rock and, as privileged groups are now allowed to see him, I am going to send an application as a follower of Òrìṣà demanding that Sango worshippers also want to see him now.' Furthermore, and in a clear allusion to the flagrant contradictions in the reports of the two groups of clerics, Soyinka noted, that 'the clerics that have visited him have been very modest in their report. One said he couldn't speak while another said he heard him grumble, but both agreed he could not use his hand.' He then suggested, half in jest, that: 'It is time a committee of Nigerian doctors actually see Yar'Adua and examine that his hand was truly raised and as well examine if the hand can be used properly.'[1]

Two themes from Soyinka's remarks are directly relevant to the analysis in this book. The first concerns the continued marginalisation of Òrìṣà worshippers (or, indeed, non-Christians and non-Muslims, a generic category that also includes humanists and atheists) from the Nigerian public space. For Òrìṣà worshippers specifically, with the ascendance of Pentecostal Christianity, the insult of demonisation has been added to the injury of marginalisation. Soyinka's tongue-in-cheek demand that Òrìṣà worshippers be allowed to see President Yar'Adua was simultaneously an acknowledgement of this marginalisation, an insistence that they be seen as civic equals worthy of the same obligations and privileges, and a reaffirmation of his decades' long pro-humanist campaign for a public sphere that is true to the secular principles supposedly enshrined in the country's constitution.

A second theme arising from the remarks is the monopolisation of access to President Yar'Adua by Muslim and Christian clerics; this is consistent with the overall dominance in political culture of the struggle for primacy between Muslims and Christians in the country. For someone who, by all accounts, was a moderate Muslim (a fact, I would argue, not vitiated by the fact that in 2000, as governor of Katsina State, after initial reluctance he joined several other Northern states in introducing sharia law), it is ironic that the last six months of Yar'Adua's short-lived tenure as president featured all the components of a spiritual drama in which sundry Muslim and Christian clerics and Islamic marabouts played a central and often confusing role. Soyinka's remarks were a direct allusion to this, and especially to the frustration among the general public that the ailing president was being held hostage by his wife, First Lady Turai Yar'Adua, working in cahoots with all manner of shadowy, and not so shadowy, religious agents.

On 23 November 2009, President Umaru Musa Yar'Adua was flown out of the country to the King Faisal Specialist Hospital in Jeddah, Saudi Arabia, after reportedly suffering a massive stroke. From that day onwards, and notwithstanding that he was flown back to the country in February 2010, he more or less ceased to function as president until his passing on 5 May 2010. Effectively, then, Yar'Adua, having been sworn in on 29 May 2007, was in power for just over two years. Because of this short duration, there is relatively little material with which to illustrate the Nigerian historical pattern of Muslim–Christian struggle for power during this period, or the framework postulated in the book concerning the overall Pentecostalisation of politics in the Fourth Republic. As a result, the strategy adopted in this chapter is to focus on three key moments with important implications for understanding the interplay of religion and politics in the Fourth Republic specifically, and in Nigerian history in general. These are: the emergence of the Muslim extremist group, Boko Haram; the constitutional crisis triggered by Yar'Adua's prolonged absence from the country, starting in November 2009 and ending with Goodluck Jonathan's swearing-in as acting president in February 2010; and, finally, and as indicated above, the jostling among religious agents for influence during the ailing president's last three months on earth.

Before moving to these incidents, and in order to afford a full appreciation of the Yar'Adua presidency, a recapitulation of his journey to power is in order.

From Obasanjo to Yar'Adua

As I have demonstrated elsewhere,[2] a sense of how Nigerians feel about Nigerian politicians and political regimes can be derived from the jokes they tell about them. Of the many about Umaru Yar'Adua, the one in which he is compared to a snail is telling. In the joke, a patron walks into a restaurant and orders rice, plantain, and two Yar'Aduas. When the attendant protests that there is no

'Yar'Adua' on the establishment's menu, the man points to a piece of snail meat bobbing around in the pot. The snail was a metaphor for Yar'Adua's seeming personal lethargy (he was also referred to as Baba Go-Slow) and the listlessness of his administration when the joke began to gain currency.

Yar'Adua got off to a rocky start. First, there was the intra-party squabbling over his choice as the presidential candidate of the ruling PDP, followed by the controversy that ensued as the 21 April 2007 presidential and National Assembly polls descended into a spiral of fraud and violence across the country.

Given the provisions in the PDP's constitution regarding the 'rotation' of key political offices, including the presidency,[3] there was little surprise when Obasanjo decided to throw his weight behind a Northern Muslim. What flummoxed many observers was the choice of Yar'Adua himself.[4] Among political pundits and the general public, the expectation was that the president would support one of the more visible PDP governors.[5] Hence, until he was more or less handpicked by Obasanjo, Yar'Adua had flown under the radar. A mild-mannered former chemistry teacher, he had not particularly attracted attention among Northern PDP governors, even though, unlike others, he seemed to have run a largely transparent administration while personally steering clear of financial malfeasance.

Yet, while his personal conduct as governor may have put him beyond reproach, he continued to be dogged by rumours regarding the state of his health. For instance, his opponents pointed out that, as governor of Katsina State, he had been hospitalised for six months in a German hospital in connection with an undisclosed ailment. The rumours gained traction after he was hurriedly flown to Germany in the middle of the presidential campaign to attend to what his spokespeople described, not particularly convincingly, as 'exhaustion' and 'a minor cold'. Nevertheless, Obasanjo remained unstinting in his support.

For many, the real reason why Obasanjo handpicked and stoutly backed Umaru Yar'Adua as his successor was because of his closeness to Umaru's older brother, the late Shehu Musa Yar'Adua, who was Chief of Staff, Supreme Headquarters to Obasanjo between 1976 and 1979 when the latter was military head of state. Both Obasanjo and Shehu Yar'Adua were jailed by a military tribunal in 1995 for allegedly plotting to overthrow Sani Abacha, but Yar'Adua died in prison in December 1997, apparently of poison administered by agents working on behalf of Abacha.[6] For those who held this view, Obasanjo's backing for Umaru Yar'Adua was an expression of his desire to compensate the family. While this is not improbable, it seems more plausible that Obasanjo was in fact motivated by a different sort of emotion – vengeance. Until the Nigerian Senate voted in May 2006 to reject a proposed constitutional amendment, Obasanjo had vigorously, if clandestinely, lobbied to run for an unprecedented third term in office.[7] Given his failure, Obasanjo's surprising support for Umaru Yar'Adua was in all probability dictated by a desire to take his pound of flesh from a political class that – with a few exceptions – valiantly rebuffed his third term overtures.

Having signalled that there was no going back, Obasanjo left no stone unturned in his determination to ensure victory for his candidate. According to political scientist Rotimi Suberu, it was Obasanjo, for instance, who 'set a thuggish tone for the electoral campaign by infamously describing the 2007 elections as a "do-or-die" affair for the PDP', thus adding 'tension to an already-fraught atmosphere that would be marred by about seventy election-related deaths, including political assassinations, in the five months preceding the voting'.[8] And, right on cue:

> The police would brazenly intimidate or detain opposition supporters and candidates, ransack the offices and campaign headquarters of opposition parties, and deny permits for major opposition rallies and meetings. Even independent organizations, including private media and civic organizations, suspected of opposition sympathies would become targets of

police and security-service harassment and intimidation. Nor would police misconduct be the end of it. The EFCC, INEC [Independent National Electoral Commission], and an ad hoc panel of presidential appointees – sometimes acting in defiance of court rulings – began issuing politically motivated corruption indictments in order to disqualify targeted candidates.[9]

Because of Obasanjo's and, ipso facto, the entire security apparatus's perceived partisanship, Yar'Adua commenced his historic tenure as president[10] under a cloud, even though, officially, he had won 70 per cent of the 21 April 2007 ballot, trouncing Muhammadu Buhari of the All Nigeria People's Party (ANPP) and Atiku Abubakar of the Action Congress (AC).[11] But even he was quick to recognise the irate mood in the country and the real credibility deficit he needed to overcome, acknowledging in his inaugural address following his swearing-in 'that our elections had some shortcomings', and urging those with grievances to pursue them through the country's 'well-established legal avenues of redress'.[12]

Although he promised in the same speech to accelerate 'economic and other reforms in a way that makes a concrete and visible difference to ordinary people', and spoke of 'comprehensive plans for mass transportation, especially railroad development',[13] Yar'Adua never came close to matching his soaring rhetoric in practice. Instead, his administration would soon settle into a ponderous routine, made worse by its egregious missteps in the fight against corruption.

In December 2007, Yar'Adua provided further ammunition to those who had accused him of not taking seriously the anti-corruption campaign initiated by his predecessor when he fired the EFCC chairman and ordered him to take a compulsory one-year course at the National Institute for Policy and Strategic Studies in Kuru, near Jos. In addition, Yar'Adua tarnished his personal image with his closeness to former governor of Delta State James Ibori, who reportedly bankrolled his election. In April 2012, Ibori received a 13-year jail sentence for fraud at Southwark crown court in London.[14]

Hence the jokes about snails and go-slows.

The rise of Boko Haram

The emergence of Jama'atu Ahlis-Sunna Lidda'awati wal-Jihad,[15] also popularly known as Boko Haram, predates the Yar'Adua regime. Linguist Paul Newman has challenged the common association of the Hausa term *boko* with the English word 'book' and has insisted instead that *boko* 'is an indigenous Hausa word originally connoting sham, fraud, deceit, or lack of authenticity'.[16] Most accounts trace Boko Haram's hazy origins to 2002, although it did not carry out its first attacks until December 2003 when a small group of militants attacked Nigerian police stations in Kanamma and Geidam in Yobe State, killing several policemen and making away with weapons and cars.[17] Perhaps emboldened by its success, the group carried out further attacks, mostly on police targets, at the beginning of 2004, and again in September and October of the same year,[18] before going into a hiatus apparently devoted to stepping up recruitment and garnering material and financial resources. Abdul Raufu Mustapha described those two years (2003–04) as the 'utopian/insurrectionary phase' in the evolution of the group.[19]

A comprehensive analysis of Boko Haram is beyond the scope of this book, the intellectual vacuum in this respect already being gradually filled by a growing number of important studies.[20] Nevertheless, a brief discussion in this chapter seems warranted for a couple of reasons.

First, it was during Yar'Adua's tenure that, on 26 July 2009, Boko Haram's first full–scale uprising was launched. Various reports put the number of Boko Haram militants and Nigerian security operatives killed in the spate of coordinated attacks on police stations and other government buildings in Bauchi, Borno, Kano and Yobe States at between 800 and 1,000. The police responded by going after the group's spiritual leader and founder, Muhammad Yusuf, capturing and then summarily executing him in Maiduguri in full view of the public.[21] In the estimation of Peter Lewis and Michael Watts, that singular act marked 'a critical turning point for Boko Haram – which adopted a new, more radical leadership – and amplified preexisting animosities toward a secular state seen to have abandoned Islam and the protection of Muslims'.[22]

There seems to be broad sympathy for this view (that a state crackdown led to greater radicalisation) across the literature, but I smell a whiff of circularity. If one of Boko Haram's founding grievances was that the state is corrupt and hence unacceptable to 'true' Muslims, why expect fair treatment of Muslims from that state? At any rate, precisely what kind of reaction was Boko Haram hoping to generate from a state whose police officers and other infrastructure it had consistently targeted? And would the trial of Muhammad Yusuf under the same 'Western' protocols Boko Haram had pointedly renounced be acceptable to the group? While the extrajudicial killing of Yusuf cannot be justified, it should be pointed out that it was Boko Haram that appears to have changed the rules of engagement ab initio with its attacks on state targets. Nor am I denying the plausibility of a situation in which, according to Alexander Thurston, the unlawful execution of Muhammad Yusuf might have 'intensified his successors' sense that the state systematically victimized Muslims'.[23] Thurston, in fact, illustrates how Abubakar Shekau, who took over leadership of Boko Haram following Yusuf's death, was able to promptly 'fit the 2009 crackdown into a larger narrative'.[24] My point is that the arc of evolution of Boko Haram's activities always pointed in the direction of increased radicalisation, whether or not there were state reprisals of dubious legality. This view is substantiated by Mustapha, who shows that Boko Haram may have entered a phase 'marked by doctrinal extremism, recruitment, indoctrination, and the radicalization of its members' right after Yusuf returned from his self-imposed exile in Saudi Arabia in 2005.[25]

Second, a discussion of Boko Haram is directly relevant because, given the focus of this book, it is hard to think of a more precise example of the close alliance of the religious and the political. Whatever one may think of the historical and more immediate socio-economic, political and demographic drivers of Boko Haram,[26] the fact that it is 'draped in the language of Islamic renewal'[27] is hardly disputable. In my approach, I take this religious/ Islamic element as a mere fact; that is, Boko Haram has clear religious motives for its campaign, motives easily discernible from, among other things, its leaders' publicly available theological assertions and remonstrations. But, while the religious aspect of Boko Haram may be clear, it is the political element that is controversial, and therefore of interest. What I mean by the political aspect is the effect of the emergence of Boko Haram on the political framing of the Yar'Adua administration, particularly the manner in which Boko Haram was promptly subsumed within the existing grid of ethno-political contention and mutual suspicion in the country.

This has largely arisen from an attempt to understand not just the meaning of Boko Haram, but, at the same time, the meaning of its mobilisation of violence, which could be quite narrowly targeted in some cases and quite indiscriminate in others.[28] Among scholars, explanations for Boko Haram's emergence and violence vary, ranging from regional demographic growth to social inequality, doctrinal puritanism, the imperviousness of the Nigerian system to calls for reform – and hence the attraction and banality of violence – political grievances, and other international factors.[29] Of these, the 'social inequality' argument seems the most intuitive and hence the most common.

The argument relates to the disparity in economic indicators between the Northern and Southern regions of Nigeria. For example, according to a 2016 World Bank report, while, since 2004, 'the total number of the poor in the south declined by almost 6 million, it increased by almost 7 million in the north'.[30] Generally, '[t]he Muslim heartlands of the north – the dominant seat of political power in the country for half a century – now appear as the most materially deprived region in the federation and singularly accounts, in large degree, to the persistence of high rates of poverty nation-wide'.[31] The same report blames the asymmetry on, inter alia, a 'higher concentration of drivers of poverty reduction in the south',[32] the fact that the Southern zones of the country 'are closer than the northern zones to the realization of the demographic dividend',[33] the fact that 'human capital is greater in the Southern states, where the labour market is more modern and dynamic',[34] and, finally, the fact that '[u]rban residence has a strong impact in reducing the risk of poverty, and the southern zones tend to be more highly urbanized'.[35] All in all, while '[t]he coastal parts of the South West and South South states can be considered middle-income economies … the upper northern states have been experiencing deep poverty, sluggish growth, and limited access to basics services and infrastructure'.[36]

Yet, the argument hardly holds up to close scrutiny. For one thing, and as Thurston argues, 'economic deprivation alone cannot explain why violent movements grow in some places and not others, or why some movements develop particular worldviews'.[37] For another, the 'social inequality' or 'economic deprivation' argument is easily contradicted by experiences from other parts of the world, where radicalisation is almost directly correlated to material comfort. This is not to deny the sociological significance of poverty in the North, and particularly in the north-eastern part of the country. What I am arguing instead is that what Mustapha calls 'the importance of the socio-economic context for understanding Boko Haram'[38] is not obvious and cannot be taken as an unproblematic given. On the contrary, the poverty or inequality thesis begs a number of critical questions. These include the following: if poverty or economic inequality is an inspiration for Boko Haram, why does it rarely feature, if at all, in Boko Haram's founding articles and its leaders' public statements? Given that the so-called 'middle-income' Southern part of the country is not exactly poverty-free, why does poverty in the South not give rise to the same kind of violence carried out by Boko Haram? Why is poverty so concentrated in the Northern part of the country anyway, and might the kind of socio-ideological infrastructure that historically has allowed groups such as Boko Haram to perennially erupt in the Northern part of the country also be an impediment to economic development? And finally, what are we in fact missing by not viewing Boko Haram's violence through the prism of Jihadist principles of martyrdom?

One group that has consistently refused to see Boko Haram as exclusively, or even primarily, driven by economic grievance is CAN. For them, Boko Haram is nothing but the latest iteration of a perceived Northern historical plot, not only to Islamise Nigeria through jihad[39] but also to 'persecute, denigrate and dehumanize' Nigerian Christians in the process.[40] In fact, it was on the basis of this conviction that CAN campaigned to have Boko Haram desig-nated a terrorist organisation. The same reading of Boko Haram's intent also informed the group's opposition to later efforts to nego-tiate. The following statement by Ayo Oritsejafor, who became CAN president in 2010, is illustrative of this sentiment:

> What I know from what some very devout Muslims have told me is that when a Jihad starts, they don't stop. The Jihad has to be completed. They either die or they achieve their goal. And the goal is to Islamize Nigeria. The real war is a war between the ideology of Sharia and the ideology of democracy. This is the war that is going on, and it is a worldwide war.[41]

Whether or not one agrees with CAN's diagnosis of Boko Haram's aims and intentions, what is important is that it makes sense against a backdrop of 'the high level of religious polarization and mistrust between Nigerian Christian and Muslim communities'.[42] Vaughan is aware of this historicity in Nigeria – of radical Islam in the North, and of Christian–Muslim rivalry – when he argues that:

While it is true that this radical group's brutal activities do not represent the myriad role of Muslim groups in Nigerian society, it would be shortsighted to dismiss Boko Haram as an aberration in Muslim Northern Nigeria. Despite the unique context in which it exploded on the Nigerian public scene, *Boko Haram is another example of militant Northern Muslim movements insisting on the radical transformation of the state in Northern Nigeria, going back several centuries.*[43]

From July 2009 onwards, Boko Haram kept up its attacks against various targets, and as the audacity and ferocity of its violence grew, so did its share of the national conversation about the interaction of religion and politics.

A crisis of absence

As discussed earlier, concerns about the health of President Yar'Adua first surfaced before he took office, as soon as it became clear that he was the one 'anointed' by then President Obasanjo as his successor. Although Yar'Adua and his spokespeople sought to reassure doubters (when Yar'Adua became ill in the middle of the campaign, Obasanjo placed a call to him in the presence of a live audience and asked: 'Umaru, are you dead?', to which candidate Yar'Adua responded, 'No, I am alive, your Excellency'), the concerns did not completely go away, with media reports continuing to be dominated by rumours that he had heart and kidney problems. In the event, Yar'Adua's brief tenure was vitiated by his poor health, for which he had to seek medical assistance intermittently.

Things came to a head in 23 November 2009 when Yar'Adua was flown out of the country for urgent medical assistance. However, perhaps not anticipating a lengthy stay outside Nigeria (or perhaps loath to hand over to his deputy, Goodluck Jonathan, as many in the opposition believed), the president did not, as required by the constitution, formally communicate to the National Assembly an intention to be away on medical leave. As time wore on, and as anxiety grew over the state of the president's health, giving rise to all manner of fantastic speculations, the country slowly descended into a constitutional crisis.

At issue was section 145 of the 1999 constitution regarding the proper transfer of power in the event of the temporary absence of the president. The section states:

> Whenever the President transmits to the President of the Senate and the Speaker of the House of Representatives a written declaration that he is proceeding on vacation or that he is otherwise unable to discharge the functions of his office, until he transmits to them a written declaration to the contrary, such functions shall be discharged by the Vice-President as Acting President.

Based on this, two communications were required of the president, one informing the Senate and the speaker of the house of an intention to be temporarily absent, and a second informing them of his return, hence bringing his absence to an end. The main problem with Yar'Adua's departure was that he did not transmit the first (never mind the second), thus throwing the country into confusion. The logical thing to do would have been to send a letter informing the National Assembly of his intention to be absent. But he didn't, his critics supposed, because, either: (1) he was already incapacitated at the time of travel, and hence unable to do so (in which case he should have tendered his resignation); or (2) he was being prevailed upon not to do so by 'a powerful Northern cabal' desperate to ensure that power remained in Northern hands.

Perhaps because of this, while a good portion of the debate that ensued in the popular press about Yar'Adua's health focused on whether or not he was incapacitated, and the constitutional provisions regarding this situation, the political elephant in the room was the second point. Since Yar'Adua was taking the Northern Muslim 'turn' in the presidency, it was obvious that his exit from office for whatever reason would be a political loss for the region – if not, in fact, the religion. Accordingly, the controversy was as much about advancing or protecting ethno-religious claims and interests as it was about constitutional propriety.

This is not to say that ethno-religious and political interests alone were at stake. Broadly, and at least publicly, President Yar'Adua seemed to have three sets of defenders: his wife and First Lady, Turai; members of the Federal Executive Council (FEC), comprising key ministers; and, at least in the beginning, the Arewa Consultative Forum (ACF), a politico-cultural organisation dedicated to the advancement of Northern interests. However, as Olusegun Adeniyi, chief media spokesperson for the president, later wrote, indicating a fluid terrain of clashing personal, political and regional interests:

> What was happening at the time was that there were ministers and other top government officials who were fighting either to retain power and privileges under Yar'Adua or to secure such under Jonathan. On the side of the president were people like the agriculture minister, Dr Abba Ruma, his FCT counterpart, Senator Adamu Aliero and Tanimu, as well as Alhaji Dahiru Mangal (businessman and friend of President Yar'Adua). They needed no one to tell them that with Yar'Adua out, they would also be left out in the cold.

He continued:

> On the other side were mines and steel minister, Mrs Deziani Allison Madueke and her Niger Delta counterpart, Godsday Orubebe, who were fighting to become the new power brokers in the villa, with strong backing from private sector people like Femi Otedola. *What was interesting about these disparate interests was that there was no coordinated group either on the side of Yar'Adua or on the side of Jonathan, but as 'cabals' go, these were*

some of the real vested interests jostling for power at a time when
alliances and counter-alliances were being forged.[44]

The reaction of the ACF was typical of this atmosphere of strategic contingency. From the very beginning, there was no doubt as to what constituted the 'Northern' interest: keeping Yar'Adua as president. The brutal logic of this was affirmed by Mohammed Alhaji Yakubu, who, speaking as youth leader for the Northern Union, argued that the North would continue to back Yar'Adua, even if he was disabled and wheelchair-bound. From this point of view, a physically challenged Northern president was preferable to any non-Northerner, even a capable one, and the ACF, primed to stand up for Northern interests, seemed to toe this line at the beginning. Thus, initially, as anxiety about the health of the president was becoming palpable, the group quickly issued a communiqué after a meeting in Kaduna at which it expressed confidence in a 'fit as a fiddle' Yar'Adua continuing in power. The ACF said:

> While the forum believes that Nigerians have a legitimate right to know what their leaders do with the mandate given them, it regretted that the undue pressure being brought to bear on the President on account of his health alone is unhelpful. Contrary to the insinuations of the critics, the ACF believes that the President is capable and is discharging the duties of his office. The forum urges all Nigerians to remain positive and give the President their total support, cooperation and encouragement in order for him to do more and achieve more.[45]

As Vaughan demonstrates, part of the reason why the ACF had to come out robustly in support of Yar'Adua was because of its legitimate eagerness to preserve its legacy of unifying 'Northern Muslims behind the Sharia' and defending 'Northern state governments' sharia policies against their Southern and Middle Belt Christian adversaries'.[46] For that reason, the ACF threw its weight behind the president.

But even such support could not possibly last, especially given the interplay of what Adeniyi (quoted above) refers to as 'disparate interests'. For one thing, internally, the ACF was susceptible to tensions between its older generation and 'disaffected Muslim youths, who had become increasingly restless since the political and economic crisis of the 1980s'.[47] For another, maintaining a common front was difficult given the ACF's frustration at the lack of information about the president's health, and the way in which his affairs were being managed by his wife and handlers. This much was clear from the statements it issued, initially after it backed a transfer of power to Vice President Goodluck Jonathan, and later after it decided to pledge its support to the acting president. In the first statement, the group directly accused members of the FEC[48] of 'a deliberate attempt to foist falsehood on the Nigerian people' and of aiming to play down 'the reality of President Yar'Adua being either on vacation or incapacitated, considering the obvious fact that the President has been away from his duty post for more than two months now'.[49] On 5 March 2010, nearly a month after Jonathan's swearing-in as acting president, the ACF again lamented 'the fissiparous tendencies that now threaten the Executive Council of the Federation and the National Assembly, but also the entire nation along ethno-religious and regional cleavages'. It also urged 'those charged with the authority and responsibility of managing the health of President Yar'Adua' to be 'forthcoming with information on the true position of Mr. President's health status and physical capacity'.[50]

In any case, and due in no small measure to its change of tune, the ACF could not maintain a common front. For example, in February 2010, following its call for power to be transferred to Goodluck Jonathan, Kano-born Tanko Yakasai, a founding member, announced his resignation, decrying the group's stance on the ailing president as 'not in tandem with the promotion of the unity of the people of the north and protection of their interest' and a deviation 'from its [the ACF's] aims and objectives'.[51]

ACF's complete volte-face was largely consistent with the overall shift in the public mood, which was signalled by a letter of 27 January 2010 to President Yar'Adua by the highly respected Eminent Elders Group (EEG).[52] In the letter, copies of which were delivered to the Senate President David Mark, Speaker of the House of Representatives Dimeji Bankole, and Vice President Goodluck Jonathan, the body urged the president 'to formally issue the necessary communication that will enable the vice president to be Acting President in accordance with section 145 of the 1999 Constitution as soon as possible'.[53]

Evidently, the change in public mood, which culminated in the swearing-in of Goodluck Jonathan as acting president, came about only after concerted pressure had been brought to bear on the National Assembly, the FEC and the PDP by the media and various civic-minded groups. The most visible and arguably the most successful among these groups was the Save Nigeria Group (SNG), led by Pastor Tunde Bakare. SNG signalled an important moment in the politics of the theocratic class in the Fourth Republic, and was a useful illustration of the capacity of religious leaders to mobilise disparate civic groups, even if momentarily, around common interests.

Prophetic politics

In December 2010, *Newswatch* magazine announced its selection of Tunde Bakare as 'Man of the Year'. Describing him as 'a personality who endeared himself to millions of Nigerians in 2010 for good governance and constitutionalism', the Lagos-based publication praised Bakare for what it called 'his show of raw courage and determination to ensure good governance through his campaigns on the streets'. The campaigns in question were the series of 'Enough is Enough' rallies led by SNG, a self-declared 'non-profit political society organisation',[54] which had been convened by Bakare in January and March of the same year. The protests, which took place in Abuja, Lagos, Port

Harcourt, London and New York, were aimed at forcing the hand of the National Assembly to swear in Vice President Goodluck Jonathan as acting president, given the uncertainty surrounding the health and whereabouts of President Umaru Yar'Adua.

As discussed in the previous chapter, Bakare had been thrust into the national limelight in 1999 on the back of his controversial prophecy that Obasanjo was not the messiah that Nigerians were hoping for, and that Obasanjo would get his comeuppance before his swearing-in as president. When the prophecy did not come to pass, Bakare was roundly criticised for lying and sowing disaffection among the general public. However, rather than balk, Bakare stuck to his guns. In February 2002, there were media reports of yet another prophecy shared by Bakare with his congregation in which God apparently reconfirmed to Bakare his original prophecy, throwing in the additional revelation that God had established 'a tender plant from the side of the north aforeprepared before the foundation of the world to steer Nigeria to her prophetic destiny'.[55] When operatives of the State Security Service and the Directorate of Military Intelligence arrested him at the Murtala Muhammed International Airport in Lagos and briefly detained him, this merely boosted his growing reputation as what a national news magazine, *The News*, called an 'activist in cassock'.[56]

By 2010, therefore, Bakare had become one of the most visible Pentecostal pastors in Nigeria. Journalists were drawn to him because he made for excellent copy, and he seems to have maintained his animosity towards Obasanjo and his administration to the present day. For instance, in a 2013 interview with *Punch*, Bakare described Obasanjo as a 'demon' who requires 'exorcism':

> I said Owu as a kingdom had produced angels in human flesh like the late Akin Olugbade, whose generosity and philanthropy benefitted a person like me ... That is why I told them that Owu kingdom has produced angels and demons such as Obasanjo, who incidentally is called *Ebora Owu*. *Ebora* means

demon and demons are to be exorcised. Our job is to cast out demons and that we would do by God's grace.[57]

As recently as 2014, Bakare told an interviewer that Obasanjo 'only wrote to me that he would like me to come and commission his ministry and I turned it down and said: "Thanks a lot."'[58]

It is interesting to speculate on the sources of Bakare's undeniable resentment towards Obasanjo. One possibility is that, not unlike a section of the Yoruba elite (see the discussion in Chapter 2), Bakare has never forgiven Obasanjo for reaping where he did not sow. This specifically refers to the fact that Obasanjo took advantage of the 12 June campaign and became president in Abiola's stead, even though he never supported Abiola, a fellow Egba (both Abiola and Bakare are Gbagura, unlike Obasanjo, who is Owu). Another possibility, implausible as it may sound, is that Bakare genuinely holds Obasanjo responsible for the country's perennial political crisis. As he said in a speech to celebrate his sixtieth birthday in November 2014: 'He who wants to hear, let him hear. I am going to drum what needs to be drummed. I think Obasanjo needs to hear some things before the house collapses on him, because he is responsible for the problems we face now.'[59] Lastly, being politically ambitious himself (which I discuss presently), Bakare probably sees Obasanjo as a legitimate political obstacle to be removed at all costs.

In his political mode, which is often inseparable from the theological, Bakare is a fiery symbol of what theologian Amos Yong has called 'prophetic politics', especially its specific iteration as 'the antithetical political stances often characteristic of pentecostalism's public announcements'.[60] By the time the controversy stoked by Yar'Adua's prolonged absence from the country gathered pace, Bakare was in a prime position to leverage his considerable social capital as someone with strong opinions about the political situation in the country.

In a 10 March 2010 petition to Goodluck Jonathan, who by then had been sworn in as the acting president, SNG described itself as 'a coalition of pro-democracy and human rights organizations and patriotic Nigerians who desire the entrenchment of a truly democratic and accountable governance' and who 'believe in Nigeria and are determined to fight to save the country from the control of groups and individuals that profit from the failure of the Nigerian system'.[61] By this time, Yar'Adua had been flown back into the country under the cover of darkness, hence the petition's demand for 'an end to the invisible Presidency of Yar'Adua by activating Section 144 of the Constitution so that presidential powers will be fully accountable', and 'the dissolution of the present Executive Council of the Federation which has largely collaborated with presidential aides to foist this crisis on the nation'.

Most of the group's truly decisive work had been done in the previous two months when it had managed to coordinate several protest rallies in Nigeria and major Western capitals. A sample of some of the banners displayed by protesters at these rallies is a useful guide to what they believed was at stake: 'Umaru, where are you?', 'What's happening to Yar'Adua? We want to know', 'We must know Umaru's health status', 'Governors are part of the cabal' and 'Enough of offshore president'. Other signs, such as 'Let's kill corruption before it kills us' and 'Constitutional reform now', were proof that the controversy surrounding the health of the president was just the latest manifestation of the political problems that preceded his accession to office, and that SNG had successfully tapped into a real archive of political grievances.

SNG owed its success to a mix of factors: Nigerians' pent-up anger at the state of affairs in the country, and the popularity of a message that linked Yar'Adua's health to the country's socioeconomic crisis; the group's ability to mobilise a wide array of interest groups, both within and outside the country; and the incorporation of civil society activists, writers and opinion leaders with credibility among the people. For instance, among other respected public figures, both Nobel laureate Wole Soyinka and radical Lagos lawyer Femi Falana were closely associated with the group and were in attendance at the group's inaugural march on Abuja on 12 January 2010.

Finally, SNG clearly benefited from the sheer force of Bakare's personal charisma, and his unique ability to ground popular issues in the language of mass spirituality. For instance, in a not atypical 'state of the nation' broadcast on 1 March 2010, instructively titled 'Biblical Answers to our National Dilemma', he alluded to President Yar'Adua being smuggled into the country 'like a thief in the night',[62] warned the president that 'what happened to Dagon when the Philistines hijacked the Ark of the Covenant of God and brought it to Dagon's temple may happen to him',[63] and reminded 'those who might be tinkering with the idea of [a] military solution … that the Jehu revolution that wiped out Jezebel and the sons of Ahab brought greater disaster to Israel than the combined efforts of Ahab and Jezebel'.[64]

In an important sense, his leadership of the group is a vivid demonstration of the new authority of Pentecostal pastors. While, for example, mainstream Christian groups such as the Catholic Church played a leading role in the anti-SAP (structural adjustment programme) campaign of the late 1980s as well as in the ecumenical struggle to reverse the annulment of the 12 June 1993 presidential election,[65] by the late 1990s the country had arrived at a Pentecostal era in which Pentecostal pastors wielded considerable socio-political leverage. I discuss further demonstrations of the scope – and limits – of this leverage in subsequent chapters.

Terminal struggle

Doubtless in response to sustained pressure by SNG and other such groups, Yar'Adua was secretly flown back into the country on the evening of 23 February 2010 without the knowledge of his deputy. He was not seen in public until his death on 5 May. The period between his return to the country and his eventual passing was dominated by a clamour among various groups either for the president's spokespeople and allies to release information about his health, for the ailing president to transfer power to Goodluck Jonathan,[66] or for him to resign. None of these happened until his eventual death, but the intervening period provides a useful example of a struggle for power in which, among other things, the enhanced influence of religious agents in the Fourth Republic was dramatically highlighted.

The first group of clerics to visit the president, then effectively holed up in Aso Villa, on 31 March 2010 comprised prominent Northern Islamic clerics.[67] If the planners of the visit had intended to reassure an increasingly restless public, they achieved the exact opposite. In the first instance, the fact that a few handpicked Muslim clerics had gained access to a president who had not been seen in public since his secret return to the country did not go down well. If anything, it fuelled speculation that the affairs of the country were being handled by a 'powerful Northern clique'. Second, the religious identity of the visitors gave the impression that Muslims were 'in charge', and that the decision not to allow Acting President Jonathan access to someone who, technically speaking, remained his boss had been taken for political and strategic reasons. This suspicion remained, despite Sheikh Musa Pantami's explanation that the clerics had not received an invitation but had sought permission from Yar'Adua's family.[68] In fact, the general sense of intrigue and conspiracy was probably deepened by Ustaz Musa Mohamed's disclosure to his congregation that the president had 'improved considerably' and 'would resume duties soon',[69] which contradicted Ibrahim Datti Ahmed's statement to the media that the president 'was pale', even though 'he was far better than what we had been led to understand'.[70]

Given the outrage provoked by the Muslim clerics' visit to Aso Villa, it was only a matter of time before there was a 'balancing' visit by Christian clerics. This took place on 5 April 2010, reportedly at the instance of Isa Yuguda, Bauchi State governor and Yar'Adua's son-in-law. The delegation included Most Reverend

John Onaiyekan, then president of CAN and Catholic Archbishop of Abuja, David Oyedepo of the Living Faith Church, Reverend Emmanuel Kure, and former Aso Rock chaplain Yusuf Obaje. The General Overseer of the RCCG, Pastor E. A. Adeboye, could not be reached.[71] Quite possibly, Adeboye was out of the country at the time. However, it is instructive that his absence also fell within an established pattern of radio silence in moments of national crisis. For instance, when Obasanjo attempted to change the constitution in order to stand for a third term (see Chapter 2), Pastor Adeboye was conspicuously silent. Again, until the clerics' controversial visit to Aso Rock, he had remained conspicuously silent, even as various Christian leaders weighed in with their views on the situation in the country. In Chapter 5, I discuss this mode of politics in detail.

The Christian clerics' visit generated as much public ire as the Muslims' visit had done, especially after the clerics declined to share details of their visit with the media.[72] Ironically, the most strident condemnation of the visit emanated from factions within CAN itself.[73]

Conclusion

> Whatever the case, power is always the fruit of a confronta-
> tion between rival factions, concealed though this is from the
> observer by the apparently monolithic character of the single
> party or the army. The ways in which these factional struggles
> are fought are many: ministerial reshuffles, coups d'état, polit-
> ical trials or assassinations, meetings of 'elites' in the provinces,
> campaigns of rumours peddled in the 'chantiers', 'maquis' and
> other 'circuits' by 'deuxièmes bureaux', *fetish gatherings* and
> ritual crimes, marriages, business associations.[74]

Shortly before the presidential election of 2007, Umaru Musa Yar'Adua, nominee of the PDP, with his running mate Goodluck Jonathan in tow, paid a widely publicised visit to Pastor Adeboye at the latter's Redemption Camp on the Lagos–Ibadan Expressway, Lagos. Yar'Adua, a Muslim, wanted Adeboye's 'blessing' in the election then approaching. Adeboye obliged, demonstrating his own renown as Nigeria's most politically connected 'Man of God'. Yar'Adua's pilgrimage to the Redemption Camp, undoubtedly the Fourth Republic's political Mecca, is indicative of the all-important rapprochement between politicians and the theocratic class since the return to civil rule in 1999, as well as an illustration of the continued impact of Pentecostalism during Yar'Adua's brief tenure. A further attestation is the leading role played by Pastor Tunde Bakare, a bona fide member of the theocratic class, in SNG's politically momentous mobilisation.

This ascendance has not gone uncontested. For Northern Muslims, the Yar'Adua presidency was a welcome opportunity to peel back some of the competition's gains, a task made all the more urgent by the ACF's perception that it had been handed the short end of the stick throughout the Obasanjo years, when a Yoruba born-again Christian ostensibly 'failed to confer on Northern Muslims the recognition commensurate to their support for him'.[75] In fact, this may have accounted in part for the ACF's initial willingness to back Yar'Adua when concerns over his illness became a cause *célèbre*. Accordingly, the struggle for access to the president, even as he remained sequestered from the general public, was a microcosm of this struggle for power.

Yet, and as would seem appropriate for a paradigm of enchantment, it was not just Muslims and Christians who sought to instrumentalise the disorder ensuing from the uncertainty over Yar'Adua's health. The sense of what, *pace* Bayart (above), might be called a fetish gathering was brought home by media reports that the president's family had also retained the services of Islamic marabouts.[76] As Nobel laureate Wole Soyinka lamented, the only people missing from these gatherings were Òrìṣà worshippers.

Because of the transitory nature of the Yar'Adua administration, we can only speculate on how it might have reacted to the

Boko Haram menace going forward. For example, if Yar'Adua had not been distracted by his personal health challenges, would he have offered the Boko Haram insurgents an amnesty deal similar to the one extended to the Niger Delta militants in 2009? Or, would he have deployed the full force of the Nigerian military against the group, despite the likely political backlash? For the successor administration of Goodluck Jonathan, these were not theoretical questions, and its response to them went a long way in determining its political fortunes, including, as I go on to argue, sealing its fate in the 2015 presidential election.

Chapter 4

2010–15: PENTECOSTALISM RE-ASCENDANT

Introduction: a president, his confidant, and a botched arms deal

On 5 September 2014, a Bombardier Challenger 601 private jet with registration number N808HG landed at Lanseria International Airport, Johannesburg, South Africa, en route from Abuja International Airport, Nigeria. On board were three Nigerian crewmembers and three passengers – two Austrians and an Israeli defence contractor. There were four pieces of luggage in tow, containing nearly $10 million in cash.[1] Upon arrival in Johannesburg, all six crew members and passengers were apprehended and interrogated by suspicious South African customs officials, who, impounding the cash, accused the six men of acting in violation of South African statutes regarding money transfer.

After news of the incident broke in the Nigerian media, most people were curious to know three things: who the Austrian and Israeli nationals on board the private jet were representing; what the large amount of cash was intended for; and who owned the jet in question. They soon got their answers. The passengers were representatives of the Federal Government of Nigeria, and the cash was intended as payment for the supply of arms to the Nigerian government. The private jet was the property of Pastor Oritsejafor, founder and senior pastor of the Warri-based World of Life Bible

Church, and, at the time of the incident, national president of CAN. The disclosures raised other puzzling questions: if the trip was truly for a legitimate government arms purchase, why the secrecy? Why was it necessary to freight such a large amount of cash when a simple wire transfer could have sufficed? Why borrow a private jet belonging to a private citizen for an official transaction – and for such a highly sensitive one, for that matter?

While rumours continued to swirl about the 'real' (i.e. nefarious) aim of the trip, Pastor Oritsejafor was compelled to issue a statement. In it, he denied that the aircraft was a gift from President Jonathan, who had been only 'a guest in our church during the anniversary celebration when the jet was presented to me by members of our congregation'.[2] Pastor Oritsejafor also denied knowledge of or any involvement in the arms deal, although he failed to explain precisely why his private jet had to be pressed into service.

The theme of this chapter is the symbolic return of Pentecostalism to the centre of political power under President Goodluck Jonathan (2010–15). Following the demise of President Yar'Adua in May 2010, Christian leaders, reminiscent of their characterisation of the Obasanjo regime, were quick to drape the administration of his successor, Goodluck Jonathan, in religious symbolism. In return, President Jonathan wore his supposed Christian and Pentecostalist credentials on his sleeve, enthusiastically embracing the clerical and popular narrative of his ascension to the presidency as a supernatural event. Furthermore, Jonathan worked hard to cultivate the leading lights of the theocratic class and would eventually develop a close relationship with many of them.

One of the things Jonathan did to remain in the good graces of the pastors was to regularly send them gifts, including, once, in the case of Pastor Bakare, an apparently unwanted Christmas cow.[3] According to Nasir El-Rufai, in November 2010, President Jonathan also attempted to bribe Pastor Bakare and the leadership of SNG with the sum of $50, 000. The envelope containing the 'transport money' was reportedly conveyed by then Niger Delta minister

Godsday Orubebe and Tony Uranta, Executive Secretary of the Pan-Niger Delta Forum.[4]

Pastor Oritsejafor, who became CAN president in July 2010 shortly after Umaru Yar'Adua's passing, just as Jonathan was finding his bearings as his successor, was gradually drawn into the new president's orbit of friends and confidants. The botched arms deal, involving a private jet registered primarily in the pastor's name, is testimony to the special intimacy that Jonathan shared with the pastor – and, indeed, with the theocratic elite to which Oritsejafor belongs.

The courtship of Jonathan and the Pentecostal elite was mutually pragmatic. With Jonathan's ascendance, Pentecostal leaders could claim that the divine masterplan that had unfolded with Obasanjo in 1999 was now being resurrected after a Muslim interregnum. At the same time, individually and corporately, it gave them the opportunity to employ the kind of social leverage that perceived proximity to power has always afforded. On Jonathan's part, simple political survival dictated that he remain in the good books of the Pentecostal elite, and early on, especially as he sought to extend his political base outside his Ijaw–South South geopolitical region, he must have felt a need to keep on his side the leading lights of an elite that boasted large congregations and deep pockets.

With Obasanjo, the fact that he had served time in jail, had 'miraculously' managed to outlive a military dictator who, by all accounts, was intent on murdering him, and, improbably, had ended up in Aso Rock as the Fourth Republic's inaugural president, was, as shown in Chapter 3, ready-made material for a prison-to-president providential narrative. Unlike Obasanjo, however, Jonathan had no acquaintance with prison and had seen none of the political adversities with which the former president appeared to have been inundated. However, whatever Jonathan lacked in political adversity, he would more than compensate for with his first name, Goodluck, his middle name, Ebele ('God's wish'), his wife's first name, Patience, and other details of his personal biography and political career.

In this chapter, I show how Jonathan went to extraordinary lengths in order to ingratiate himself with the Pentecostal elite and live up to his designation as the 'Chosen One'. Primarily, this involved the staging of political performances intended to keep the powerful pastors and their millions of congregants in a permanent state of seduction. However, given that performances always have their limitations, and the imperatives of the country's geopolitics, Jonathan's efforts at keeping his Pentecostal base happy always had to be balanced with finding a proper response to the well-founded misgivings of the Northern power elite. In the end, and for reasons discussed later, it would seem that Jonathan ultimately lost the trust of both.

Between North and South

Right from the beginning, Jonathan was torn between, on the one hand, keeping the Pentecostal elite and their large constituencies happy, and, on the other, ensuring that a Northern elite that understandably felt politically bereft following the death of Umaru Yar'Adua was pacified. The tension thus created was the unchanging backdrop to the entire Jonathan presidency.

When Yar'Adua took over from Obasanjo in 2007, the tacit understanding among the leaders of the PDP – if not among the Nigerian power elite as a whole – was that, as a 'candidate of the North', he would complete two terms of office. However, having been taken ill and eventually passing away in May 2010, Yar'Adua failed to complete his first term of office. Because he had taken up the North's slot, his death was a political disaster (for the North, that is), and in retrospect Northern concerns about the region's immediate political prospects probably explains Northern leaders' initial desperation to keep Yar'Adua in power, despite credible media reports suggesting that he was permanently incapacitated. In any case, Jonathan had his work cut out in putting the North's political luminaries[5] at ease. More than anything else, he needed to convince them that, beyond seeing out Yar'Adua's first term, he had no desire to consolidate his position in power, a move that would not only effectively kill the North's desire for a quick return to power in 2011, but also upend the more or less established elite consensus on power rotation.

Perhaps driven more by a desire to win their political backing and less by the merits of their reasoning, Jonathan entered into a secret gentleman's agreement with some Northern governors just before the 2011 presidential election. The essence of that agreement was that he would serve just one term of four years (2011–15) and would refrain from seeking a second term in 2015. Early in 2013, as indications increasingly pointed to the possibility of Jonathan running for a second term of office, Mu'azu Babangida Aliyu, governor of Niger State at the time and chair of the Northern States Governors Forum, reminded Jonathan of his pledge and warned him against reneging on it.[6] Although the president promptly denied having entered into any agreement with the Northern governors, he would later admit to it when justifying his decision to back out with the argument that: 'You can make a political promise and change your mind, so long as it is within the law.'[7]

Ultimately, and his most desperate efforts notwithstanding, Jonathan failed to recapture the trust of the Northern power bloc when he needed it most. But that was only at the end. In the beginning, across the religious and political spectra, he managed to win many hearts with his performances as a pious, politically unambitious man of humble origins.[8]

The 'lucky' one

Shortly after President Jonathan took the oath of office on 6 May 2010 to complete the rest of Yar'Adua's tenure, jokes began to circulate across social media about his mode of ascension to the nation's highest office. Almost invariably, the punchline of most of the jokes involved the danger of having someone named 'Goodluck' as your 'assistant', deputy or second in command. The following was typical:

> In your own interest, no matter the position you are offered in any organisation, if your deputy is named Goodluck, please decline. Even if it is UN Secretary General or Head of the African Union, just decline. Why? Check out these facts: Goodluck Jonathan was assistant head boy in his primary school days. The head boy was expelled and Goodluck took over. Goodluck was assistant senior prefect in secondary school. After the senior prefect died, Goodluck took over.[9] Goodluck was deputy local government chairman. The chairman was implicated in corruption allegations and Goodluck took over. Goodluck was deputy governor to Diepreye Alamieyeseigha. He took over after the latter was engulfed in an oil concession corruption scandal. Goodluck was vice president to Umaru Yar'Adua – Pericarditis![10] A friend just called off his wedding because his best man was named Goodluck!

Jokes like this captured genuine public perplexity about Jonathan's unusual 'fast track' to the Nigerian presidency. From the relative obscurity of the deputy governorship of the oil-producing south-eastern state of Bayelsa, Jonathan, a one-time environmental protection officer, had emerged in 2010 as the occupant of the highest office in the land. On his dramatic ascent to the presidency, he had profited from the impeachment of Governor Diepreye Alamieyeseigha in December 2005, and then assumed the reins as Yar'Adua succumbed to illness. Because of this series of fortunate (for Jonathan, that is) events, it quickly became common to read Jonathan's path to power – if not the totality of his personal biography – as proof of divine intervention. In short order, a political mythology would coalesce around the idea of the president as an innocent political outsider who was extremely reluctant to accept the responsibility of being president – who, in fact, had done his utmost to turn down the burden – but who had the presidency thrown in his lap nonetheless.

This mythology was a godsend to many religious leaders, and they were soon stepping over one another in a rush to slap more flesh on its bones. A 13 May 2010 article written by Kaduna-born Father Matthew Hassan Kukah, and published in *The Guardian* newspaper, captures something of the emerging mood. In the article, titled 'The patience of Jonathan', Kukah, then secretary general of the Nigerian Catholic Church, expressed the idea that the then newly sworn-in president was a 'miraculous' figure with an unprecedented pedigree and a unique political mission. In Kukah's view, other than sheer luck, or what he called 'a monumental act of divine epiphany', there was no rational sociological explanation for Jonathan's journey to the summit of political ambition in Nigeria. As he put it: 'This man's rise has defied any logic and anyone who attempts to explain it is tempting the gods.' For Kukah, there is no better demonstration of the divine provenance of the Jonathan presidency than the fact that he still became president even though, apparently, he had:

> never spent any money to purchase a form of [sic] declaring his intention to run for public office in politics. This man does not seem to have been sponsored into politics by any known god-father. Like the rest of us who are considered children of lesser gods, he comes from an insignificant family and a village that hitherto, could not easily be found on the national or state map. He does not seem to have invested heavily to become either Deputy Governor or Governor.[11]

In Kukah's telling – which, it must be said, is consistent with the general sentiment in the first flush of the Jonathan presidency – the president's success owed nothing to any calculable agency on his part, but instead resulted from a series of coincidences. By just being there, Kukah seems to suggest, 'all these events have cascaded on his laps [sic] within a period of a mere 12 years'. In fact, 'Dr Jonathan has done absolutely nothing to warrant what has befallen him. I am sure he can safely say he has neither prayed, lobbied nor worked for what has fallen on his lap'.[12]

At least two readings of Kukah's article are possible. In one sense, and as indicated above, Kukah was merely codifying a sentiment that was already in the public realm regarding Jonathan's extraordinary good luck. As I said earlier, this was a godsend for Christian Pentecostal leaders, especially insofar as it could be presented as 'proof' that unseen forces were actively shaping the country's political fortunes and that the destiny of the Fourth Republic was in God's hands.

At the same time, it is not implausible to surmise that, in portraying Jonathan in this flattering light, Kukah, a native of Zangon Kataf in predominantly Christian Southern Kaduna, was attempting to keep the region and the cause of its ethno-religious minorities on the new president's radar, though whether he needed to locate Jonathan's political trajectory in a realm beyond rational comprehension in order to achieve this aim is a different matter.

In fairness to Kukah, and pursuant to the above, his ardour may have been fired by the realisation that, for a Kaduna Christian, Jonathan's ascension to the presidency had set off arguably the most important 'power shift' in the state's history; this occurred when Patrick Ibrahim Yakowa became the state's first Christian governor after incumbent, Namadi Sambo, was appointed vice president by Goodluck Jonathan. The symbolism of Yakowa's governorship for the state's Christian community can be seen from the homily Kukah delivered at Yakowa's funeral following his tragic death in an air crash in December 2012. Kukah noted:

> From the creation of Kaduna State in 1987, the Northern ruling class, by policy seemed to have erected an invisible sign that read: No Christians Need Apply to enter what would later be called Kashim Ibrahim House or represent the State at the

highest levels. Despite the fact that all states were opened to Christian military officers, it was only Kaduna and perhaps Sokoto states that were never governed by non-Muslims.

This policy of exclusion against non-Muslims turned Kaduna State into a political mecca and laid the foundation for the unnecessary and sad religious tensions that have continued to dog the state. This is why, a routine change like a Deputy Governor taking over from a Governor would generate such ripples across the country. It also has created the climate for the anxiety, fear and suspicion that destroyed the foundations of Christian–Muslims relations.[13]

At any rate, Kukah was by no means the only one involved in the creeping sacralisation of the Jonathan presidency. At the time, the notion that nothing except a combination of luck, coincidence and providence could 'explain' Jonathan's rapid ascendancy to the presidency was broadly popular. Statements such as the following by Orji Uzor Kalu, governor of the eastern state of Abia (1999–2007), were quite common:

> Those who followed consistently the metamorphosis of President Jonathan from a university lecturer to a deputy governor, then governor, vice president and now president, will see a definite pattern – a pattern never witnessed in the annals of the country. The enigma of the man Jonathan does not lie in his meteoric rise to the apogee of the nation's political hierarchy. It lies rather in the hand of God upon his life. Anybody may say or write whatever he likes about him, but one thing nobody can dispute is his manifest covenant with God. It is epitomized succinctly in Jonathan in practical, unambiguous terms. Can anybody tell the difference between Goodluck Jonathan and David the son of Jesse?[14]

Not unlike Kukah, Kalu was in all probability scheming to position himself in an emergent political dispensation under a brand-new president. Also, because there was famously no love lost between himself and former President Olusegun Obasanjo, Kalu did not need any motivation to aggrandise Jonathan as a way of drawing an invidious comparison between Jonathan and Obasanjo. For example, his comparison of the two in another article published a few years later is quite revealing:

> What many people might not have known is that President Jonathan is a totally different person from Obasanjo. While one is brash, extroverted, loud and outlandish, the other is introverted, calm, calculated and collected. This does not mean that the latter is a saint, because there are no living saints. The comparison is only intended to paint a distinct picture of each man in terms of carriage and mien.[15]

Nevertheless, it is not unreasonable to point out that Kalu could very well have drawn that comparison and spoken glowingly about Jonathan without automatically invoking religious symbolism or portraying Jonathan's story as belonging outside the secular course of events – just as Kukah could have done. That Kalu did so is what makes it interesting, and the argument is that his statement is best seen as part of the moment's emerging glorification of Jonathan. While the question of the role 'luck' played in the rise of Jonathan is philosophically interesting, it falls outside the purview of this work.[16] Of direct relevance, however, is how luck was discursively incorporated into a broader religious narrative on the assumed uniqueness of President Jonathan. This, as suggested earlier, was a boon for the Pentecostal elite, if not for the country's Christian constituency as a whole; they could also point to the rise of Jonathan as an example of a 'divine breakthrough'. Nor, significantly, were Jonathan and his immediate circle of advisers loath to promote this discourse or to prime the electorate to perceive Jonathan's presidency in this light.

Bio-politics

Many Nigerians were genuinely thrilled when Jonathan eventually became president. For one thing, the new president seemed the very opposite of the man whose deputy he had once been, and about whom eyebrows were already being raised even before he became ill. The main problem had been Yar'Adua's perceived ponderousness. In contrast, Jonathan was a youngish 53, and many saw his relative youth as a plus. Also, the fact that Jonathan was the holder of a PhD (in zoology) was a dream come true for many Nigerians, who assumed that a well-educated leader[17] would bring greater sophistication to the Nigerian presidency and the administration of the country. Furthermore, many seem to have been taken by the new president because they found the purported 'grass-to-grace' arc of his life (for example, the oft repeated story that Jonathan had grown up without a pair of shoes to his name) truly inspiring.

Shrewdly banking on the political capital accruable from the emerging narrative surrounding his 'good luck', Jonathan and his immediate circle of advisers took careful steps to bolster that narrative. Accordingly, it might be argued that much of Jonathan's self-presentation as president was aimed at embodying this biographical construction. Here he is, for example, on 18 September 2010, while declaring his candidacy for the presidential primaries of the PDP:

> I was not born rich, and in my youth, I never imagined that I would be where I am today, but not once did I ever give up. Not once did I imagine that a child from Otuoke, a small village in the Niger Delta, will one day rise to the position of President of the Federal Republic of Nigeria. *I was raised by my mother and father with just enough money to meet our daily needs. In my early days in school, I had no shoes, no school bags. I carried my books in my hands but never despaired; no car to take me to school but I never despaired. There were days I had only one meal*

*but I never despaired. I walked miles and crossed rivers to school
every day but I never despaired. Didn't have power, didn't have
generators, studied with lanterns but I never despaired.* In spite of
these, I finished secondary school, attended the University of
Port Harcourt, and now hold a doctorate degree. **Fellow Nigerians, if I could make it, you too can make it.**[18]

In the quote above, and as on numerous other occasions throughout
his presidency, Jonathan was giving credence to the story of his
humble origins, and at the same time seeking to extract political
capital from it.

Common inspiration aside, there seems to be a totally different
reason why many Nigerians, especially Pentecostals, were drawn
to Jonathan's 'no shoes, no school bags' story. The reason, I would
argue, is that it meshes seamlessly with the ethos of the prevailing
prosperity gospel, which prizes the heroic achievement of the individual. In so doing, the prosperity gospel discounts power relations,
if not the political in toto, and dislocates the individual believer
from the social matrix within which his or her agency is forged.[19]
In the above excerpt, for instance, President Jonathan, in a line that
would not look out of place in any conventional prosperity gospel
literature, challenges his audience that 'if I could make it, you too
can make it'. With this singular flourish, Jonathan celebrates the
miracle of the heroic all-conquering self-possessing individual, one
who wins against all the odds. Pentecostals might say of such an
individual that they prevailed because they found 'divine favour'.

Bowdlerised or not, Jonathan's biography provided a ringing
endorsement of the principles of the prosperity gospel, and for that
reason he was a firm favourite of the country's leading Pentecostal
pastors. On his part, Jonathan courted them aggressively, giving
them symbolic gratification with his constant displays of open piety
and, when necessary, seeking to induce them with hard cash.[20]

Performing piety

In order to remain in the good books of the leading Pentecostal pastors while at the same time reaching out to their large congregations, President Jonathan sought to bolster the popular narrative that saw him as an especially lucky man whose good fortune was made possible by 'divine favour'. Of a piece with this, and with the same objective, was his self-presentation as a humble and pious man. In his typically ostentatious performances of piety, Jonathan routinely exceeded Obasanjo, whose relative restraint was most probably due to the staid conventions of his Baptist upbringing. For Jonathan, being *seen* to be pious and humble was integral to his overall identity as president, and his presidency was punctuated by several telling moments.

Preparing to take charge of his first FEC meeting as the country's substantive president after Yar'Adua's passing, Jonathan, no doubt conscious of the symbolism of the moment and the intense gaze of the press cameras, removed his trademark fedora hat, clasped his hands, and closed his eyes in prayer. This was a calculated performance of piety and humility, an overture to the Pentecostal constituency signalling that he, as 'one of them', was 'in charge' (behind him, strategically positioned, was the crest of the Federal Republic of Nigeria). At the same time, it was a gesture of ostentatious humility choreographed for the consumption of Nigerians more widely.

Jonathan would often repeat this pose of gratuitous modesty and pornographic piety. For example, as president, Jonathan visited several times with the General Overseer of the RCCG and the symbolic godfather of the theocratic elite, Pastor Enoch Adeboye. On at least two of these occasions, in December 2012 and February 2015 (the latter, as we shall see, was part of a desperate appeal for votes in the approaching presidential election of March 2015), he knelt down before Adeboye, who then prayed for him, his family, and the country. Jonathan's words to Adeboye were: 'I am your sitting president, pray for me so that I will not deviate from the fear of God.'[21]

Another demonstration of Jonathan's desire to be seen as humble and pious took place in October 2013 when he became the first Nigerian head of state to go on a pilgrimage to Jerusalem.[22] At the Wailing Wall, Jonathan knelt down for prayers before Pastor Oritsejafor and other members of the presidential entourage. The special moment was captured by his press corps for distribution to journalists around the country.

The power of moments like these as well-timed demonstrations of Jonathan's humility, piety and, no less importantly, willingness to submit cannot be overemphasised. As previously argued, such performances were directly correlated to his political ambition. Nevertheless, there is a larger logic that must be grasped: integral to Jonathan's performances is a kind of calculated self-abjection, whereby a political actor confesses to his 'ignorance' in matters of governance and humbly asks for God's 'wisdom'. This wilful repudiation of the very basis of his authority (an admission of incapacity, in fact) can be a project of avoidance, the staging of a ruse that subtly extends the ideology of the state, disguises its impunities, and hence furthers its legitimation.

Queer politics

In addition to symbolic gestures such as openly kowtowing to powerful pastors, President Jonathan enacted policies that could easily be construed as being driven by a desire to retain the goodwill of the Pentecostal elite and their congregations. One such move was the signing into law in January 2014 of the Same Sex Marriage (Prohibition) Act of 2013, which criminalises marriage or civil union between people of the same sex and prescribes lengthy jail terms for anyone who either directly violates the law or facilitates the union of two people of the same sex.[23] The latter is defined broadly to include 'a person or group of persons who administers, witnesses, abets or aids the solemnization of a same sex marriage of civil union, or supports the registration, operation and sustenance of gay clubs, societies, organizations, processions or meetings in Nigeria'.[24]

There are good grounds for supposing that the enactment of the legislation was politically motivated. One is the timing. Although Jonathan did not officially declare his intention to run for a second term until November 2014, there were already clear signals at the beginning of the year that he would. As a result, with opposition preparations already at full throttle, and with national elections just over a year away, it seemed like the perfect opportunity for Jonathan to claim the moral high ground, particularly regarding an issue on which public moral revulsion could not be more palpable. Furthermore, by January 2014, Jonathan and the ruling PDP were facing intense pressure as a result of a perceived lack of progress on the economic front. By signing the Same Sex Marriage (Prohibition) Act into law, and hence stirring up intense debate across local and transnational civil society, Jonathan may have hoped to create a temporary diversion from his regime's economic struggles.

If Jonathan's aim was to extract political capital from public revulsion, he could not have chosen a better subject, for in Nigeria's recent history it is difficult to find an issue around which, in the main, a rare alliance of religious leaders, the political elite and print media has coalesced. I say 'in the main' because some qualification is warranted. For instance, it is true that there is a variance between elite and public perceptions of and discourses on homosexuality in Nigeria. For ordinary people, homosexuality is a route, albeit a reprehensible one, to power and its rewards, and, in this respect, it is what 'those in high positions – the cream of the military establishment, the political elite and wealthy businessmen – do'.[25] The fact that politicians invoke homosexuality from time to time as a way of damaging an opponent's reputation is proof that they are conscious of this discourse.[26]

Furthermore, there is considerable variance in regional discourses on homosexuality in Nigeria. As anthropologist Rudolf

Gaudio has observed: 'Many southern Nigerians ... who scoff at the suggestion that there might be men or women in their region who engage in homosexual behavior claim that it's only "those Muslims" up north (as well as decadent Westerners and Arabs) who do that sort of thing.'[27] In this economy of blame, Northern Muslims are hoarders of political power who do not readily acquiesce in its 'sharing' unless one is willing to partake in their quaint ways, meaning homosexual sex and its 'depraved' affiliates. Hence, it seems necessary to underscore that fact that homosexuality is a subtle, if persistent, component of the popular discourse on and understanding of socio-economic and, in particular, political power in the country.

Interestingly, in the North, a similar degree of nebulousness is encountered. On the one hand, Northern Muslims 'are less inclined to deny the existence of homosexuality in their society than they are to gossip about it, usually in disparaging terms'.[28] In fact, 'homosexuality is not seen to be incompatible with heterosexuality, marriage, or parenthood, which constitute strong normative values in Hausa society', and at some point in their lives 'most of the men ... marry women and have children, even as they maintain their more covert identity as men who have sex with men'.[29] Nevertheless – and this is the rub – although the general culture appears to be tolerant of the *yan daudu* (as Hausa men who have sex with other men are called), '[c]onservative religious and political leaders periodically condemn *yan daudu* as purveyors of immorality, and actively encourage the abusive treatment, including arrest, extortion, and physical violence, that *yan daudu* often experience at the hands of police and young hooligans'.[30]

In their condemnation, conservative Islamic leaders thus find common ground with Southern Pentecostals, and in finally signing into a law[31] legislation proscribing same-sex marriage, Jonathan had identified a way to kill two birds with the same stone, politically speaking – handing a sop to a Northern Islamic establishment seething with disaffection, while appeasing Southern Pentecostals whose abhorrence for homosexuality is well documented.[32]

Since Jonathan would ultimately fail in his second-term bid, it is legitimate to ask whether the Same Sex Marriage (Prohibition) Act achieved what it was arguably intended to: that is, unite the country around a common grievance while constructing Jonathan as a model of ethical leadership. What seems beyond doubt is the reaction that was provoked by the passing of the legislation into law. For one thing, if the aim of the law was to keep gay people out of the public gaze, it most definitely backfired. For some individuals, the signing of the Act was the cue they needed to come out of the closet. One example is Kenyan writer Binyavanga Wainaina, who not only came out as gay, but also spoke of his determination to continue to visit Nigeria despite the possibility of arrest and a prolonged jail term.[33] Therefore, by putting homosexuality on the public agenda and increasing homosexuals' public visibility, thereby complicating the link between sex and citizenship, the law arguably achieved the very opposite of what Jonathan and its other proponents presumably wanted. Nor was it homosexuality alone that the law, counterintuitively, helped put on the front burner. As I have argued elsewhere,[34] the deliberative exuberance around homosexuality ultimately set the stage for a questioning of otherwise settled assumptions regarding gender relations, sexual relations, sexual rights and reproduction.

Although the Act did not achieve its short-term political goal for President Jonathan, it remains a reminder of the combined power of religious leaders (Christian Pentecostal as well as Islamic) and offers a narrative woven around the visceral power of religious symbolism.

Politics of insurgency

On Monday 18 June 2012, President Jonathan flew to Brazil to participate in the year's United Nations Earth Summit. There was nothing unusual about the trip, other than the fact that, over the preceding weekend, there had been reports of violent attacks consistent with the activities of Boko Haram in Kaduna and Yobe

States. By the time Jonathan and his entourage boarded the plane for Rio de Janeiro, the air was still thick with uncertainty, with the number of fatalities from the attacks still to be determined. Thus, when news broke that the president had flown out of the country even though he had been briefed about the attacks, he was roundly criticised. The spokesman for the House Representatives, Zakari Mohammed, appeared to capture the mood of a cross-section of Nigerians when he suggested that: 'A trip like that could have been delegated by Mr President so that he can stay at home to take charge of security.'[35]

There is an argument to be made that, while Jonathan was fixated with the forest, he tended to leave individual trees unattended. The trip to Brazil is a perfect encapsulation of this personal tendency. While Jonathan did everything to keep the Pentecostal elite on his side, and while he often went out of his way to court prominent Northern politicians, he was paradoxically remiss when it came to taking action on matters that directly affected the geopolitical interests of either of these constituencies. In so doing, he left himself and his administration open to vehement criticism. The Boko Haram crisis and the political turmoil that followed the abduction of an estimated 276 girls (many of whom were Christians) from the Government Secondary School in Chibok, Borno State, by Boko Haram militants, are illustrative.

The sociology of Boko Haram's emergence has been analysed in Chapter 3. What warrants discussion here is the fact that, for a crisis that predated the Jonathan presidency, the Boko Haram insurgency played such a crucial role in how the Jonathan administration came to be 'framed' and perceived. For, while Jonathan did in fact inherit the insurgency, as he strove to make clear on several occasions, there is little evidence to suggest that he truly apprehended the severity of the situation – despite the fact that in several official speeches he made pointed references to the group and assured the Nigerian public of the Federal Government's determination to wipe it out. All in all, Jonathan sent out conflicting signals about

Boko Haram. On the one hand, he could not wait to see the group eliminated because of its repeated assaults on ordinary citizens. At the same time, he gave a distinct impression of not wanting to hurt members of the group because, as president, he was reluctant to lose the life of a single Nigerian. The following response to a journalist's question about his administration's handling of the insurgency illustrates his indecision:

> Security issues are not issues that we are going to discuss in details [sic]. The issues of dialogue continue to come up. Some people feel that government should not dialogue with terrorists. That is the position of some, particularly in the West. But to us in this country and to me in particular, the Boko Haram members are Nigerians and I don't want to lose the life of one Nigerian. I will love a situation where the Boko Haram people will stop the rubbish that they are doing so that they can be trained in business skills that will enable them to become productive and contribute to our economy ... We want them to change, we want them to become decent citizens; to become top businessmen in this country.[36]

The problem, however, was that 'the rubbish' that 'the Boko Haram people' were doing was grisly,[37] and either Jonathan did not know how to contain it or he was hamstrung by religio-political calculations. One strand of analysis, generous to Jonathan, might suggest that, being a Southern Christian, he dreaded the political consequences of pacifying a group of insurgents who, when all is said and done, organised under the banner of Islam. This probably accounts for his constant references to the insurgents as compatriots who needed to be brought back inside a common civic tent and his general care in distinguishing between them and everyday (Northern) Nigerian Muslims. Another strand of analysis, perhaps not as generous, goes something like this: by letting Boko Haram wreak havoc on the north-eastern part of the country, Jonathan was counting on the security situation in the region deteriorating to the extent of preventing elections taking place there – whereas normally he would count on the antipathy of voters (at the time, Adamawa, Borno and Yobe States were under the control of the opposition APC).

There is a third possibility: that Jonathan held back because he actually believed that 'powerful' Northern interests were behind Boko Haram. There is no evidence to back up this claim, and, apart from widespread rumours, it was only sporadically made by close allies of the president, apparently in order to whip up sympathy for him. For instance, for Pastor Oritsejafor:

> Boko Haram is a terrorist organization. The activities of Boko Haram are not fueled by poverty, but by a religious fundamentalist ideology. *Boko Haram is being funded from within by people who desire to use them to create political space for themselves* and funded from without by those who want to see Nigeria divided along religious-ethnic lines.[38]

While the first explanation sounds plausible and the second sounds like a conspiracy theory, the overall effect is that the Boko Haram insurgency left Jonathan trapped between a rock and a hard place. He could not go after the insurgents due to his fear of stepping on the toes of Northern Muslims who might have a glimmer of sympathy for them. Nor could he afford not to, for that would expose him to attacks by Christian leaders, many of whom had been left fuming by Boko Haram's attacks on churches and killings of Christians, and by Jonathan's failure to deal with the situation.

Proof that Jonathan may have failed in his balancing act and exhausted Christians' patience came in August 2012 when the Northern CAN issued a press release calling on him to resign. Citing a statement credited to Jonathan that he could not crush Boko Haram because '[t]hey are our siblings and you cannot set the army to wipe out your family', the association accused the president of having failed Christians and Nigerians, and wondered whether

'Christians are not members of this family he is talking about'.[39] Although the release was later challenged by other Christian leaders, including a former secretary of the Kaduna State CAN, Reverend Joseph Hayab,[40] it was clear that, among Northern Christians especially, frustration with Jonathan was growing. In any case, as time went on, it was not Christians alone who were calling for the president's head, as Muslim leaders such as Sheikh Ahmad Abubakar Mahmud Gumi, son of the late Sheikh Abubakar Gumi, soon joined calls for Jonathan's resignation.[41]

News of a kidnapping

On the night of 14–15 April 2014, Boko Haram militants stormed the students' hostel at the Government Secondary School in Chibok, Borno State, in north-eastern Nigeria, and abducted an estimated 276 girls. In retrospect, this particular incident was a turning point in the Jonathan presidency. Until that moment, Jonathan had been able to count on lingering sympathy among those who genuinely believed that, in Boko Haram, he was faced with a politically intractable crisis, and among others who believed that the insurgency itself was the handiwork of unnamed 'political enemies', but his handling of the fallout from the Chibok schoolgirls' kidnapping massively depleted the ranks of his supporters.

Everything that could have gone wrong politically for Jonathan with regard to the incident did go wrong – and much of it was self-inflicted. For at least two weeks after the mass kidnapping, President Jonathan and members of his immediate circle stuck to their improbable story that reports of the attack had been concocted by the opposition in order to denigrate the Jonathan administration.[42] In addition, even after the Obama administration decided to share satellite imagery from US surveillance drones showing the militants setting up temporary camps and moving through isolated villages,[43] the Nigerian government's response did not match the severity of the situation in terms of the urgency required.

Jonathan's handling of the Chibok affair will most likely be remembered for the same mix of sporadic illumination and utter bewilderment that had long been the hallmark of his approach to the Boko Haram insurgency. For example, in early May 2014, the president sent a signal of his administration's readiness to liberate the schoolgirls from their captors when he boasted that: 'I believe that the kidnap of these girls will be the beginning of the end of terror in Nigeria.'[44] Yet, two months later, at a meeting in Abuja with the young Pakistani activist Malala Yousafzai, Jonathan seemed to waver on his earlier determination with his statement that 'terror is relatively new here and dealing with it has its challenges'.[45] Nor did his wife and First Lady, Dame Patience Jonathan, help matters. On 3 May 2014, having summoned to Abuja the Borno State Police Commissioner, the Divisional Police Officer for Chibok, the Borno State Commissioner for Education, and the school principal, among others, she conducted a macabre 'investigation' during which she broke down in tears on national television.[46]

Part of the problem for President Jonathan, and a nagging source of exasperation for many Nigerians as well, was that, while all this was going on, Abubakar Shekau, the leader of Boko Haram and mastermind of the kidnappings, continued to taunt the Nigerian government and the abducted schoolgirls' parents. In one video, for example, he boasted: 'I abducted your girls. I will sell them in the market, by Allah … There is a market for selling humans. Allah says I should sell. He commands me to sell. I will sell women. I sell women.'[47]

Intended or not, Shekau's boast about the kidnapping being licensed by Allah had the effect of foregrounding a barely subsumed religious dimension to the crisis. While, initially, the religious identity of most of the abducted schoolgirls did not explicitly feature in media commentary, as time went on, and as the frustration of the schoolgirls' parents mounted following reports that many of them had been forced into sexual slavery,[48] their identity as Christians became a focus of attention. For parents of the kidnapped schoolgirls and for Northern Christian opinion leaders, the cavalier attitude of the Jonathan government was consistent with the historically discriminatory treatment of minority Christian communities across Northern Nigeria.

The impression that the attack on the school might have been carried out for religious reasons was further strengthened when CAN released the names of 165 Christian girls (compared with 15 Muslim girls) reportedly abducted by Boko Haram. In a 3 May 2014 statement signed by Evangelist Matthew Owojaiye (president and founder of Old Time Revival Hour, Kaduna, and one-time chairman of the Northern States Christian and Elders Forum, a CAN affiliate), CAN pointed out that 'Chibok Local Government is 90 percent Christian' and the 'majority of the girls abducted are Christian', and wondered why the militants did not attack 'other Local Government Girls Secondary Schools in Borno State'.[49] Urging 'every Christian home' in the country to 'raise a lamentation to heaven daily', the association also demanded that the Federal Government pay 'a N50m damage [sic] as trauma compensation to each girl' and 'take each girl to an overseas university on government scholarship by September 2014'.[50]

CAN's statement was proof, if any were needed, that Jonathan had lost considerable ground among his Christian supporters, many of whom had initially warmed to him because of his apparently sincere religiosity and down-to-earth humility. They did not necessarily believe that he had abandoned these personal virtues, but it was becoming increasingly difficult to defend – never mind stand behind – a president who could not be counted on to protect fellow Christians, including defenceless women and children, from the attacks of Islamist radicals.

Conclusion: a lesson in performance

After a brief honeymoon period in which he was the darling of a cross-section of Nigerians, President Goodluck Jonathan gradually frittered away his considerable political capital. As the PDP candidate in the April 2011 presidential election, he had won 23 states in total, including 16 out of the 17 Southern states, seven Northern states (Kwara, Kogi, Nasarawa, Benue, Plateau, Adamawa and Taraba) and the Federal Capital Territory, Abuja. Although he won 31 per cent of the vote in 32 states, thereby outperforming the constitutional requirement for at least 25 per cent of the vote in at least 24 states, he fell short in Bauchi, Borno, Kano and Yobe States. Still, for someone who had to deal with a Northern political elite who mistrusted his designs on power, and whose opponent, the Congress for Progressive Change's (CPC) Muhammadu Buhari, captured only 12 states, all of them in the North, this was as close as he could possibly get to securing a broad national mandate.

Yet, for a variety of reasons, Jonathan failed in his attempts to balance his romance with the Pentecostal elite with his wooing of the Northern political establishment. While, initially, many Nigerians were won over by his gratuitous displays of piety and humility, eventually even they would lose patience with him. His refusal to publicly declare his assets, as well as his decision to pardon his one-time boss, Diepreye Alamieyeseigha, convicted of embezzling millions of dollars, must have cost him a few friends. *The Economist* captured something of the popular frustration with President Jonathan when it described him in a biting editorial as 'an ineffectual buffoon'.[51] Over time, the trope of a total outsider who merely 'lucked' his way to the nation's highest office would wear thin, as Jonathan showed himself more than capable of the scheming and gamesmanship that he had tried to distance himself from at the start, and in opposition to which he had struggled to construct a political persona. Yet, for all that scheming, he was neither able to mine Nigeria's religious divisions successfully nor mobilise the country's almost limitless presidential power to construct a winning coalition.

As his mask slipped, he turned in desperation to the same Pentecostal elite that he had always struggled to keep on his side, not only for their social influence, but also as the most direct route to their vast congregations. How he went about it, and why he eventually failed, is what I now turn to.

Chapter 5

ELECTORAL THEOLOGIES

Introduction: a royal blessing

As would seem appropriate, arguably the defining image of the March 2015 presidential election campaign has President Goodluck Jonathan at the centre of a spiritual performance. I am alluding to the picture taken on 7 March 2015, at the palace of the Ooni of Ife, the late Oba Okunade Sijuwade. In the picture, Jonathan, swaddled in a grey Yoruba *agbada*, is perched on a low stool, hands clasped together in prayer. He is surrounded by a gaggle of Yoruba Obas and other high-ranking chiefs who collectively point their staffs of office towards him. While the idea of sitting down for a royal blessing was reportedly the late Ooni's, the act is consistent with the pose of extravagant humility that Jonathan had always seemed liable to contrive.

The image generated mixed reactions among the Nigerian public. It most certainly did not go down well with Jonathan's friends in the Pentecostal community, not least because of their well-documented aversion towards all things 'traditional', which are regarded as 'demonic'.[1] For members of this community, Jonathan had gone rogue by his evident willingness to 'submit' to such spiritually dubious 'powers' and 'principalities' as traditional rulers. Other Nigerians took umbrage at what they saw as Jonathan's desperation, denoted by his obvious willingness to throw himself at anyone who might help him in his bid to retain power. At the same time, there were others who expressed doubt that what Jonathan was getting from the Obas was genuine blessing, something that apparently could only be conferred through an Oba's *irukere* (horse whisk) as opposed to the staff of office or walking stick, which is thought to be reserved for more sinister purposes.

As the 2015 presidential election approached, Jonathan had redoubled his overtures to different segments of Nigerian society. After the election originally scheduled for 14 February was moved to 28 March, he used the intervening period to ratchet up his election-eering. While, throughout 2014, he had looked quite formidable, as 2015 drew to a close, and bad news poured in from all directions, he saw his electoral prospects fading. As he dwindled in popularity, so his desperation mounted; and as his desperation mounted, so, reported-ly, did his eagerness to splash the cash to keep his old coalition together.[2] The March 2015 visit to the palace of the Ooni of Ife, one of many undertaken by Jonathan in a desperate bid to reach out to poles of authority across the country, and, through them, to their publics,[3] was emblematic of the dire straits in which he found himself.

This chapter focuses on the March 2015 presidential election, which is symbolic for having marked an important breakthrough in Nigeria's political history – the peaceful transfer of power from an incumbent to his challenger from an opposing party. The election is also notable for marking the transfer of political power from a Southern Christian to a Northern Muslim. Against this backdrop, the analysis here navigates around three crucial themes: (1) the role of religion and sundry spiritual agents in the election, won by the All-Progressives Congress (APC) presidential candidate, Muhammadu Buhari; (2) the role of religion and religio-political calculations in Buhari's selection of his running mate and public appreciation of the two contrasting tickets; and (3) the specific role of Pentecostal pastors. In focusing on the latter especially, we are afforded the opportunity of examining agents who, on the one hand, are implicated in driving a particular narrative about power in the Nigerian Fourth Republic, but who, at the same time, are driven – if not divided – by varying corporate and personal calculations.

Religion talk

As the 2015 election loomed, supporters of President Goodluck Jonathan – or, more precisely, opponents of the APC candidate, General Muhammadu Buhari – circulated an old interview of his with the popular BBC programme HARDtalk.[4] In the interview, conducted in 2004, nine months after the conclusion of the 2003 presidential election that he contested and lost as the presidential candidate of the ANPP, Buhari is seen ostensibly defending his record as a military dictator and showing no remorse for the fact that he had put the media through the wringer with his infamous Decree No. 4 of 1984, which severely limited press freedom. As the election approached, Buhari's popularity had surged, driven mostly, but not exclusively, by the perception that he was the kind of morally disciplined leader who could effectively take over the reins of power from a slovenly incumbent. In circulating the video, Buhari's political opponents aimed to check his surge in popularity by reminding Nigerians of the horrors he had perpetrated the last time he was entrusted with power.

But this was by no means the biggest challenge confronting Buhari. In addition to questions about his political pedigree, his religious credentials also came under close scrutiny. Given the prevailing mood in the country, 2015 was not a good time for anyone – let alone a serious aspirant to the nation's highest office – to be accused of siding with Islamic fundamentalists or taking a hard line on religious matters. Yet, this is precisely what Buhari's opponents accused him of, tendering as proof various statements he was reported to have made in the past. For example: 'I will continue to show openly and inside me total commitment to the Sharia movement that sweeping all over Nigeria [sic]. God willing, I will not stop the agitation for the total implementation of Sharia in the country.'[5] Or: 'Muslims should vote for fellow Muslims who can defend their faith.'[6] Unsurprisingly, Buhari promptly denied ever having made such statements.

There is an important irony here. Just as, before the election, the allegation against Buhari was that he was too religiously conservative, once he became president-elect, the frustration of sworn religious conservatives was that he was not conservative enough. For instance, when, on Friday 15 May 2015, as a guest at the wedding ceremony of then Edo State governor Adams Oshiomhole, Buhari was caught on camera shaking hands with the bride, Lara Oshiomhole, he was denounced by religious conservatives as 'un-Islamic'.[7]

With the struggle for power intensifying in the dying embers of the Jonathan administration, and both sides attempting to undercut the candidacy of the other, religion became weaponised. The foregoing provides an illustration of the extent to which they went, while simultaneously invoking religious sentiments. While the personal attacks launched at each other by both candidates were especially virulent, it was nonetheless understandable given what was at stake. For Buhari, who was taking his fourth shot at the presidency (having run unsuccessfully in 2003, 2007 and 2011), it seemed highly improbable that he would ever run again if he lost.[8] Even so, this was hardly just about Buhari's personal ambition. In geopolitical terms, what was embodied by the 2015 presidential election was the perennial North–South struggle for power. On one side of the equation, there was the possibility that, in President Buhari, the largely Muslim North would be getting back what it had lost with Umaru Yar'Adua's demise in 2010. On the other, if Jonathan rode the power of incumbency to victory, as many initially thought he might, the largely Christian South stood to enjoy another four years in the saddle. This was the larger political imperative pushing an embattled incumbent and his beleaguered opponent as they jostled to mobilise symbolic and actual capital.

Acts of faith

Doubtless, both candidates were also responding to a sociological fact – the rise of Pentecostalism as a political force since the dawn of the Fourth Republic in 1999. As shown in Chapter 4, that reali-sation was arguably the driving force behind President Jonathan's crude ingratiation with the leading Pentecostal pastors, and much of his ostentatious performances as president.

Buhari, in contrast, seems to have come to that realisation late in the day, at least if his choice of running mates during his first two presidential campaigns is anything to go by. In both 2003 and 2007, with his choice of Chuba Okadigbo and Edwin Ume-Ezeoke respectively (incidentally, both came from Anambra State), he seems to have calculated that the most promising route to the presidency lay in an alliance with the Igbo political class. Having lost badly on both occasions (by at least 12 million votes in 2003 and more than 18 million votes in 2007), he changed tack in 2011 when he opted for Pastor Tunde Bakare, founder and overseer of the Lagos-based Latter Rain Assembly. Bakare represented a change of direction in an ethno-regional sense, allowing Buhari to appeal to a Yoruba ruling class mostly influenced by Asiwaju Bola Ahmed Tinubu, former governor of Lagos State and the very definition of a secular Muslim. But Bakare symbolised a change of direction in arguably a more important religious sense. As one of the conveners of SNG, he had gradually established a niche as one of the country's most outspoken activist pastors, and Buhari's selection of him as his running mate was in part an acknowledgement of his rising status as a man of the cloth with a progressive political vision.[9] Beyond the individual, tapping Bakare was also, logically, an acknowledgement of the growing influ-ence of the pastoral class to which Bakare belongs.

Although the Buhari–Bakare ticket lost at the ballot (Goodluck Jonathan and his running mate Namadi Sambo eventually won by more than 10 million votes), it did not make Buhari repent of his conviction that the path to Aso Rock was through an alliance with the influential Pentecostal elite, largely Yoruba, and dynamically connected to the traditional power elite. The issue, it would then seem, was not to jettison the choice of a pastor, but to find the right one.

In retrospect, Bakare may have been the wrong choice for various reasons. First, although he was a co-convener of SNG and can rightfully claim plaudits for forcing the hand of a dithering National Assembly in swearing in Goodluck Jonathan as acting president in February 2010, history – in Nigeria as elsewhere – shows that such associations, forged in the heat of the political moment, do not necessarily last, and are hardly ever converted into long-term political movements or goals. Instructively, the reaction of SNG to the choice of Bakare as Buhari's running mate was to disown him on the grounds that the group had not been informed.[10]

Besides, despite his influence and visibility, Bakare could not automatically count on the support and loyalty of fellow Pentecostals, let alone Yoruba voters in general. For one thing, he does not command the kind of cachet normally associated with, say, Pastor Adeboye, the doyen of the Pentecostal class, and someone with whom he has not always had the most cordial of relationships.[11] Nor, crucially, did he have the support of Bola Tinubu, the wily Yoruba power broker who decided at the last minute to throw in his lot with the incumbent, Goodluck Jonathan.[12] Lastly, and as noted above (and discussed later), the fact that Bakare is a well-known Pentecostal pastor still begs the broader question of whether there is indeed a Pentecostal vote to be captured.

None of this is meant to suggest that Buhari's choice of a running mate for the 2015 election was straightforward. The range of candidates that Buhari reportedly considered[13] before eventually deciding to go with Yemi Osinbajo, former Lagos State attorney general and a leading pastor of the RCCG, speaks to the difficulty of arriving at the most suitable candidate.

By all accounts, Buhari's original preference was Bola Tinubu, a choice probably recommended by his status as one of the most important political kingmakers in Yorubaland, if not Nigeria, since the inception of the Fourth Republic. If Tinubu himself is to be believed, Buhari had already decided to select him, before being prevailed upon by both Nasir El-Rufai (former Minister of the Federal Capital Territory under Obasanjo, now governor of Kaduna State) and Bukola Saraki (former governor of Kwara State (2003–11), now President of the Senate) – allegedly because the former in particular was backing Tunde Bakare for the same position.[14] While it is indeed possible that Buhari wanted Tinubu as his running mate, since this would have been his surest guarantee of 'locking in' the Yoruba vote, he may have been forced to rescind the decision for reasons other than El-Rufai's and Saraki's dissuasion. For one thing, a Buhari–Tinubu ticket would have meant a Muslim–Muslim ticket, and while there is no reason to believe that it would not have worked (after all, it famously did with Abiola and Kingibe in 1993), it would have played straight into the hands of opponents who had already labelled Buhari an incurable Islamic hardliner. Accordingly, not only did Buhari need to dispel concerns about his purported religious conservatism, he needed to shore up his candidacy with a ballast that only a Southern Christian, ideally a Pentecostal, could provide.

Buhari might have considered Tinubu too politically risky, but he still realised that he could not do without him – or his vast political network and folkloric political sagacity. Hence, it was to Tinubu that Buhari would turn in asking for three nominations from which Buhari would pick one. Tinubu forwarded only one name: his one-time attorney general and Commissioner of Justice, Yemi Osinbajo.[15] For Tinubu, having a political associate a heartbeat away from the presidency was the next best thing to being there himself.

For Buhari, though, Osinbajo was acceptable for other reasons. First, as a senior pastor of an RCCG parish, Olive Tree House of Prayer for All Nations in upscale Banana Island, Lagos, he met the Pentecostal criterion, and to the extent that it makes sense to speak of a 'Redeemed' vote (separate from the larger Pentecostal vote), he seemed, at least on paper, the best way to access it. (As we shall see presently, this was hardly a straightforward matter.) Furthermore, Osinbajo's image (even among non-Christians) as being generally above board was a plus.[16] Third, at 58, he had a certain youthful quality, and a connection with young people that Buhari, at 72, seemed to lack. Evidence of the goodwill that Osinbajo enjoyed with members of the younger generation could be seen in the fervent support given to his candidacy by Generational Voices, a non-partisan pan-Nigerian movement of individuals (mostly professionals) between the ages of 18 and 40.[17] Finally, it did not hurt that his wife 'Dolapo is the granddaughter of the late Obafemi Awolowo, the revered Yoruba philosopher and statesman.

Compared with Buhari, who needed to build new alliances within the Pentecostal community, all that Jonathan had to do was continue to service the relationships he already had. Buhari's choice of Osinbajo as his running mate made Jonathan's need to remain in the good graces of the Pentecostal community imperative. It meant, first, that he could no longer take the solidarity of that community for granted. Second, with Osinbajo now at his side, charges of Islamic fanaticism against Buhari became less plausible. Proof that Buhari's choice of Osinbajo may have had the desired effect came in January 2015, when, during a secret meeting in Abuja with a group of Pentecostal pastors, Jonathan agonised that 'Osinbajo is my problem'.[18]

Therefore, between January and February 2015, in order to strengthen what he saw as his loosening grip on the Pentecostal vote, Jonathan embarked on a series of 'courtesy visits' to Pentecostal churches, primarily along the Lagos–Ibadan axis, but also in other parts of the country. Before embarking on the visits, he had based his decision on the need to 'go round and continue to appreciate what our brothers and sisters have been doing', promising that 'from now onward, until I leave the State House, every last Sunday of the month, I will go to different churches'.[19] To make good his word, he visited, among others, the RCCG, Lagos–Ibadan Expressway; Winners Chapel in Ota, Ogun State, where Bishop Oyedepo reportedly assured him that '[w]e will open the gate of hell on those who oppose you';[20] the RCCG, Olive Tree Parish, Ikoyi, Lagos; and the Dunamis International Gospel Centre, Abuja.

President Jonathan also attended a meeting on Monday 12 January 2015 at Obasanjo's Presidential Hilltop Estate in Abeokuta, Ogun State, at which both Pastor Adeboye and Bishop Oyedepo were in attendance.[21]

Such was Jonathan's desperation to remain in good standing with the leading Pentecostal pastors that, in September 2014, after a guesthouse collapsed within the premises of the Synagogue Church of All Nations, Lagos, killing at least 115 people, mostly South African nationals, President Jonathan was among the first group of political dignitaries to visit and 'express my personal condolences to Prophet Joshua, the Synagogue of All Nations and of course the bereaved families'.[22] Instructively, President Jonathan's visit came days after the incident, when its cause had yet to be fully established, and amid growing calls for the criminal prosecution of Pastor T. B. Joshua for having deliberately misled the public.[23]

The tour of churches was merely one element of Jonathan's political strategy;[24] he also tried everything possible to cut into Buhari's perceived overwhelming support among Muslims. (I should point out one of the paradoxes of ethno-regional politics in Nigeria: while Buhari could more or less take the support of Northern Muslims for granted, Jonathan could not afford to do the same with the electorate in the South.) His success in this regard was limited. For instance, early in March 2015, Aso Rock aides attempted to initiate a conversation between President Jonathan and Moroccan monarch King Mohammed VI. Over the years, diplomatic relations between Nigeria and Morocco have been frosty because of the former's support for the Polisario Front in its efforts to create the Sahrawi Arab Democratic Front in Western Sahara. Since 1975, Morocco has claimed the territory as its own. Reaching out to the Moroccan monarch was a last-ditch attempt by Jonathan to curry favour with the influential King Mohammed VI, and ipso facto, with Northern Nigerian Muslims. But the move was rebuffed by the Moroccan Ministry of Foreign Affairs, which 'deemed it inappropriate on grounds of the upcoming elections in Nigeria'.[25]

Game of robes

All this had the effect of underscoring the political clout of the Pentecostal elite, and, as the 2015 election approached, all eyes were on them as influential power brokers who controlled congregations running into hundreds of thousands, exercised symbolic authority over millions more, and boasted financial wealth in the billions of dollars. In 2015, five of the ten richest pastors in the world were Nigerians.[26] Understandably, many of the most influential pastors felt morally obligated to President Jonathan. Not only had he gone out of his way to woo them, as already shown; there were also unconfirmed reports that many of them had received financial inducement for their support. For instance, in the run-up to the election, several news sources in the country published reports alleging that the president had made a large donation (up to $30 million, according to some accounts) to the Ayo Oritsejafor-led CAN. Presumably, the money was meant to buy the loyalty of CAN's top echelon.[27]

Ultimately, no financial largesse was enough to guarantee the political allegiance of either CAN or the Pentecostal elite to one candidate. In this regard, the 2015 presidential election confirms that, while, in formal terms, Pentecostal pastors or religious leaders may constitute a class, that does not mean that they are politically or ideologically homogeneous. Accordingly, while some pastors refused to show their hand, at least in the initial stages, others came out very early in support of their preferred candidate. The point to keep in mind is that, in nearly all cases, pastors' political preferences seem to have been determined not by some vague national interest or even by denominational loyalty (not that these can be ruled out completely) but by a mix of corporate (not excluding financial) interests, location, personal relationships, and complicated projections and permutations regarding which of the two candidates would best assure that they benefited in the post-election period.

Among the leading pastors, only Sunday Adelaja, founder and senior pastor of the Ukraine-based Embassy of God openly – and consistently – backed General Buhari. As Adelaja himself told me in an interview conducted via email, in backing Buhari, he was answering to his 'logic and mind', which made it difficult for him to support an administration that 'squandered the economy and the treasury of our country'.[28] While the integrity of his position should be respected, it is not unreasonable to surmise that the fact that he resides outside the country may have made his decision to declare his hand early in the campaign process easier.

Compared with Pastor Adelaja, the home-based pastors enjoyed no such luxury. As discussed above, many of them were already cosy with President Jonathan, and more than a few of them had welcomed him as a special visitor to their churches, sometimes on more than one occasion. They also appear to have been constrained (but only to some extent) by the fact that Buhari's running mate, Yemi Osinbajo, a leading member of the RCCG and a pastor in his own right, was one of the tribe.

But there was real division among the leading pastors that not even Osinbajo's identity as a pastor himself was able to conceal, and it finally burst open in late January 2015 when, following a secret meeting held at the RCCG camp in Lagos, both CAN and PFN came out to endorse President Goodluck Jonathan. In attendance at the meeting, convened ostensibly to ask God's blessing for a successful general election, were Pastor Adeboye, Bishop David Oyedepo, PFN President Reverend Felix Omobude, Pastor Paul Adefarasin of the Lagos-based House on the Rock Church, and other important Christian leaders. Osinbajo was present in his dual capacity as Pentecostal pastor and vice-presidential aspirant of a major political party.[29] According to media reports, the decision to endorse Jonathan was taken after Oyedepo addressed the gathering and assured it that God had led him to this option. Before then, Adefarasin had pressured Adeboye to make his choice for president known, only for Adeboye to announce that 'he is a man under authority and … since he is under the authority of CAN and PFN, whoever they endorsed, he would go with them'.[30]

CAN's endorsement of Jonathan came as no surprise. Given the close relationship between President Jonathan and Pastor Oritsejafor, it would have been a massive shock if CAN had gone in the opposite direction. In fact, even before that fateful late January 2015 meeting, CAN (then no different from Oritsejafor himself) had made its preference for Jonathan and disdain for Buhari known through a series of texts and WhatsApp messages to its members. Here are two examples:

> During Babangida's regime [sic], he sold Nigeria to OIC in order to Islamise Nigeria with an agreement that OIC will be supporting Nigeria financially and materially to accomplish their mission. And every year, Nigeria will be paying interest to OIC. So from IBB's regime, Nigeria has been paying, until 1999 when Obasanjo who is a Christian came and stopped it for eight years. Then, in 2007 Yar'Adua came in and paid the outstanding debt of Obasanjo to OIC, with an interest and apology, he also paid his own from 2007–2010 and died. Goodluck Jonathan came in and stopped it for six years now and [the] OIC constitution said that any member nation that stopped this payment for 10 years will be automatically excommunicated. Now GEJ [Goodluck Ebele Jonathan] has ruled Nigeria from 6th May, 2010–2015. He is seeking for 2nd tenure that will make it 10 years so that Nigeria will be delivered from the blood sucking Islamic religion.[31]

> Remember Nigeria's 100 years centenary was in 2014. And any religion that starts to rule from this 2015 will take dominion till the next 100 years. Note: I am not campaigning for GEJ, but I am just revealing a secret to my fellow Christians *to vote for religion*. Forget Boko Haram. OIC masterminded it to distract us, it will soon be over. Nigeria did not have the monopoly of terrorism, Iraq, Iran, Afghanistan, Egypt, Pakistan, Kuwait, Somalia, etc. have. This entire nation has been fighting terrorism since in the

8os yet ... Don't personalize this secret please! [sic] Make sure you send it to all your friends and everybody around. May God bless you, as you will vote for a Christian President in Nigeria election – 2015. Remember, God will judge you for using your thumb to dig the grave of his Church.[32]

CAN's messages fell back on the familiar prosody of Christian anxieties about Islam and narratives about the political designs of Northern Muslims. Tellingly, they included, in a radical departure, an exhortation to Christians to vote for a Christian candidate because, presumably, whichever faith won the day in 2015 was destined to rule the country for the next century. But CAN was too riddled with contradictions to successfully create a pan-religious platform. For one thing, and as already noted, its head, Ayo Oritsejafor, was perceived by many to be a stooge of the president. Second, a vote for Buhari could not be represented as a vote for Islam against Christianity, since Buhari's running mate was a Christian – and a pastor in the country's pre-eminent Pentecostal church at that. In addition, CAN's image among the general public had been eroded because of the alleged involvement of some of its members in the scandal surrounding the receipt of financial inducements from the Jonathan government.

The leading Pentecostal pastors were not without their own differences and contradictions, and perhaps no one embodied that internal turmoil better than Pastor Adeboye, the widely adored RCCG leader. For him, the choice of Osinbajo ought to have been obvious. Not only was Osinbajo a pastor in his church, he had approached Adeboye and spoken to him twice about his candidacy. Yet, when the time came to make a selection, and in Osinbajo's presence, Adeboye opted for Jonathan, in part because of assurances he had reportedly received from the president regarding import licences for steel and other building materials for the new 12 million capacity auditorium that the RCCG had been struggling to complete.[33] Adeboye may also have found it difficult declaring for Osinbajo, given that he had received Jonathan in person at his Lagos–Ibadan Expressway Redemption at least twice, and on one of those occasions, in December 2012, he had prayed for the president that: 'All those who wish him well, let it be well with them.'[34] But there was also, for Adeboye, a kind of moral consistency in not backing Osinbajo (even though he had given him 'his blessing') on the one hand, and, on the other, not endorsing Jonathan openly (it was a secret meeting). As the doyen of the Pentecostal class and an icon of the Pentecostal domination of public life, he is, ironically, careful to be seen as transcending political allegiances.

Unlike Adeboye, Bishop David Oyedepo could not afford to hedge his bets, and his open support for Jonathan (recall his resolve to open the gate of hell for opponents of the president) may have been predicated upon hopes of material support for Canaanland, his 560-acre mega-church project currently under construction in Ota, Ogun State.

If anyone truly hedged their bets, though, it was Pastor Tunde Bakare, Buhari's running mate in 2011. Although he participated in the national conference organised by President Jonathan in 2014 as one of the South West geopolitical zone's 15 official delegates – a fact that might have predisposed him to the president – he was quick to condemn both CAN and PFN for their endorsement of Jonathan.[35] While Bakare reportedly denounced 'the compromising leaders' and 'palace prophets' who 'were only after their pockets',[36] it should be noted that, as a one-time running mate of Buhari and as someone whose name was being put forward yet again by a group led by Nasir El-Rufai, he had a dog in the unfolding fight. Thus, although he may have appeared to back Buhari when he decried the abandonment of Osinbajo by CAN and PFN, he would later execute a complete turnaround by asking for the postponement of the presidential election until Nigeria addressed:

the underlying problems by joining forces to deal with insurgency, seeking national reconciliation and integration, forging a new people's constitution, developing a blueprint for development along zonal lines, organizing an accurate census and establishing a truly independent Electoral Commission whose head is not appointed by the President and whose financial allocation will be obtained from the first line charge of the Federation Account before the election.[37]

Although he added that 'the proposal for suspension of elections is not with a view to giving the president an avenue for undue tenure elongation but for the purpose of building a coalition that will bring lasting solutions to our problems',[38] the fact that he appeared to defend President Jonathan against charges of incompetence and favourably compared him with Abraham Lincoln left him open to accusations that he was acting as a secret agent for the president.

The 2015 presidential election in Nigeria is a perfect illustration of what happens when the theological meets the political, and when religious leaders (in this case Nigeria's increasingly influential Pentecostal elite) are dragged into the cauldron of party politics even as they seek to maintain the façade of bipartisanship. Among other things, we are confronted with the sheer complexity of Pentecostal praxis, and the fact that religious agents are insinuated in overlapping layers of class, location and interests – personal and corporate – that seem to dictate how they act and what they say in changing social circumstances.

We see this mercuriality demonstrated most eloquently in the affair that involved President Jonathan and his wife Patience, and Reverend Father Ejike Mbaka, founder of Adoration Ministry, Enugu. On New Year's Eve 2014, as he addressed his congregation, Father Mbaka launched an unprovoked attack on President Jonathan and vowed to vote for Buhari, his Islamic faith notwithstanding.[39] Said Mbaka:

I love President Goodluck Jonathan and I used to be his ardent fan, but I want good [sic] for my people and that's why I want

Nigerians to vote out Goodluck and vote General Muhammadu Buhari. I don't care if Buhari is a Muslim and from the
North; all I care about is that Buhari can save Nigeria.[40]

The attack was surprising, considering that, about seven weeks
earlier, on Sunday 9 November, Father Mbaka had anointed and
prayed for Mrs Jonathan,[41] who was visiting the church in the
company of Ike Ekweremadu, deputy senate president at the time.[42]
During the November visit of Mrs Jonathan, Father Mbaka had not
only endorsed her husband for re-election, he had also commended
the Jonathan administration for 'doing well' and insisted that it
could have done more were it not for those 'distracting' it.[43]

Following his about-turn, which might have had something to
do with his anger at apparently being slighted by the Jonathans,[44]
Father Mbaka remained a steadfast Buhari loyalist. As a guest of the
latter at the presidential villa in December 2015, President Buhari
made sure to thank Father Mbaka 'for not only criticizing some
policies of the former President Goodluck Jonathan but also moving
against the latter's re-election bid in the 2015 presidential poll'.[45]

Conclusion

In the end, the March 2015 presidential election in Nigeria was a
perfect anti-climax. This was because not only did the widespread
post-election anarchy confidently foretold by leading commentators,
politicians on both sides of the political divide, and some pastors
not materialise (Bakare had forecast a 'catastrophic Euroclydon' if
the election were not postponed),[46] but the election was peacefully
conducted, by and large, and managed to produce a clear winner,
the APC candidate General Muhammadu Buhari. As a result, as the
incumbent placed a congratulatory call to the APC candidate, what
in some sections of the media had been framed in generational terms
as a showdown between youth and old age (Jonathan and Buhari were
57 and 72 years old respectively) ended up falling short of its billing.

Still, the election will continue to be remembered for the role played by some of the leading figures among the country's increasingly influential Pentecostal pastorate. As shown, one role in which this pastorate has distinguished itself is in framing elections and the politics of electoral contestation in spiritual terms. For instance, as discussed in Chapter 2, the election that landed Olusegun Obasanjo the Nigerian presidency in May 1999 was narrativised in Pentecostal circles as the consummation of a 'power shift' from a Muslim North to a Christian South.

Not too dissimilarly, the 2015 election was framed as an opportunity to keep an underwhelming Southern Christian in power, but only as a way to ensure that power did not go to an unreconstructed Muslim hardliner who, however improbably, would inaugurate a 100-year Islamic reign. But this narrative did not stick, and the fact that it did not do so is testimony to the inherent difficulty of constructing essentialist frames in a multi-religious and multi-ethnic context in which, among other key factors, elite interests are always transgressive. As a result, neither CAN nor PFN, let alone the powerful Pentecostal pastors, could speak with one voice, their best efforts notwithstanding. In addition, and as mentioned earlier, the political masterstroke of selecting Osinbajo as a running mate guaranteed that Buhari could not be boxed in, religiously speaking.

This is not to say that the Pentecostal class was any less powerful; rather, it affirms that its corporate, personal and political entanglements may have led it to compromises that limited the extent of its influence. Nor, again, is it to definitively conclude that there is no such thing as, in this case, a Pentecostal vote (given that Buhari won by a large majority in the Yoruba Pentecostal heartland, with the exception of Ekiti State);[47] rather, it is to state that, ultimately, religious voters may not define their interests exclusively in notionally religious terms. In the case of the 2015 election, for many Christians, and for Pentecostals especially, the symbolism of Osinbajo as a vice president seems to have sufficed to assuage their anxieties about religious marginalisation or Islamic domination. But it is also plausible that, beyond the two leading contenders' religious proclamations, voters found Buhari, with his austere exterior, more credible than Jonathan, who, especially in the closing moments of the presidential campaign, seemed to be increasingly desperate and appeared to take a Manichaean view of religion. In the end, after all the votes had been tallied, the Nigerian electorate had put its trust in a Northern Muslim president, whose running mate was picked singlehandedly by a Southern secular Muslim power broker, but whose choice (Osinbajo) was at best received lukewarmly by someone (Adeboye) who was regarded as the iconic religious personality of the Nigerian Fourth Republic.

Considering the focus of this book, the question of why the Pentecostal narrative failed in this instance and why congregants did not simply do their leaders' bidding is an interesting one to ponder. One answer, already implied by the analysis above, is that the fact that there is a Pentecostal laity does not automatically imply the existence of a Pentecostal vote. Furthermore, the experiences and perspectives of the Pentecostal laity differ from those of the theocratic class, members of whom, as already shown, have differing ambitions, tendencies and relational commitments. This is not to say that Pentecostal and/or Christian unity is impossible; the point is that such unity cannot be assumed, but depends on the interplay of issues and forces at play in any given situation.

Chapter 6

'KILL THEM BEFORE THEY KILL YOU': ON VIOLENT PENTECOSTALISM

Introduction: the pastor as fortune teller

As Bola Tinubu's second term in office as governor of Lagos State (2003–07) gradually wound down, the intra-party struggle to succeed him ratcheted up. One of those who expressed a firm interest was Tinubu's deputy, Femi Pedro. Pedro had been deputy governor since April 2003, the beneficiary of Kofoworola Bucknor-Akerele's decision to resign in December 2002 after relations between her and Tinubu had broken down irretrievably. But Tinubu did not want Pedro, who would end up being impeached by the State House of Assembly in May 2007,[1] to succeed him; in retrospect, he may have made up his mind as to his choice of successor from the very beginning. Be that as it may, it is what he did next that is interesting for our analysis of the overlay of the political with the religious in the Nigerian Fourth Republic. As I gathered from several informants, Tinubu approached Pastor Adeboye, gave him the names of three gubernatorial prospects, confessed to his dilemma in making the right choice, and solicited Adeboye's guidance.

The important thing for my analysis is not the outcome of the meeting, or the distinct possibility that Tinubu, having apparently already made up his mind to back Babatunde Raji Fashola (like him, a Muslim), was using the visit as a smokescreen to reassure his Christian constituents, who, like millions of Nigerian Christians, held Pastor Adeboye in high esteem. What is important here is the status of Pastor Adeboye as a revered political broker, and the fact that Tinubu, an astute power broker in his own right, felt the need to seek his approval in regards to a secular (at least in theory) matter. It was not the only time that Tinubu had consulted with Adeboye. For instance, even after picking Osinbajo as Buhari's running mate for the 2015 election, he still had to put the choice before Adeboye for the latter's arbitration.[2]

In seeking Adeboye's imprimatur, Tinubu was doing what nearly every significant player in the politics of the Fourth Republic, regardless of faith or denominational affiliation, had done and continues to do. As noted in Chapter 2, there is a sense in which the Redemption Camp on the Lagos–Ibadan Expressway is regarded as the political Mecca of the Fourth Republic. If the Redemption Camp is the political Mecca of the Fourth Republic, Pastor Adeboye is its spiritual lodestar. When Obasanjo needed 'spiritual clarification' on whether or not to run for the presidency in 1999, Adeboye was one of the religious counsellors he turned to, and the one whose word, according to Obasanjo's account, mattered the most. Shortly before the presidential election of 2007, Umaru Musa Yar'Adua, nominee of the PDP and a Muslim, paid a widely publicised visit to Pastor Adeboye to request his 'blessing' in the approaching election. As has been noted, his successor, President Goodluck Jonathan (2010–15), was a frequent visitor to the Redemption Camp, and, on at least two occasions, had publicly knelt down before Adeboye for prayer.

Consultations like these are best seen as facsimiles of endogenous spiritual practices in which important matters are referred to or cleared in advance with one or a combination of traditional religious actors, including seers, diviners and fortune tellers. In this sense, the contemporary Pentecostal pastor extends the legacy of endogenous spirituality.[3] A comparison could easily be made with the way in which Yoruba Obas usually present their candidates for any chieftaincy to Ifa diviners for divine confirmation, or the way in which the Obas themselves are subject to this process.

If, in the context of the Fourth Republic, Pentecostal pastors have emerged for all practical purposes as 'consultants' who are entrusted with the final choice on the most important matters – parochial, political or pietistic – Pastor Adeboye is the very embodiment of this sociological dynamic. As courtier and spiritual godfather to politicians and technocrats within and outside Nigeria, he operates as a statesman without portfolio – and is more or less accepted as such. For instance, he is the person to whom politicians are most likely to turn to broker intractable intra-elite feuds.[4] Among the Nigerian theocratic class, Adeboye more or less stands alone in paying well-publicised 'official visits' to state houses across the country, and undertaking 'official' tours of government establishments and parastatals. In this capacity, he is rightly regarded as an itinerant soothsayer for the Nigerian ruling elite.

The foregoing prompts a series of questions: if Pastor Adeboye is so influential, why could he not bring that influence to bear on the outcome of the 2015 presidential election? Put differently, judging by the discussion in Chapter 5, are there not grounds for supposing that the power of the Pentecostal elite is hyperbolised? Why, if indeed they exert so much influence, could the same elite not prevent the defeat of President Goodluck Jonathan, a man who could not keep his Christian faith under wraps, to a Northern Muslim?

One could readily point out that, as demonstrated in Chapter 5, the electoral context was not an uncomplicated Christian–Muslim showdown in which people simply voted according to their religious allegiances. If many Christians, particularly in the south-west, voted for Buhari, it was not simply because he had a Christian running mate. At the same time, because most people were genuinely put off by his political incompetence, his failure to rein in corruption, and the unending shenanigans of his wife,[5] Jonathan's religious affiliation and spiritual posturing were inadequate to hold down the 'Pentecostal vote'. Furthermore, just as the election never boiled down to a clean Muslim–Christian divide, key religious figures, as we have seen, are themselves constantly balancing various personal and political considerations. Hence, they could not be solidary in their allegiances, which inspires the key insight that the agency of religious actors is not always based on – or necessarily driven by – religious motives and considerations alone, however those may be defined.

An even more crucial point, perhaps, is that ambiguities like the above betray a misunderstanding of the way in which this elite exercises its influence, and that it is misleading to judge their social influence solely by the outcome of a single election, however momentousness it might appear to be. A central argument of this book is that a better and more illuminating place to look is in the narratives and discourses that key religious leaders craft – about the destiny of the nation, the character of the Fourth Republic, the democratic process, particular elections, individual candidates, the supposedly unique agency of pastors themselves, and so forth. To the extent that these pastors might be said to have cast a spell on the Fourth Republic, it is through such narratives and discourses. Viewed in this way, Tinubu's decision to present a list of gubernatorial prospects to Adeboye for his ratification becomes a demonstration of the power of these narratives (this, and good old political pragmatism), and the imprint this leaves on the social imaginary.

As advanced in Chapter 1, one of the most important discourses promoted by the Pentecostal elite, echoing Paul Gifford[6] on the enchantment of the political process, is that political power and those who exercise it constantly operate under the shadow of invisible and ubiquitous diabolical forces, forces that can be disciplined – but never completely extinguished – only by agents endowed with the appropriate spiritual know-how. I suggest that the successful mobilisation of this discourse allows the Pentecostal elite to legitimate both its expertise and its identity as a class. Furthermore, it enables it to form alliances with the political elite to such an extent that the Pentecostal elite is justly regarded as an extension of the ruling class.

In what follows, I use excerpts from the writings of D. K. Olukoya,[7] General Overseer of the Lagos-based MFM, to analyse this discourse of the ubiquity of diabolical forces, and to argue that, for the Pentecostal elite to which Pastor Olukoya belongs, the power of the discourse ultimately emanates from the discursive atmosphere that it helps create. Since, for Olukoya, ubiquitous evil can be effectively challenged only through violent prayer, I explain why a (mostly) symbolic recourse to violence makes sense against the backdrop of military rule and the banalisation of violence in post-independence Nigeria.

Ubiquitous evil: the cosmos of Pastor D. K. Olukoya

Given my contention that Pastor Adeboye is the spiritual lodestar of the Fourth Republic, it would seem logical to make him the centre-piece of my analysis of the discursive influence of Pentecostal pastors. But I have chosen not to do so for two key reasons. The first is that a lot has already been written about Pastor Adeboye. For example, in his excellent study of the RCCG, Asonzeh Ukah describes him as 'a political figure whose present role in Nigeria could be aptly compared to the role of Billy Graham in the religious politics of the United States of America';[8] while Ruth Marshall acknowledges his pioneering role in the modernisation of the RCCG and the evolution of a specific born-again spirituality.[9] Olukoya, in contrast, does not appear to have enjoyed the same intensity of scholarly scrutiny.[10] Moreover, compared with Adeboye, Olukoya is relatively obscure – though it is fair to say that every Nigerian Pentecostal pastor is obscure in comparison to Adeboye. Crucially, unlike Adeboye, Olukoya is rarely seen in the company of major politicians or key political figures in the Fourth Republic.[11] Yet – reason number two – it seems to me that, for all his relative anonymity, Olukoya cannot embody the Nigerian Pentecostal zeitgeist more perfectly. Among the Pentecostal elite, he stands out for his consistent exposition of the belief that the Republic, the country, the African continent and the black race are under permanent spiritual siege, the solution to which is a combination of different strategies of prayerful counter-violence.

At the centre of Pastor Olukoya's Pentecostalist *Weltanschauung* is the figure of 'the enemy' – persistent, ever-foraging. This enemy – sometimes just the devil, at other times a range of visible and invisible agents – is invariably behind all the believer's woes. Such woes range from 'health attacks', having the 'spirit of seduction' and 'attacks from the womb' to 'being in a "wrong marriage"' and 'ignorance of one's destiny and identity'.[12] The usual recommendation – consistent, it must be said, with a theology whose centrepiece is 'ceaseless prayer' (as per 1 Thessalonians 5.17) – is prayer. But the prayer required is no ordinary prayer. Because 'Satan is an obstinate fighter, who yields only when he must',[13] and because '[t]he enemy has poured a legion of angry spirits into the world' who 'act in rage and exhibit unthinkable madness and wickedness', 'spiritual violence is needed'.[14] Hence, the born-again Christian 'must have violent vigilance' and 'must burst forth with holy anger, violent determination and faith'.[15] Above all, he or she 'must not hold your peace'.[16]

These exhortations to rage and violence are believed to be rooted in the Bible, and one of the most frequently cited verses in defence of such aggressive supplication is Matthew 11.12: 'And from the days of John the Baptist until now the kingdom of heaven has been suffering violence, and the violent take it by force.'[17] Olukoya also likes to cite Psalm 2.8–9: 'Ask of me, and I shall give thee the heathen for thine inheritance, and the uttermost parts of the earth for thy possession. Thou shalt break them with a rod of iron; thou shalt dash them in pieces like a potter's vessel.'[18]

For Olukoya, therefore, not only is violent prayer biblically justified; crucially, it is mandated by the reality of a world in which the believer must continually struggle against a community of hostile spirits. Among the 70 individual spirits listed in *Prayer Warfare* are: 'seductive spirits', 'womb polluters', 'desert spirits', 'wicked spirits', 'backsliding spirits', 'coffin spirits' and 'business bewitchers'.[19] To combat these 'mad spirits', prayer is essential, and the prayer has to be aggressive because '[t]he arms of God respond to violent prayers'.[20]

Because these 'familiar spirits' must be engaged vigorously, and because God responds to violent prayers, the language of 'prayer points' must be accordingly robust. Consider the following sample from *The Tragedy of Stealing*: 'Every power that has turned my life upside down, *roast* by fire, in the name of Jesus';[21] 'Holy Ghost Fire, *burn* away every satanic deposit in my life, in the name of Jesus';[22] 'Every satanic investment in my life, *be wasted* in the name of Jesus';[23] 'Satanic agenda for my life, *vanish*, in the name of Jesus';[24] 'Axe of God, *cut down* every witchcraft tree of stealing battling my life in the name of Jesus';[25] 'Every cage of witchcraft fashioned to suppress my star, I *smash* you to piece [sic] in Jesus name';[26] 'Every power behind destructive habit [sic] in my life, *die* in the name of Jesus';[27] 'The Adam in me, come out and *die by fire* of God of Elijah in Jesus name.'[28]

The way Olukoya sees it, the Christian journey only makes sense in terms that are purely and fundamentally martial, and the onus is on every believer to master what he calls 'the terms of the battle', for '[n]o king goes to war, unless he understands the terms of the battle and the powers of the enemy. He has to understand his strength, resources and the value of what is at stake.' 'Likewise,' he continues, 'we must evaluate our lives and see how well we are performing in the spiritual warfare.'[29] There is no escaping warfare. It is:

an intrinsic part of your life as [a] child of God. No matter what you know about holiness, you cannot possess your possessions without warfare. The devil will not contend with you when you try to hold on to the doctrines of the Scriptures. But one fact is clear, you are not exempted from battles or warfare.[30]

Ultimately, therefore: '*Violence is the only language the enemy under-stands* – Violence is required for total victory.'[31] Total victory here is not merely 'possession of the self', but ultimately – and consistent with the Pentecostal world view – conquest of the world for Christ.

Olukoya's quasi-animism, and his conviction that violent prayer is the only effective solution for fending off ubiquitous evil, is, as suggested earlier, broadly shared across an otherwise diverse Nigerian Pentecostal community. For instance, Nigerian Pentecostal cinematic production upholds a world of 'contrary spirits' and 'occult forces' that can be combated only with aggressive prayer.[32] In this sense, there is more than a Freudian slip involved in Matthews Ojo's description of the charismatic movement in Nigeria as an 'end-time army'.[33]

How do we make sense of the emphasis on violent prayer (not just by Pastor Olukoya. but, as I show presently, across the Pentecostal belt) to combat ubiquitous evil? And how, if at all, might Nigeria's recent political history, shed light on this?

On the violent heart of Pentecostal praxis

> In the Mountain of Fire and Miracles Ministries we do battle violently. When you talk about spiritual warfare, you need to go aggressive. Holy violence must be involved. (Pastor Ruth and Wole Adewoye, MFM, Italy)[34]

On Tuesday 3 July 2014, 21-year-old Tolani Ajayi, a History and International Relations major at the Redeemers University, Lagos–Ibadan Expressway, Lagos, Nigeria, slaughtered his father, Mr Charles Ajayi, a Senior Advocate of Nigeria, in a fit of oedipal fury. Flashing a kitchen knife, he reportedly lunged and slashed at his 60-year-old victim several times, before eventually finishing him off with a machete. Mission accomplished, Tolani carefully packaged his father's remains in a box, which he then dragged into a nearby bush within the Redemption Camp where the family lived and owned a home. In the course of interrogations following his eventual arrest by the police, Ajayi, according to reports in the media,[35] told the police that the ultimately fatal showdown with his late father was due to the latter's frustrations at his son's failure to respond positively to the family's prayer points.

Incidents such as this happen all too frequently in contemporary Nigeria, and, as one pattern within the larger mosaic of urban violence, they probably speak to the stresses of family life against the backdrop of deepening economic insecurity. Given the thrust of this chapter, what makes it interesting is the fact that it took place in the context of a father–son disagreement regarding prayer, and within the premises of the Redemption Camp, a 'prayer city'[36] touted as a world apart from the chaos and discontent of Lagos. As an instance of the affinity between prayer and violence, it foregrounds at least three distinct ways in which violence appears baked into the Nigerian Pentecostal imaginary. These are: (1) an understanding of prayer in relation to aggression (physical and otherwise); (2) violent *performance* of prayer, especially in a way that seems to suggest a belief in a correlation between violence and efficacy; and (3) the imagery of violence as a recurrent element in prayer.

Although this militant element – and specifically the pervasiveness of imprecatory prayer to combat the intensity of 'spiritual warfare' – has received some attention in the relevant literature,[37] the question of what the intimacy between violence and Pentecostal prayer suggests, and how it might illuminate a sociological understanding of both, remains largely neglected. Theologian Emmanuel Katongole puts it down to a reluctance among African scholars to perpetuate a notion of violence as something arising 'spontaneously out of some incomprehensible contradictions within "African culture"'.[38]

Even when the reluctance is overcome, rarely does it translate into a systematic engagement with the persistent violence – in the imagination, if not in practice – of Pentecostal prayer, let alone an exploration of Pentecostalism as a tradition that appears inexorably steeped in violence. As a result, even when the violent exploits of explicitly Christian charismatic groups such as Alice Lakwena's

Holy Spirit Movement and Joseph Kony's Lord's Resistance Army in Uganda, Christian militias in the Central African Republic, and Nigerian Pentecostal 'That Witch Must Die' campaigns[39] against innocent children are brought into focus, their violence tends to be attributed to an elusive 'traditional' essence in their formation, rather than to the muscularity of their interpretation of Christianity. Yet, focusing on the prevalence of violence in Pentecostal prayer opens an analytic window onto Pentecostalism, and, more broadly, onto the social matrix in which it has become indisputably influential.

To pursue this, we need first to account for the place of violence in the Nigerian socio-historical process.

Quotidian violence in Africa: between the epochal and the episodic

If Katongole (see above) is to be believed, one explanation for the apparent reluctance of many African academics to tackle the subject of violence is the fear of perpetuating essentialist notions of the continent as irrecoverably mired in the 'mindless' violence of a 'Dionysian nightmare'.[40] The reluctance creates at least two problems. In the first instance, it often translates into neglecting the reality of everyday violence across postcolonial Africa, a violence seen in citizens' vulnerability to state coercion and intimidation on the one hand, and to other non-state forms of violence, such as armed robberies and abduction, and violence involving armed militias on the other. In addition, there is the kind of 'targeted' violence in which women, children and the socially 'marginalised' in general are almost always the targets of 'random' physical and psychological abuse. For Jean and John Comaroff, such is the ubiquity and intensity of violence in Africa that, effectively, it has become:

> a currency of politics and economic enterprise; in which government both abhors the threat of disorder, yet uses it for

its own ends; in which citizens are at once repelled and fasci-
nated by lawlessness; in which other urgent threats, like poverty
and ill-health, are eclipsed, making it more likely that violence
serves as a routine mode of production and representation.[41]

Furthermore, a reluctance to indulge in a Western metaphorisation
of Africa as the locus of dystopic lawlessness, while understandable,
can very quickly become a forfeiture of the opportunity to study and
understand the various ways in which, amid evidence that 'the line
between the political and the criminal is fast eroding',[42] violence is
used by subalterns to negotiate the asperities of daily life, open up
new political spaces, and create oases of dignity and opportunity
– in short, the way in which violence is increasingly mobilised for
the purpose of self-recuperation and assertion. For young people
especially, violence is tied to the process of 'becoming', particularly
in spaces where access to life-giving and employment-providing
networks of patronage is often a matter of life and death.[43] Henrik
Vigh's study[44] of the role of violence in young people's 'social navi-
gation' in Guinea-Bissau in the early 2000s suggests a phenomenon
with regional ramifications.

These anxieties repeatedly overshadow attempts to historicise
and understand 'African violence'. Such attempts, animated by frustration at African countries' failure to achieve sustainable 'order',
often take as their point of departure the impregnation of (colonial)
social life in Africa by violence. Literary scholar Ato Quayson is
representative:

> In Africa, both before and after colonization, 'state power
> enhanced its value by establishing specific relations of subjec-
> tion'. In the colonial era these relations of subjection derived
> from the violence inherent in governing the colonized in the
> first place. The act of colonial governance drew upon a prior
> act of linguistic and conceptual violence in which the native
> was situated not just as wholly other, but also as bestial and

uncivilized, assumptions that were then used in various guises to justify acts of expropriation.[45]

Although a similar logic of coercive non-accountability continues to dominate state–citizen intercourse in the postcolonial era, the relevant scholarship is divided on how to judge the exact influence of this legacy on the contemporary moment. What seems beyond dispute is the role of neoliberalism in galvanising two opposing dynamics across Africa: popular 'resistance' to state 'capture' versus an official resolution to 'incorporate'. To take one example, the resurgence of identity politics has been met mostly by vicious state pacification, unprecedented even by Africa's standards of draconian repression. Meanwhile, the surge in identity politics aggravates the need for the state to make itself more legible, affirm its authority over its 'subjects', and recapture one of its fundamental postulates. The recurrent production of social violence in Africa unfolds within this framework.

In Nigeria, quotidian violence is further negotiated against the specific backdrop of prolonged martial rule, the paradox of which was the mismatch between the promise of security and the reality of insecurity and generalised uncertainty. I would argue that Pentecostalism is best seen as part of the emergent apparatus of escape from this all-consuming uncertainty, not least 'the harshness in daily social relationships'[46] experienced by the system's 'necropolitical casualties'.[47] Crucially, as an apparatus of escape from violence and insecurity, Pentecostalism is inescapably alloyed with what it purports to be, and is widely seen as, a liberation from. This probably explains its immersion in the daily 'flow of violence',[48] an immersion that is on display in its iconography, the 'war paradigm' of its cinematic production,[49] the virulence of its portrayal in the media, and the muscularity of its entire devotional assemblage – most importantly, prayer.

Violent Pentecostalism?

How, then, to account for the apparent imbrication of Nigerian Pentecostalism in symbolic violence, a violence rendered with such poignant vividness in Pastor Olukoya's writings? The analysis in this chapter presumes a correlation between, on the one hand, societal decomposition in Africa (reflected in the unravelling of social norms and rules of civility) and the quest for security and protection (especially 'spiritual' security); and between systemic violence and what I have called the violent imaginary of Pentecostalism on the other. In other words, the violence of Pentecostal prayer has to be seen as being intertwined with the violence of everyday life. This violence is simultaneously produced and reinforced by a situation in which '[p]eople generally pay little attention to state laws and legal principles of action, and social interaction is mainly regulated by neo-customary norms where social hierarchies based on wealth, seniority or gender define inequalities'.[50] As a consequence:

> local rule tends to be the unpredictable fallout of patronage domination and the poorest people often only survive as subjects bound to powerful protectors. In most cases, the competition is between judicial, traditional and religious authorities' rules, and in each of these 'systems' there is a claim to the signification of violence and 'normality'. This results in a situation of legal uncertainty for ordinary people who are no longer sure of the legitimacy of their rights and do not know who to turn to if they have been violated. They cannot even begin to predict what will happen if they do not meet their social obligations. Ordinary violence also has its roots in the plurality of the prevailing moral standards and is continuously fed by the failure of the authorities to regulate violence.[51]

It is this violence that, I suggest, bleeds into and permeates Pentecostalism, whose performative cornerstone is prayer. Furthermore, this violence is by no means incidental, but is integral to the construction of the discourse through which Pentecostals seek to 'make a break with the past',[52] discard their 'old selves', dispose of 'the old way' (of acting, eating, dressing and 'relating'), and assume a new identity as 'born-again' Christians. On this basis, it is difficult to accept Gifford's claim that 'the morality Olukoya inculcates is entirely personal' or that his 'concerns are individual and spiritual, not social and political'.[53] In fact, it would seem that Olukoya's morality is corporate – meaning that it is instantiated across the Pentecostal belt – while his seemingly individual concerns are deeply woven into and always framed by the fabric of the social and political.

It is this socio-political fabric that explains some of the key elements of violent Pentecostal prayer in Nigeria – for example, the vocabulary.

Encountering phrases such as 'spiritual insecticide', invoking a 'decree' in the course of prayer, 'demonic pollution', 'the traffic jam of life', 'satanic roadblocks', 'revoking evil decrees' or going for a 'spiritual check-up', one is in no doubt that moments from postcolonial Nigeria's landscape of anguish have been reformulated and transplanted into the charismatic milieu. Political scientist O. B. C. Nwolise's advocacy of 'Strategic Spiritual Intelligence', discussed in Chapter 1, crystallises this social anguish. With respect to 'demonic pollution', for instance, it is not difficult to conjure an image of actual pollution in many Nigerian urban centres. In the same vein, 'evil decrees' recall the era of decrees and the legislative anarchy of the military era of the not too distant past, while 'the traffic jam of life' and 'satanic roadblocks' are 'scripts' from Nigeria's perennially unruly highways. Lastly, anyone who has lived in Nigeria for any significant amount of time and has tried to access healthcare from any of the country's hospitals would understand the yearning for a 'spiritual check-up'. While, as I have argued, these Pentecostal-inflected terms draw directly from the lived experience of religious citizens in the Fourth Republic, they are also therefore remarkably effective tools for expressing, articulating and analysing their feelings and experiences.

Conclusion

Muscular readings of Christianity abound, with most of them relating to the link between Christianity, the idea of empire, and the employment of Christianity in the service of imperial rule.[54] My analysis of violent Pentecostalism differs in tone, focus and emphasis, not least because the violence that I reference is, for the most part, discursive. Drawing on the extensive writings of Pastor D. K. Olukoya, I have tried to argue that the recurrence of violence in Pentecostal prayer is far from being coincidental; rather, it is indicative of a deeper connection between both. I have postulated a correlation between the aftermath of martial rule and an ensuing economy of 'ordinary violence'. The omnipresence of evil or malevolent forces that militate against particularly *material* success in civic life fans the embers of a theology of conflict and violence. It becomes evident that Pentecostalism and the socio-political process in Nigeria have evolved in parallel.

Yet, though key, this is only a subsidiary argument. My primary aim is to show how the creation and acceptance of a cosmos of ubiquitous evil, extirpated solely through the agency of violent prayer, creates a discursive ecology that bolsters the authority of its proponents – in this case powerful Pentecostal pastors. I argue that the maintenance of this discourse gives the pastors considerable leverage as mediators of people's experience of the state, especially insofar as it amounts to a re-narrativisation of state power within the democratic process. I focus on this all-important political effect in the concluding chapter. The question is rightly asked as to how the Pentecostal elite is able to sustain this discourse, and hence maintain its power. One answer, flagged above, is that the narrative maps on to the assumptions of endogenous African metaphysics.

Theologian Allan Anderson is not alone in suggesting this as one of the reasons for the historical success of Pentecostal churches in Africa. In his view: 'They are essentially of African origin (even when founded by western Pentecostal ministries) and fulfil African aspirations, with roots in a marginalized and underprivileged society struggling to find dignity and identity in the face of ... oppression.'[55] A second answer is that the social standing of the pastors (including the fact that they are well-educated and, usually, well-spoken) lends a certain weight, if not prestige, to their claims, whether those claims concern spiritual or secular matters. For instance, the authority of Pastor D. K. Olukoya may not be unconnected to the fact that he is the holder of a PhD in molecular genetics. After all, who better to speak authoritatively about a demon-saturated world than the holder of the highest possible qualification in one of the more abstruse subject areas in the physical sciences? By positioning ultimate power in an invisible world, the Pentecostal elite is able to exert authority on secular democracy.

Chapter 7

CONCLUSION

Introduction: a political bromance

On Sunday 31 July 2016, I attended morning service at the Latter Rain Assembly in Ikeja, Lagos. My decision to be present at the service was a last-minute thing. I was doing fieldwork in Ibadan, an hour's drive away (if you are lucky), and had no intention of visiting Lagos for at least another week or so. However, late on Saturday 30 July, I got to know through an informant who is also a member of the church that an important politician would be worshipping with them the following morning.

At first light, I was off to Lagos.

The important politician turned out to be none other than Kaduna State governor Nasir El-Rufai, a close friend of Pastor Tunde Bakare, Latter Rain Assembly's ubiquitous general overseer. I wasn't at all surprised that Governor El-Rufai was the august visitor in question, since it wasn't his first visit. During a previous visit in November 2012, he had tweeted: 'In Latter Rain, after an emotional presentation by children, I teared up … gifts given, cakes being cut … no jets as gifts … proud.'[1] Apparently, he was also on his way to Latter Rain in December 2013 when an Aero Contractors Boeing 737-500 plane in which he was travelling crash landed at the Murtala Muhammed International Airport in Lagos. Since their first face-to-face meeting in Dubai in March 2010,[2] El-Rufai's friendship with Bakare (whom he affectionately calls 'my *egbon*'[3]) – all the more remarkable because one is a practising Muslim and the other a well-known Pentecostal pastor – has been one of the more eye-catching examples of elite fraternisation in the country in recent times.[4]

If anything, it was the timing of the visit that had me scratching my head, and my suspicions as to its purpose were confirmed as soon as Governor El-Rufai took the microphone following an introduction by Pastor Bakare. In July 2016, President Buhari had been in power for more than a year; but because there had been no significant alteration in the country's economic circumstances, a certain despondency had begun to set in among the people. Given the president's many promises on the campaign trail, many were shocked by the disarray that characterised Buhari's first year in office, and the tone of media criticism of the administration was becoming increasingly nasty.

On that Sunday, the essence of El-Rufai's message to Bakare's congregation – delivered, so he assured them, in his capacity as an observer who happened to be familiar with President Buhari's well-meaning attempts to turn things around in the country, and who appreciated the odds he faced in the process – was that it was too early to give up on the president. Clearly alluding to the dire economic situation during Buhari's first period in power as military head of state (1983–85), El-Rufai spoke of his 'pity' and sadness for a man who always seemed destined to inherit a country in trouble:

> When we sit down with President Buhari these days, I pity him. I pity him because he has always become president anytime [sic] Nigeria is in trouble. First, it was after the NPN [National Party of Nigeria] government had almost grounded the economy [sic] in 1984 and now, after a massive looting of the nation's treasury, and he has to lead the team to fix it.

El-Rufai also invoked the unique situation apparently created by the country's empty coffers following 'massive looting of the nation's treasury', while assuring the congregation that Buhari possessed the mettle to repair the damage done by the previous administration and to restore the economy to good health.

In short order, it became clear that El-Rufai had been dispatched to Lagos by the Buhari administration to douse the fire of rising popular discontent, and his visit to Latter Rain Assembly was part of a carefully coordinated charm offensive.

It is also possible that El-Rufai intended to use his visit to kill two birds with one stone. At the time, he was enmeshed in a controversy with a section of the Christian community in Kaduna State over his proposal of an executive bill to regulate religious preaching in the state. While the 'Bill for a Law to Substitute the Kaduna State Religious Preaching Law, 1984' had been applauded in some quarters, it was condemned by most Christian groups as an assault on their rights to propagate their religious beliefs.[5]

Nor should we be surprised by the use of Pastor Bakare's church as a staging post for the Buhari administration's strategy. Bakare was a known ally of President Buhari and, as discussed in Chapter 4, had stood next to him in 2011 as the CPC's vice-presidential candidate. Both had remained close despite their loss to Goodluck Jonathan, and, in fact, a group led by El-Rufai had pressured Buhari to select Bakare again as his running mate in the 2015 election. Although Bakare's open condemnation of both CAN's and PFN's decision to support Jonathan (see Chapter 5) had seemed to indicate a fervent support for Buhari (something he confirmed in an interview with Sahara TV on 22 December 2014),[6] his later call for a postponement of the same election made his overall position rather ambiguous. In any event, Bakare was soon restored beside Buhari, and was part of the latter's official entourage during his state visit to Washington in July 2015. Others on the trip were: former Rivers State governor, Chibuike Rotimi Amaechi; governors Abiola Ajimobi, Rochas Okorocha and Adams Oshiomhole of Oyo, Imo and Edo States respectively; governor of the Central Bank of Nigeria, Godwin Emefiele; and permanent secretaries of the Federal Ministries of Defence, Foreign Affairs, Industry, Trade and Investment.

The image of El-Rufai, a Northern Muslim politician, sharing the pulpit with Bakare, a Southern Pentecostal pastor, offers a compelling visual microcosm with which to analyse the religio-political alliance that, I claim, has been the engine of democratic politics in the Nigerian Fourth Republic.

Spiritual radicalism

In Chapter 2, I described the growing recognition by Nigerian Christians, beginning in the 1970s, of a need to play a more assertive role in politics; and subsequently the establishment of the Christian Association of Nigeria (CAN) in 1976 as the institutional crystallisation of this transformation. Symbolically, the original CAN comprised only the Catholic Church and 'orthodox' Protestant groups. In time – and perhaps inevitably, given their growing influence on the religious landscape – the ranks of CAN would be swollen by the inclusion of Pentecostal groups. This new Christian assertiveness had two complementary elements: a resolve to counter and roll back perceived creeping Islamisation; and a determination to insinuate Christianity (whenever possible via agents inspired by a decidedly Christian ethos) within the fabric of a reimagined public sphere.

Subsequently, opportunities would arise for this new Christian commitment to play out. Among such opportunities were the contest over Nigeria's backdoor incorporation into the OIC by the Babangida regime in 1986; the political crisis triggered by the introduction of sharia law by several Northern states, starting with Zamfara in October 1999;[7] and the brouhaha that ensued in 2002 after Isioma Daniel, a *This Day* reporter, wrote an article that was perceived by many Muslims to be derogatory towards Prophet Muhammad.[8] But as far as opportunities for political muscle flexing by determined Christians were concerned, arguably no occasion would be more epochal than the annulment of the 12 June 1993 election. The protracted crisis that followed the annulment – and, significantly, the opportunity it handed the church to present itself as the country's moral compass – was a key milestone in the creation of political Christianity in Nigeria, and, in retrospect, seems to have been an important precursor to Christian influence in the democratic politics of the Fourth Republic.

The backdrop to this brings up two important points. The first, as suggested before, is that the crisis lent itself to ethical narrativising, especially when seen as a struggle for moral redress by a political agent (Chief M. K. O. Abiola) aggrieved by a totally arbitrary change of rules right at the end of a political game. Christian leaders, especially progressive-minded Catholic priests, were crucial to the articulation and promotion of this moral discourse. The second was that it occurred at a propitious global moment, particularly with the growing popularity of liberal democracy, which had seized the imagination in the aftermath of the collapse of the Berlin Wall in 1989. Cashing in on the momentary paralysis of many civic institutions as a result of the political crisis, the church transformed, momentarily at least, into a surrogate political force, in which role it helped create a discursive milieu in which both secular democracy and political liberalism were elevated as ideal national goals.[9]

If there were ever a definitive emblem of this pivotal moment in the history of Christian involvement in politics, and subsequently the politicisation of the church, it was the pulpit. From it, sundry religious leaders, in particular Catholic leaders, undertook the cerebral and emotional project of freighting an ostensibly secular struggle with a sacral aura. As the pulpit became a political platform, a 'safe space' from which otherwise state-sanctioned speech could be uttered, even if necessarily disguised in aphorisms and parables, the church was sucked deeper into the vortex of political radicalism.

A reactionary turn

I suggested earlier that the joint presence of Pastor Tunde Bakare and Governor Nasir El-Rufai in the same pulpit is symbolic of the rapport between the theological class and the political elite in the Fourth Republic. To fully appreciate the significance of this moment, a founding hypothesis of this book must be accepted: that is to say that following in the footsteps of the ideological retooling of Nigerian Christianity as a political force, Pentecostalism moved into pole position as the dominant form of Christian praxis. While the reasons for this have been discussed elsewhere,[10] what is important for our analysis here is its overall political effect: namely, (1) the blunting of political Christianity's more radical edge (as noted above), epitomised, inter alia, by the absorption of the Pentecostal elite (perhaps it is more accurate to speak of the mutual absorption of both) into the ruling class; and (2) the de-radicalisation of the pulpit, illustrated by the way in which it has frequently been turned over to members of the ruling elite. Apart from the incident involving Pastor Bakare and Governor El-Rufai, I have referenced other examples (for instance, regarding Pastor Adeboye) in previous chapters.

I want to note in parenthesis that it is not difficult to see how this kind of intra-elite and inter-religious realignment could be celebrated as a possible harbinger of inter-religious harmony, which in turn could be leveraged to facilitate political integration. I do not deny this, but the problem – and the reason why inter-religious alignment is not automatically conducive to political cohesion – is that the agents involved are often acting on various personal calculations; hence the ironic coexistence, in Nigeria at least, of a high level of inter-elite cordiality and nagging socio-political disharmony. Not only that, the same cordiality can lead to situations in which specific agents align with positions that are at cross-purposes with those of their primary (religious or political) constituencies.

I invoke, as an example, Pastor Bakare's uncharacteristically lame response to the killings of Christians in Southern Kaduna in late 2016, regarding which Christians across the country were understandably exercised, with some leading pastors, angered by the perceived maltreatment of their Christian compatriots, going to the extent of praying for Nigeria to break up, 'if it's God's will'.[11]

In contrast, speaking about the killings in January 2017, Bakare was strangely conciliatory, assuring vaguely that 'peace will return to Southern Kaduna' based on 'some other things that I know that made me say peace will return there'.[12] He also prayed, in atypical officialese, that: 'All things will work together for the good of our country and especially Kaduna State.' Another example is the silence of the same Pastor Bakare regarding President Buhari's repeated trips abroad for medical treatment, prompting criticism that Buhari was too sick to discharge the arduous responsibilities of office. In sharp contrast to the passion he displayed when President Yar'Adua was hospitalised between 2009 and 2010, Bakare decided to bite his tongue. In both of these cases, it can be argued that Pastor Bakare's inter-religious alliances (with El-Rufai and Buhari respectively) mitigated his reaction.

The above parenthetical note confirms one of my key arguments regarding Pentecostalism's blunting of political Christianity's pugnacious edge. Nevertheless, I can imagine a pushback to my conclusion along the following lines. One, the question might be posed as to whether, on the basis of the evidence presented here, a conclusion may be drawn about the character of Pentecostal politics, or Pentecostalism *tout court*. Second, notwithstanding its decisive influence on politics and sociality in Nigeria and a growing number of African countries (again, as amply demonstrated), it could be argued that it is premature to pronounce definitively on the character of Pentecostal politics, and that the conclusion that Pentecostalism carries an immutable authoritarian gene is precipitate. A third possible line of attack is that the relationship between religion and (democratic) politics is always contingent, and that, as we saw with the example of the church and the 12 June crisis, religious leaders and associations can successfully press claims for social justice and the expansion of democratic space.

While these are valid objections, I insist that the alliance between the Pentecostal elite and the Nigerian ruling class bodes ill, especially insofar as it cements the emergent status of political

Christianity as guarantor of the status quo, and Pentecostalism as the purveyor of religious reason in defence of the state. There is an obvious irony here: namely that churches and other religious organisations in Nigeria are in fact among the prime beneficiaries of the turn to democracy, taking full advantage of what political theorist John Keane calls 'the openness, pluralism and sense of contingency that democracy unleashes through such mechanisms as press freedom, elections and freedom of association [and the way in which this] clears spaces for the experience of freedom of religion'.[13] We can confidently predict that, as people continue to seek meaning – a quest that democracy itself more or less underwrites when, contrary to its most earnest promises, it fails to deliver security, economic prosperity and stability – religious experience will remain attractive.

This is what makes elite discourse such a potent force. In Nigeria, part of what lends the discourse of ubiquitous evil its immense power is that it enfolds the entire democratic process into its episteme, foretelling of its possibilities and promises, and always hinting darkly at its perils. For precisely this reason, Pentecostalism is a ballast that gives Nigerian democracy stability. The real question is whether it is stability or rupture that the system requires, and my answer is that rupture is highly unlikely for as long as the entente between the ruling class and the theological elite remains in place.

Final thoughts: democracy and invisible power

Running through this book is the theme of power – its ultimate residence, its ends, and how it is distributed and shared. The central conceit of democracy as a system of rule is its openness and rational transparency. It is the assumption that the people are the ultimate source of power, which they are at liberty to dispense or withdraw as the spirit (pun not intended) leads. This formulation places democracy and religion at cross-purposes, especially insofar as the latter entails an appeal to a higher 'reason', and hence to an alternative source of power beyond the regular demos. Yet, and as a quick glance at history confirms, actually existing democracies scarcely map on to this theoretical template, not least because, as previously stated, the relation of religion to democracy is always contingent. As shown in the example of the struggle for the validation of the 12 June 1993 election, religious authorities may appeal to a higher reason to justify the truth of a claim to democratic redress.

But the fact that religious power and religious appeals to 'external' reason do not always constitute a menace to the democratic process is no reason to let our guard down. The most critical threat, judging by the evidence so far from the mobilisation of Pentecostal power in the Nigerian Fourth Republic, comes from the tendency to elide the separation between church and state, a pivotal liberal democratic principle. As I have suggested, the power to do this derives in part from Pentecostal leaders' successful establishment of a narrative that erects Nigeria's democratic destiny on a metaphysical scaffolding. Should this continue, not only will it make democratic deliberation within the public sphere less susceptible to rational argumentation, it will probably escalate the perennial power struggle between Christians and Muslims in Nigeria.

I should like to close with a caveat. Although Pentecostalism is clearly the *idée fixe* of the Fourth Republic, it is worth remembering that its apparent political triumph is by no means irreversible. For one thing, it is not inconceivable that its alliance with the state could spell the beginning of its political doom. As I have argued, if the events surrounding the 2015 presidential election tell us anything, it is that the Pentecostal elite, far from being cohesive, is eminently prone to personal and political differences. Nor, being politically ambitious themselves, are members of that elite satisfied to merely act as cheerleaders for the political class. For instance, in January 2018, Pastor Bakare surprised his congregation – if not Bakare watchers – with the announcement that God had told him to run for the presidency. Going down the list of the 12 important things he said God had revealed to him would happen in 2018, Bakare said:

This twelfth one is a difficult one for me. It may draw excitement or condemnation. I have tried my best to keep it to myself, but the Holy Spirit will not allow me to do so. In my study around 4am on Sunday morning, God told me 'you cannot bring your political career to a close; there is still more to do. Run for the presidency. I will do it at the appointed time.[14]

If, hoping to parlay their visibility and influence, more members of the Pentecostal elite embrace party politics by presenting themselves as candidates in elections, they will most certainly surrender some of the social prestige that currently accrues to them as men of the cloth. They can also count on a degree of hostility from professional politicians whose current deference is partly dictated by political realism, and partly by an understanding that they will not have to compete with religious leaders for office.

At any rate, Pentecostalism could very easily fall victim to Nigeria's continually evolving political realignments. Beyond the personal magnetism of its leading lights, it is not altogether clear what Pentecostalism's theory of politics is – or, indeed, whether it has any. As historian Femi Kolapo argues: 'For its members who are in government or in politics, Nigeria's Pentecostal movement does not have a framework to positively influence policies in a wholesome manner as does a political party or structured social movement.'[15] Now, I agree with the comparison, but it is difficult to see Nigerian Pentecostalism permanently declaring kinship with a political party, as is the case with evangelicals and the Republican Party in the United States. This is not just because of the fissures to which it is prone. It is also because it is not, strictly speaking, ideological – and even if it were, the political landscape is constantly shifting.

There is another possibility – a remote one, admittedly – that internal doctrinal changes could force a shift in Pentecostalism's political strategy. On the other hand, it just might exhaust itself as an ebullient movement within the Christian tradition.

Finally, and keeping in mind that the struggle for state power in (Nigerian) politics is never won definitively because the socio-political milieu is continually evolving, a lot hinges on how the Muslim competition responds. When Boko Haram first appeared on the radar, a common interpretation among the Southern political classes was that it was nothing but a vehicle for reclaiming political power by Northern elites. This interpretation was largely due to cynicism, and the trajectory of the group since then shows that it (the interpretation) could not have been less accurate. The interpretation was also motivated by what strikes me as a failure to appreciate the global impact of Pentecostalism and the ramifications of its political involvement. Although I am not necessarily recommending it, my work on the rise of 'charismatic Islam' in Western Nigeria[16] offers a model of how Pentecostal influence can be successfully countered via imitation. Whatever form it takes, the character of the response will determine the shape of the struggle for state power for the foreseeable future.

NOTES

Introduction

1   For an excellent historical analysis of the role of evangelicals in American politics, see Fitzgerald (2017). For a comparative perspective on evangelical politics in Asia, Africa and Latin America, see the analysis in Freston (2008).

2   See, for instance, Wariboko (2008; 2012; 2018).

3   See Obadare (2016a). See also Ibrahim (2017).

Chapter 1

1   Abati (2016).

2   See Agande (2016). If the account of Major Debo Bashorun, Press and Public Affairs Officer (Military Press Secretary) to President Babangida is to be believed, his boss in fact consistently consorted with marabouts while in office. Bashorun writes:

> Two incidents stood out conspicuously in my memory about the general's obsession with marabouts. The first was the housing of twenty-one Malians in a government guest house on Victoria Island for what could be termed a marathon prayer session. These foreigners could only be visited after sun down for their meals which also were being prepared under the supervision of a cleric with Nigerian roots in the State House kitchen. They were kept indoors for a month offering prayers round-the-clock and burning tons of incense that were brought only in the evenings. The sessions were usually rounded up with the slaughtering of a ram every three days in the guest house premises after which the same Nigerian would take its remains away in a mini-truck attached to him. The second experience was the burial alive of another ram within the State House grounds after some Mallams had taken it through another prayer session on a particular Sunday morning. (Bashorun 2013: 165)

Not only is the suspicion that politicians consort with marabouts rife among the general public, politicians themselves are wont to accuse one another of seeking them out for nefarious ends. For instance, after their relationship had apparently broken down irretrievably, President Obasanjo accused Atiku Abubakar, his vice president, of 'wishing him dead and consulting Islamic holy men on the date of his demise'. In return, Abubakar accused Obasanjo of using 'Christianity as a smokescreen while engaged in occultism and diabolical acts', adding that: 'The next occupant of the State House ... will need to spiritually cleanse the presidential lodge to make it habitable for normal people' (BBC News 2007). It was in the same vein that Lauretta Onochie, personal assistant to President Buhari, accused the president's enemies of hiring marabouts to pray for his death (Adetayo 2017).

3   Ibid.

4   Ibid.

5   This is a recurrent trope in countless Nollywood movies. Interestingly, it is also the main focus of a book by Wale Adedayo, one-time Director of Organisation of the PDP, Ogun State, who writes about 'rituals of appeasement' undertaken in the small hours by politicians, and the latter's belief in the potency of 'spiritual appeasement' to do a variety of things, including, notably, controlling the people they govern (Adedayo 2010).

6   See Ellis (2008).

7   Mbembe (1992: 9).

8   See Obadare (2015).

9   See Apter (2005).

10 Abati (2016, italics added).

11 Ibid. (italics added).

12 Gifford (2016: 157).

13 Adesina (2016).

14 Ibid. (italics added).

15 Kawonise (2016).

16 Ibid. (italics added).

17 Fani-Kayode (2016).

18 Adelakun (2016).

19 Adeniyi (2016).

20 Personal correspondence, 14 October 2016.

21 It is also, instructively, not limited to Nigeria. For more on everyday understandings of malevolence in Africa, see Olsen and Van Beek (2015).

22 Nwolise (2014: 93, bold in original).

23 Ibid., p. 13 (italics added).

24 Ibid., p. 95 (bold in original, italics added).

25 Ibid., p. 124.

26 Ibid., pp. 113–14 (italics added).

27 There are two currents of Pentecostalism in Africa. The first, the 'classic' version, refers to African Initiated Churches (AICs), which flourished in the early part of the twentieth century. The second is the contemporary

charismatic revival, which began in the late 1970s and early 1980s. My reference throughout is to the latter. For an analysis of the African charismatic revival which situates it within a global framework, see Anderson (2004). For an analysis of the different strands within African Pentecostalism, see Ukah (2007: 1–20).

28 Obadare (2016a).

29 See Peel (2016).

30 For an overview of Christian–Muslim relations in Nigeria, written from the standpoint of 'a theological reflection on interreligious dialogue', see Nwanaju (2005).

31 Haynes (1995).

32 Falola (1998: 104).

33 Taylor (2003).

34 See Kellerman (2016: 87).

35 Ellis and ter Haar (1998: 188).

36 Ibid., pp. 188–9.

37 Obadare (2016a).

38 Post and Vickers (1975).

39 Kendhammer (2016).

40 For a flavour of this debate, see, for instance, Asad et al. (2009). Cf. Taylor (2007), Agrama (2012) and Warner et al. (2010).

41 Nigeria's dynamic religious milieu has stimulated a sizeable academic corpus. For instance, and perhaps not surprisingly, the Pentecostal explosion and its socio-political and cultural ramifications have received generous scholarly attention. Cutting-edge work in this area includes, in no particular order, Wariboko (2014), Marshall (2009), Ukah (2008), Adogame (2011) and Ojo (2006). Other studies with a decidedly comparativist intent have situated Christianity in Nigeria within the matrix of its unceasing competition and cooperation with Islam and traditional Òrìṣà religion. Two leading studies in this area are Jacob Olupona's *City of 201 Gods* (2011) and what was effectively J. D. Y. Peel's last testament, *Christianity, Islam, and Orisa Religion* (2016).

42 See Berger (2012).

43 See Manaugh (2006).

44 Burgess (2015: 42).

45 See Zink (2012). Cf. Asamoah-Gyadu (2013).

46 See Gifford (2016) and Kolapo (2016).

47 For more on this, see Obadare (2013b). For an African perspective, see Ranger (2008).

48 Wariboko (2014), Marshall (2009) and Ukah (2008).

49 Haynes' concern is the effect of Pentecostalism on Yoruba ecumenicalism (see Haynes 2016).

50 Boyd (2015).

51 Reflecting on the attraction of the charismatic church for the new black middle class in South Africa, Roger Southall alludes to its penchant to 'legitimise the political order and the high levels of inequality over which it presides' (2016: 192).

52 Freeman (2012).

53 See, for instance, Ilesanmi (1997), Korieh and Nwokeji (2005), Falola (1998), Kukah (1993), Enwerem (1995) and Nwanaju (2005). Cf. Paden (2008).

54 Newell (2007).

55 Gifford (2004).

56 See Cooper (2017).

57 Maxwell (2006).

58 See Phiri (2003).

59 As the Boko Haram insurgency has morphed into a full-blown threat to the territorial integrity of the country, scholars have weighed in with various approaches. Examples of works in this emergent literature are Mustapha (2014), Comolli (2015), Smith (2016) and Pérouse de Montclos (2015).

60 See Deneen (2018). Cf. Luce (2017) and Lilla (2017).

Chapter 2

1 See Ibeh (2014).

2 Nigerian parlance for (monetary) inducement.

3 This is probably a reference to the fact that, since the birth of the Fourth Republic in 1999, the state's three civilian governors (Olusegun Osoba, Gbenga Daniel and Ibikunle Amosun, the incumbent) have all been Christian.

4 See *Nigerian Times* (2011).

5 See Agbese (2017).

6 Obasanjo was Nigerian Head of State from 1976 until 1979, when he handed over power to Shehu Shagari.

7 See Adogame (2006: 130).

8 See Ukiwo (2003: 115). See also Olaniyan (2010).

9 *The Cable* (2017).

10 Kingibe, of course, was not Abiola's original choice for running mate. He would have preferred a Northern Christian, and had in fact chosen labour leader and Adamawa-born Paschal Bafyau, but he was eventually prevailed upon by SDP governors who made their collaboration contingent upon the selection of Kingibe. For more on this, see Kokori (2014). Kokori is former General Secretary of the Nigeria Union of Petroleum and Natural Gas Workers. He was jailed by Abacha for his role in the 12 June struggle.

11 See Bah (2005: 57).

12 For an account of resistance to the military by NADECO and other opposition groups, see Edozie (2002).

13 See, for instance, the testimony of Barnabas Jabila, popularly known as Sergeant Rogers, before the Oputa Panel. The Oputa Panel, also known as the Human Rights Violations Investigations Commission, was set up in June 1999 by then newly sworn-in President Olusegun Obasanjo. The full testimony is available at https://www.youtube.com/watch?v=zC7rkcS6Q3A (accessed 19 May 2017).

14 The full text of the speech is available at http://www.waado.org/nigerian_scholars/archive/docum/genabdu.html (accessed 19 May 2017).

15 Ibid.

16 For a discussion of the mutual hostility between Soyinka and Obasanjo, including the roots of Soyinka's resentment of Obasanjo, see Iliffe (2011).

17 For quite possibly the best account of the cultural, political and historical backdrop to the division among the Yoruba elite with respect to Falae versus Chief Bola Ige, see Adebanwi (2014). Ige never quite overcame his loss to Falae, and lingering bitterness at his perceived mistreatment may have been a factor in his surprising decision to accept Obasanjo's invitation to head the troubled Ministry of Mines and Power.

18 See Bienen (1986: 60).

19 Robertson (1989: 12).

20 Ellis and ter Haar (2004: 100).

21 For a global perspective, see Anderson (2004); for an African perspective, see Maxwell (2006).

22 For two excellent overviews of the North–South division over the secular status of the Nigerian state, compare Suberu (1997) and Ibrahim (1997). See also Obadare (2004). For a legal perspective, see Sampson (2014).

23 Sanneh (2003: 241).

24 See the text of the 1990 press statement issued by the Council of Ulama, quoted in Sanneh (2003: 236).

25 Quoted in Kane (2003: 186, emphasis added).

26 See Paden (2002: 2).

27 See Vaughan (2016: 131). See also Falola (1998). For an excellent survey of the contrasting attitudes to secularism by Christians and Muslims in Nigeria, see Ilesanmi (1997).

28 Ranger (2008: 232).

29 CAN statement, quoted in Adogame (2006, emphasis added).

30 Apparently the first ever cleric to contest the Nigerian presidency on the platform of a major party, Dr Akande enjoyed qualified success, winning the Oyo State primaries and 174 official delegates. For more on his motivation, the initial opposition he faced from fellow Baptists, and other details of his campaign, see Egbeyemi (1996).

31 For more on this, see Kukah (1993).

32 Babangida's decision deepened Christian–Muslim tension in the country and spawned a protracted public debate. While Muslims defended full OIC

membership on the grounds that it was no different from the country's largely uncontroversial diplomatic relationship with the Vatican, Christians considered it egregious that a secular country would openly align itself with an organisation set up primarily to propagate Islam. For a detailed analysis of the OIC controversy, see Oyeniyi (2009).

33 See Adebanwi (2010).

34 See Obadare (2013b).

35 Adogame (2006: 132).

36 Adebanwi (2010).

37 See Ojo (2004).

38 See Peel (1983).

39 See Agbaje et al. (2005).

40 Obasanjo (2014: 435–6).

41 Ibid., p. 447.

42 A solitary detention centre between Obalende and Ikoyi, Lagos, where Obasanjo was briefly kept as he awaited confirmation of the terms of his imprisonment.

43 Obasanjo (2014: 448).

44 Ibid., p. 462 (emphasis added).

45 Ibid., pp. 462–3 (emphasis added).

46 See Gaiya (2002).

47 Or 'black magic'. Here, I am referring to Obasanjo's call, in 1986, as part of an international advisory group on the situation in South Africa, for the use of African juju to combat the apartheid regime.

48 *The Guardian on Sunday* (2006, emphasis added).

49 Oyetime and Okonoboh (2016).

50 Ibid.

51 Obasanjo (1998a; 2000a; 2000b; 2001) and the semi-fictional *The Story of Baba Ali Pastor Sunday Gula Theman* (2012).

52 Obasanjo (1998b: ix).

53 Ibid., p. vi.

54 Ibid., p. x.

55 In a book published in 2006, a year before Obasanjo's second term as president expired, Ukeje Nwokeforo compared Obasanjo with the biblical King David, describing him as a man 'on a divine mission to lead Nigeria, out of the bondage of corruption and underdevelopment, into the *Promised Land* of unity, discipline, social stability, economic development, prosperity and national greatness' (Nwokeforo 2006, italics in the original); cf. Ogunranti (2011) and Avwenagbiku (2000).

56 Obasanjo (2014: 438).

57 Bishop Wale Oke claims to have visited the villa 'over 40 times'. See Oyetime and Okonoboh (2016).

58 Ojo (2004: 2).

59 Ibid.

60 Later, Chris Okotie was the presidential candidate of the Justice Party and Fresh (Faith, Responsibility, Equality, Security and Hope) Party, which he founded, in the 2003 and 2007 elections respectively.

61 See Aribisala (2012).

62 1 Samuel 15.33 (NKJV).

63 He was already a prominent figure before his controversial prophecy (hence the attention it generated), but the incident and Bakare's refusal to stand down gave him instant visibility as one of the leading critics of the Obasanjo regime. In 2011, he would enter the political fray himself as running mate to Muhammadu Buhari of the Congress for Progressive Change. Before then, in January 2010, he was the brains behind the establishment of the Save Nigeria Group (SNG), which spearheaded civil society mobilisation to force the National Assembly to declare Goodluck Jonathan acting president.

64 See *The Sun* (Lagos), 10 April 2006. Among religious leaders who publicly pushed back against Bakare, by 'praying his prophecy away', issuing contradicting prophesies or generally denouncing him, were Anthony Olubunmi Okogie, Catholic Archbishop of Lagos and one-time president of CAN (1988–95); Esther Obono of the Christ Miracle Centre Point, Ilorin, Kwara State; Archbishop Omolaye Olorunwo, Cathedral of Cherubim and Seraphim, Gbagada, Lagos; and Adebanwo Towolawi of the Evangel Pentecostal Church, Okota, Lagos.

65 See Comaroff (2010: 19).

66 'Inaugural speech by His Excellency, President Olusegun Obasanjo, following his swearing-in as President of the Federal Republic of Nigeria on May 29, 1999.' Available at http://nigeriaworld.com/feature/speech/inaugural.html (accessed 30 May 2017).

67 Ibid.

68 Haynes (1995: 89–108).

69 Ellis and ter Haar (2004: 99).

70 See Asamoah-Gyadu (2005: 93).

71 See, for instance, the work of J. D. Y. Peel, especially his *Religious Encounter and the Making of the Yoruba* (2001).

72 Adebanwi (2010: 123).

73 Larkin and Meyer (2006: 310).

74 Kalu (2004: 246).

75 Ellis and ter Haar (2004: 101).

76 See Akinola (2006).

77 See Birai (1993: 187).

78 For an exploration of how disputes over architecture feed into issues around social citizenship and power relations, see the essays in Diouf and Fredericks

(2014). For a specific discussion of architecture and politics in Nigeria, with a focus on Abuja, see Elleh (2017).

79   For an incisive treatment of this question and anxieties about its demographic implications, see Stonawski et al. (2016).

80   Mobolaji Ajose-Adeogun, the first Minister of the FCT (1976–79) remains, to date, the only occupier of the office to have hailed from the Southern part of the country. There have been two Christians: John Jatau Kadiya (1979–82) and Jeremiah Timbut Useni (1993–98), both from Plateau State. See Odunsi (2012).

81   See Obasanjo (2016, emphasis added).

82   Nasir El-Rufai reports, for example, that Oby Ezekwezili and Finance Minister Ngozi Okonjo-Iweala were daily attendees (El-Rufai 2013: liv).

83   *The Guardian on Sunday* (2006, emphasis added).

84   Her husband is Chinedu Ezekwezili, described by Nasir El-Rufai as 'some kind of honorary deputy chaplain of the Presidential Villa, ministering on Wednesdays, so he had a dual relationship with Obasanjo – as Oby's husband and as once-a-week pastor to Obasanjo' (El-Rufai 2013: 502). Mr Ezekwezili was also instrumental in reconciling El-Rufai and Obasanjo after their relationship had broken down (ibid.: 175).

85   'The rest of us' were Nasir El-Rufai, Minister of the FCT, Ngozi Okonjo-Iweala (Finance), Nuhu Ribadu, head of the anti-corruption agency the Economic and Financial Crimes Commission (EFCC), Bode Agusto, Director-General of the Budget Office of the Federation, and Charles Soludo, Executive Director of the Central Bank of Nigeria.

86   *The Guardian on Sunday* (2006).

87   Haynes (1995).

88   Ellis and ter Haar (2004: 101).

89   Oha (2005: 36).

90   Located in Ota, Ogun State, and established in 2002.

91   See Obasanjo (2004).

92   Ibid.

93   See, for instance, Ukah (2008).

94   Murphy (2006).

95   Gifford (2016).

96   See Obasanjo (2006a).

97   See *Saturday Sun* (Lagos), 8 April 2006.

98   For a comprehensive report on Obasanjo's attempts to persuade various political constituencies to accept the idea, see Adegbamigbe (2006). See also Isike and Idoniboye-Obu (2011).

99   See Suberu (2010: 226).

100 For a critical examination of these tensions, see Ilesanmi (2011). See also Adebanwi (2002).

101 Kendhammer (2016: 117).
102 See Kane (1994).
103 Kendhammer (2016: 117).
104 *Talakawa* means 'of or pertaining to the poor'.
105 Suberu (2010: 225).
106 Vaughan (2016: 207).
107 Ibid., p. 208.
108 Ibid., p. 211.
109 Obasanjo (2014: 438–9).

Chapter 3

1 See Nairaland Forum (2010b).
2 Obadare (2016b).
3 The two relevant clauses are from the preamble:

> To create socio-political conditions conducive to national peace and unity by ensuring fair and equitable distribution of resources and opportunities, to conform with the principles of power shift and power sharing by rotating key political offices amongst the diverse peoples of our country and devolving powers equitably between the Federal, State, and Local Governments in the spirit of federalism.

And Article 7.2 [c]: 'In pursuance of the principle of equity, justice and fairness, the party shall adhere to the policy of rotation and zoning of party and public elective offices and it shall be enforced by the appropriate executive committee at all levels' (see http://nairametrics.com/wp-content/uploads/2013/01/Constitution-PDP.pdf, accessed 12 June 2017).

4 For Obasanjo's explanation of his choice, see volume 2 of *My Watch* (2014). See also Adeniyi (2011: 205–6).
5 Donald Duke (Cross River), Peter Odili (Rivers), Ahmed Makarfi (Kaduna), Saminu Turaki (Jigawa) and Ahmadu Adamu Muazu (Bauchi) were frequently mentioned.
6 See Obasanjo (2014: Vol. 1, 444). See also Agbo (2007).
7 For a comprehensive account of all the secret manipulations undertaken by Obasanjo and his representatives, see El-Rufai (2013). See also Timberg (2006).
8 See Suberu (2007: 97–8).
9 Ibid., p. 98.
10 His election marked the first time in Nigerian history that a civilian president would hand over power to another democratically elected civilian.
11 Similar to 1999, when the two main candidates were Yoruba Christians, the three leading candidates in the 2007 election were Northern Hausa-Fulani Muslims. Abubakar, the AC's flag-bearer, was Obasanjo's running mate,

but they had fallen out over key appointments and Abubakar's presidential ambition.

12 See the text of Yar'Adua's inauguration speech at http://allafrica.com/ stories/200705300790.html (accessed 13 June 2017).

13 Ibid.

14 See Tran (2012).

15 This is Arabic for 'People Committed to the Propagation of the Prophet's Teachings and Jihad'; the Hausa colloquial translation is 'Western education is forbidden' or 'Western civilisation is forbidden'.

16 Newman (2013: 2).

17 See 'Timeline of Boko Haram activity' at http://www.irinnews.org/ news/2011/10/07-0 (accessed 14 June 2017).

18 Ibid.

19 See Mustapha (2014: 148).

20 See, for instance, Mustapha (2014); cf. Mustapha and Ehrhardt (2018). See also Smith (2016), Walker (2016), Varin (2016) and Comolli (2015). See also Kendhammer (2016). For an excellent analysis that locates the Boko Haram insurgency in the *longue durée* of the history of violence in Central Africa, see MacEachern (2018).

21 A Borno State High Court also found the police guilty of unlawfully executing Yusuf's in-law, Baba Fugu, and awarded 100 million naira in damages to his family (see Adeniyi 2011: 113).

22 See Lewis and Watts (2015: 55).

23 See Thurston (2016: 17).

24 Ibid.

25 Mustapha (2014: 149).

26 For an understanding of Boko Haram against the backdrop of Islamic reformist movements in Northern Nigeria, see the account in Last (2014).

27 Lewis and Watts (2015).

28 Over time, Boko Haram has targeted police stations, military barracks, government offices, churches, mosques and bus stations.

29 Compare, for instance, the explanations by Mustapha (2014), Last (2014), Thurston (2016) and Vaughan (2016). See also Lubeck (2014).

30 See World Bank (2016). For a detailed discussion of the 'poverty and inequality' argument, see Mustapha (2014: 169–77). Cf. David et al. (2015).

31 World Bank (2016).

32 Ibid.

33 Ibid.

34 Ibid.

35 Ibid.

36 Ibid.

37 Thurston (2016: 7).

38 Mustapha (2014: 176, italics in original).

39 See Naij.com (n.d.).

40 See Oritsejafor (2012).

41 Eyoboka (2014).

42 Mustapha (2014: 158).

43 Vaughan (2016: 223, emphasis added).

44 Adeniyi (2011: 273, emphasis added).

45 See Mamah (2008).

46 Vaughan (2016: 178).

47 Ibid.

48 Speaking through Attorney General of the Federation Michael Aondoakaa, the FEC had insisted that: 'The president is not incapable of discharging the functions of his office, and that the [sic] medical treatment outside the country does not constitute incapacity to warrant or commence the process of the removal of the president from office, under section 144 and 146 of the 1999 constitution' (see Ogala and Archibong 2010).

49 See Owete (2010).

50 Mamah (2010).

51 Muhammed (2010).

52 The EEG was led by former Head of State Yakubu Gowon and included former President Shehu Shagari, former Interim President Ernest Shonekan, former Vice President Alex Ekwueme, former Chief Justices Mohammed Uwais and Legbo Kutigi, former Minister of Defence T. Y. Danjuma, and Professor Jerry Gana.

53 Fatade (2010).

54 See http://savenigeriagroup.com/who-we-are/ (accessed 30 May 2017).

55 Ajiboye and Abiodun (2002).

56 *The News* (Lagos), 6 August 2012.

57 See Information Nigeria (2013).

58 See Bakare (2014: 16).

59 See Ikeke (2017).

60 See Yong (2010: 12).

61 See Sahara Reporters (2010).

62 This is a reference to 1 Thessalonians 5.2: 'For yourselves know perfectly that the day of the Lord so cometh as a thief in the night.'

63 See 1 Samuel 5.1–6.

64 See Bakare (2010).

65 See the analysis in Obadare (2013b).

66 On 9 February, both houses of the National Assembly had passed an unprecedented motion to have Jonathan assume full power as acting president pending Yar'Adua's full recovery. However, the legality of that motion was never fully resolved (see BBC News 2010a).

67 These included Ibrahim Datti Ahmed, chairman of the Supreme Council for Sharia in Nigeria, Ustaz Musa Mohamed, Chief Imam of the Abuja national mosque, and Sheikh Musa Pantami (see Adeniyi 2011: 264). See also BBC News (2010b).

68 Adeniyi (2011).

69 Ibid.

70 BBC News (2010b).

71 See Adeniyi (2011: 266).

72 See Ajakaye et al. (2010).

73 See Ebimomi et al. (2010). See also the analysis in Obadare (2013b).

74 Bayart (2003: 40, emphasis added).

75 Vaughan (2016: 178).

76 See Nairaland Forum (2010a).

Chapter 4

1 See Ibekwe (2014).

2 See Binniyat et al. (2014).

3 See Odey (2013).

4 See El-Rufai (2013: 439).

5 Mainly Alhaji Adamu Ciroma, Dr Iyorchia Ayu, Alhaji Lawal Keita, Alhaji Bello Kurfi, Ambassador Yahaya Kwande and Alhaji Bashir Ibrahim Yusuf. Their position was that, since the late Umaru Yar'Adua was a Northerner, it was logical that his successor in 2011 should hail from the same region as the deceased president (see Adeniyi 2017: 7).

6 See Opara (2013). Governor Aliyu's claim that Jonathan had entered into a secret agreement was backed by other prominent Northerners, including Adamawa governor Murtala Nyako, and Dr Junaid Mohammed, a member of the National Assembly during the Second Republic (1979–83), who said he had been shown a copy of the signed agreement (see Odunuga 2013).

7 See Omipidan and Musa (2017).

8 One of Jonathan's first acts as president was to create a Facebook fan page. According to Jonathan, he wanted to use the medium for young Nigerians to 'give me the privilege of relating with them without the trappings of office' (see Adunbi 2017: 2–3).

9 In his biography of President Jonathan, written apparently with the subject's authorisation, Charles A. Imokhai makes no mention of Jonathan having been either an assistant head boy in primary school or assistant senior prefect in secondary school. In secondary school, he was secretary of the Food Committee, prefect of Masterson House, and, later, 'Chair of Prefects' (see Imokhai 2015).

10 This is the name of the heart condition that reportedly caused President Yar'Adua's death.

11   Kukah (2010).

12   Ibid.

13   See Kukah (2012).

14   Kalu (2013a).

15   Kalu (2013b). The waters of the conflict between Kalu and Obasanjo run deep. If Kalu is to be believed, it started in 1999 when he borrowed the sum of 500 million naira from the defunct Hallmark Bank and lent it to the PDP, only for the latter to default on the loan. It is also possible that Kalu holds Obasanjo responsible for his arrest in July 2007 by the EFCC in connection with an alleged 5.6 billion naira fraud. See Ozor (2014) and also Sahara Reporters (2007).

16   For a theological analysis in which 'luck' and 'chance' are critically compared, see Michael (2009). Cf. Obadare (2013d).

17   For many Nigerians, it has been a lingering source of exasperation that while it boasts so many educated people, including millions of university graduates, many of its leaders since independence have been men without a university degree to their names.

18   See https://es-la.facebook.com/notes/goodluck-jonathan/speech-by-president-goodluck-ebele-jonathan-declaring-his-candidacy-for-the-pdp-/155774224450221/ (accessed 3 September 2017, italics added, bold in the original).

19   For a critical analysis of the prosperity gospel in Africa, see Obadare (2016c).

20   See Chapter 5.

21   Jonathan's decision to kneel before Pastor Adeboye caused a furore, and not every member of the theocratic elite approved of the president's gesture. For Pastor Tunde Bakare, President Jonathan's action belittled the office.

22   In his entourage were Information Minister Labaran Maku; Special Adviser on Media and Publicity Reuben Abati; state governors Gabriel Suswam (Benue), Theodore Orji (Abia), Peter Obi (Anambra) and Godswill Akpabio (Akwa Ibom); executive secretary of the National Christian Pilgrims Commission Kennedy Okpara; and then president of CAN Pastor Ayo Oritsejafor.

23   For more on the law, the political backdrop (both domestic and global) to its signing, and the ensuing controversy, see Obadare (2015).

24   See http://www.placng.org/new/laws/Same%20Sex%20Marriage%20(Prohibition)%20Act,%202013.pdf (accessed 4 September 2017).

25   Obadare (2015: 67).

26   For more on this, see Currier (2010).

27   Gaudio (1998: 115).

28   Ibid., p. 116.

29   Ibid., p. 118.

30   Ibid., p. 122.

31   The idea was first mooted during the Obasanjo administration.

32   Obadare (2015).

33   See Kulish (2014).

34   See Obadare (2013a).

35   See Odebode et al. (2012b).

36   See Odebode et al. (2012a).

37   In 2011, it is estimated that Boko Haram carried out 32 attacks. On the whole, the numbers escalated over the course of the Jonathan presidency as follows: 148 in 2012, 108 in 2013, 220 in 2014, and 270 in 2015. In 2011, 114 people were reported to have been killed in the 32 attacks. The numbers rose even more dramatically to 910 in 2012, 1,008 in 2013, 3,425 in 2014, and 6,006 in 2015, making a total of 11,463 deaths in a five-year period (see Uhrnacher and Sheridan 2016).

38   See Ikuomola (2012, italics added). Along the same lines, it has also been suggested that Jonathan's zeal to see the insurgency brought under control might have been tempered by the fact that it was confined to a relatively economically unimportant part of the country.

39   See Attah (2012).

40   See Ikuomola and Akowe (2013).

41   Ibid. See also Liman (2014).

42   In one of the most bizarre official responses to news of the kidnapping, four days after the abduction, the Nigerian military announced through spokesperson Major General Chris Olukolade that it had rescued nearly all the girls, only to retract the claim a day later (see Adewunmi et al. 2014). The administration was not alone in insisting that no kidnapping took place. For example, up until 2016, Ekiti State governor Ayodele Fayose remained unconvinced. See Ogundele (2016) and also Ukpong and Ibekwe (2016).

43   See Bennett (2014).

44   See BBC News (2014a).

45   BBC News (2014b).

46   See Tukur (2014a). Mrs Jonathan might have calculated that her tears would impress on the watching public how much her husband's administration cared about the missing girls. But the spectacle backfired, and instead she became the subject of vicious internet memes.

47   See Abubakar and Levs (2014).

48   See Amnesty International (2015).

49   See Ayansina (2014).

50   Ibid.

51   *The Economist* (2016).

Chapter 5

1   As signalled in Chapter 1, this should not occlude the ontological proximity between universes of 'tradition religion' and Pentecostalism, seen, inter alia,

in the way in which the latter's doctrinal obsession with the former has been integral to its explosion as a social force over the past three decades. For more on this theme, see, for instance, Kalu (2007). Cf. Peel (2016).

2   According to a 19 April *Sunday Punch* frontpage report, President Jonathan may have spent close to 2 trillion naira on the March 2015 presidential election. Although the presidency denounced the report as baseless, other newspapers later published articles on the huge sums of money distributed by Colonel Sambo Dasuki, at the time National Security Adviser to the president. For instance, after rumours circulated on social media that she had collected the sum of 240 million naira from Colonel Dasuki, popular Lagos-based blogger Linda Ikeji confessed to having received an unspecified amount of money, but only for the use of 'advertisement' space on her blog. See *Premium Times* (2015b) and also Odunayo (2016).

3   According to media reports, Jonathan did not travel empty-handed and gave various sums of money, ranging between $10,000 and $250,000, to different traditional rulers based on their status and perceived popularity (see Nwodo 2015).

4   The interview is available at https://www.youtube.com/watch?v=jBkmrHg N10I&sns=fb (accessed 14 September 2017).

5   See Momodu (2014).

6   Ibid. Accusing Buhari of being a Muslim irredentist may have been intended to damage him personally, but it may also have been aimed at arousing perennial Southern fears of Islamisation by the North.

7   See Ochonu (2015).

8   In fact, just before the 2011 election, Buhari, perhaps confident of victory, had vowed that: 'This campaign is the third and last one for me since, after it, I will not present myself again for election into the office of the president' (see Aziken 2016).

9   Buhari's choice of Bakare, and the latter's decision to accept, split the Nigerian Christian community right down the middle. While some people argued that it was wrong for a pastor of his eminence to serve under a Muslim, others defended it as a strategy for introducing 'righteous people' into politics (see *PM News* 2011).

10 See Omonobi (2011).

11 Bakare did say that he sought Adeboye's blessing after Buhari had asked him to be his running mate (see AllAfrica 2014).

12 See Sahara Reporters (2015).

13 At different points, Buhari considered Babatunde Fashola (former Lagos State governor), former Edo State governor Adams Oshiomhole, former governor of Rivers State Rotimi Amaechi, and former Ekiti State governor Kayode Fayemi. All were eventually ruled out for various reasons (see Tukur 2014b).

14 See Odebode et al. (2017).

15 See Soniyi (2017).

16 In 2007, together with his wife 'Dolapo (also a pastor), he established the Orderly Society Trust, an NGO devoted to, among other things, '[t]he dissemination of ethics [sic] of integrity, patriotism, respect for civic obligation and etiquette'. See http://orderlysocietytrust.org/index.php/about-us/ (accessed 15 September 2017).

17 I am grateful to Omolara Balogun for this angle. For more on Generational Voices and its 'non-partisan' activities, see https://www.facebook.com/pg/GenVoices/about/?ref=page_internal (accessed 17 September 2017).

18 The meeting was reportedly organised by the Executive Secretary of the National Christian Pilgrims Commission, John Kennedy Okpara, and had in attendance several leading Pentecostal pastors, including Bishop David Oyedepo of the Living Faith Church Worldwide International (aka Winners Chapel), who chaired the meeting (see *Premium Times* 2015a).

19 See Nzemeke (2014).

20 See *Vanguard* (2015b).

21 See *Vanguard* (2015a).

22 See *The News* (2014).

23 Before Jonathan, Lagos State governor Babatunde Raji Fashola had dropped by to 'commiserate with' Pastor Joshua. Generally, a pilgrimage to Joshua's Lagos-based Synagogue is de rigueur for leading sports stars, celebrities, and political office holders and aspirants from other African countries, especially Ghana, South Africa and Zambia. For instance, in the run-up to the December 2017 Liberian general election, presidential candidate Yormie Johnson and eventual winner George Weah both dropped by (see *Vanguard* 2017).

24 As part of this strategy, we must include his decision to convoke a national conference in Abuja in March 2014. Rejecting (mostly Northern-centred) criticism of the national conference as a wasteful distraction, President Goodluck defended it as 'an essential part of the process of building a more united, stronger and progressive nation' (see *Vanguard* 2014). In all probability, Jonathan calculated that convening a national conference would gain him the acceptance of a broad section of the elite (among whom the popularity of the idea of a national meeting ebbs and flows), and among long-standing advocates of political 'restructuring' across the country.

25 See Ibekwe (2015).

26 These were, in order of estimated wealth (first being the richest), David Oyedepo of the Living Faith World Outreach Ministry (aka Winners Chapel), Chris Oyakhilome of Christ Embassy Church, T. B. Joshua of the Synagogue Church of All Nations, Matthew Ashimolowo of Kingsway International Christian Centre, London, and Chris Okotie of the Household of God Church International Ministries. See http://www.fullnetworth.com/top-10-richest-pastors-in-the-world/ (accessed 14 November 2015). See also Nsehe (2011).

27 See, for instance, *Osun Defender* (2015) and *First Weekly* (2015). See also Alabelewe (2016). Cf. Abimboye (2015).

28 Personal communication, February 2015.

29 See Ugbodaga (2015).

30 Ibid.

31 Ibid.

32 Ibid. (emphasis added).

33 See Anjorin (2015).

34 See https://www.youtube.com/watch?v=wsBmugKjFkY (accessed 21 September 2017).

35 See Akinola (2015).

36 Ibid.

37 The full text of the statement is available at Samuel (2014).

38 Ibid.

39 The full text of Father Mbaka's address to his congregation is available at https://theeagleonline.com.ng/full-transcript-of-rev-mbakas-new-year-message-calling-on-president-jonathan-to-quit/ (accessed 21 September 2017).

40 See Ezeamalu (2015).

41 The video of Father Mbaka praying for a kneeling Mrs Jonathan is available at http://www.dailymotion.com/video/x2vbz7x (accessed 21 September 2017).

42 See Isine (2015).

43 Ibid.

44 His account of what transpired between them, including how he declined Jonathan's dollar gift, can be found in Uzodinma (2016).

45 See Funke (2015).

46 See note 35 above.

47 This probably owes more to the power and personality of the state governor, Ayo Fayose, a sworn opponent of Buhari.

Chapter 6

1 The decision was later invalidated in December 2015.

2 See Soniyi (2017).

3 For more on this theme, see Gifford (2001).

4 See, for example, Andrews (2009). For an anthropological treatment of the clergy as 'apostles of peace' in Yorubaland, see Adebanwi (2010).

5 The extent to which Mrs Jonathan was a millstone around the neck of her husband's administration cannot be overemphasised. She was always in danger of saying the wrong thing, and, as time went on, she became the butt of many vicious jokes (see Obadare 2016b: 65).

6 Gifford (2016).

7   In all, I have drawn on eight of his books. These are, in no particular order: *The Mystery of Water Cure* (2014b); *Open Heavens Through Holy Disturbance* (2005); *Prayer Warfare Against 70 Mad Spirits* (2003); *The Tragedy of Stealing* (2014c); *What to Do When Trouble Comes* (2014f); *The Hour of Freedom* (2014d); *Watching the Serpents of the Magicians* (2014e); *Spiritual Warfare to Tackle the Enemy* (2013); and *Violent Prayers to Disgrace Stubborn Problems* (1999). These works represent only a small sample of Olukoya's publications. According to information on the website of the church, Olukoya 'has over 70 scientific publications to his credit' (see https://www.mountainoffire.org/about/dr-daniel-and-sis-shade-olukoya). More impressively, his book *Spiritual Warfare to Tackle the Enemy* (2014a) credits him with authorship of 224 books written in English, three in Yoruba and 36 in French. It is not clear whether the French books were originally written in French or are translations of others written in English and Yoruba.

8   Ukah (2008: 295).

9   Marshall (2009).

10 Two important exceptions that focus respectively on deliverance rhetoric and discourses of demonisation in Olukoya's church are Adogame (2005) and Hackett (2003).

11 On a personal note, I can also confirm that he is almost impossible to get hold of. After getting his number from a journalist friend, I sent him a polite text introducing myself and asking (or rather begging) for an audience. To my surprise, he responded almost immediately, asking, because of my last name, if I were related to the late Christ Apostolic Church televangelist Prophet T. O. Obadare. I enthusiastically replied that we hailed from the same town, but nothing more. After that, I heard nothing from Pastor Olukoya, and after several promptings I gave up. I now wonder whether I should have lied about my relationship with the late prophet.

12 Olukoya (2014f).

13 Olukoya (2003: 17).

14 Ibid.

15 Ibid.

16 Ibid.

17 King James Version.

18 Ibid.

19 Olukoya (2003: 21).

20 Olukoya (2005: 9).

21 Olukoya (2014c: 121, emphasis added in all quotes in this sentence).

22 Ibid., p. 121.

23 Ibid.

24 Ibid., p. 122.

25 Ibid., p. 47.

26 Ibid.
27 Ibid.
28 Ibid.
29 Olukoya (2013: 69).
30 Olukoya (2014b: 66).
31 Olukoya (2014g: 130, emphasis in original).
32 See Haynes (2016). Cf. Meyer (2015).
33 See Ojo (2006).
34 See the 2013 film *Enlarging the Kingdom: African Pentecostals in Italy*, directed and produced by Annalisa Butticci and Andrew Esiebo.
35 See, for instance, Awoyinfa (2014).
36 The website of the RCCG describes the Redemption Camp as the 'largest "City of God" on Earth' and as a 'former den of robbers' and 'wild animals' that 'became a place of worship'. See https://trccg.org/rccg/redemption-camp-largest-city-of-god-on-earth/ (accessed 1 October 2017).
37 Respectively as part of a broader treatment of political spiritualities (Marshall 2009), interpretations of contemporary Christianity from an African context (Asamoah-Gyadu 2013), or a specific study of an African Pentecostal church, in this case the RCCG (Ukah 2008). Cf. Adeeko (2013).
38 See Katongole (2005).
39 These were possibly inspired by the text of Exodus 22.18 ('Thou shalt not suffer not a witch to live') and prosecuted most vigorously by self-consecrated 'lady apostle' Helen Ukpabio, leader of the Calabar-based Liberty Foundation Gospel Ministries (see Oppenheimer 2010).
40 See Wickramasinghe (2001: 45).
41 Comaroff and Comaroff (2006: 28).
42 Ibid., p. 6.
43 For more on this, see Iwilade (2014). Cf. Obadare (2013c).
44 Vigh (2006).
45 See Quayson (2001: 155).
46 Ayimpam (2014: 116).
47 Vogler and Markell (2003: 7).
48 Ayimpam (2014).
49 See Oha (2000: 192–9). Cf. Shaw (2007).
50 Bouju and de Bruijn (2014: 3).
51 Ibid.
52 See Meyer (1998).
53 See Gifford (2014: 128–9).
54 See, for instance, van der Veer (2001). Cf. Hall (2006).
55 Anderson (2004: 122).

Chapter 7

1   See https://twitter.com/elrufai/status/267568926093869056 (accessed 6 October 2017). 'No jet as gifts' was most probably an indirect reference to the controversy then raging in the country regarding the acquisition of private jets by some pastors.

2   El-Rufai describes the encounter in his book *The Accidental Public Servant* (2013: 434):

> Pastor Bakare and I finally met face-to-face at the end of March 2010 in Dubai. We bonded almost instantaneously. I found in Tunde Bakare a forthright and intelligent man, a gifted speaker, passionate patriot and one of the most honest men I know. He is straight and courageous in thought, speech and action. I knew I had found another elder brother to add to the blessings of Bashir, Ali and Sani Maikudi.

3   Senior brother, in a social sense.

4   For an excellent analysis of political friendships, including their promises and perils, see Adebanwi (2013).

5   See Shiklam (2016). El-Rufai may have calculated that being seen in church, and in the company of a leading Pentecostal pastor at that, was a perfect way to rebut charges of being anti-Christian.

6   See '"I am 100% with General Buhari", says Pastor Tunde Bakare' at https://www.youtube.com/watch?v=SXez8f8KWOI (accessed 6 October 2017).

7   See Obadare (2004).

8   Ibid.

9   For more on this, see Obadare (2013b).

10 See, for instance, Obadare (2016a).

11 See Bishop David Oyedepo making such a supplication at https://www.youtube.com/watch?v=xYK6mE_xlKw (accessed 7 October 2017).

12 See *Premium Times* (2017).

13 See Keane (2015: 80).

14 See Oni (2018).

15 Kolapo (2016: 379).

16 Obadare (2016a).

REFERENCES

Abati, Reuben (2014) 'The spiritual side of Aso Villa', *The Guardian* (Lagos), 14 October.

Abimboye, Micheal (2015) 'N6 billion gift: Pastor Adeboye wants accused pastors to return money', *Premium Times*, 5 February, https://www.premiumtimesng.com/news/top-news/176306-n6-billion-gift-pastor-adeboye-wants-accused-pastors-return-money.html (accessed 2017).

Abubakar, Aminu and Josh Levs (2014) '"I will sell them," Boko Haram leader says of kidnapped Nigerian girls', CNN, 6 May, https://www.cnn.com/2014/05/05/world/africa/nigeria-abducted-girls/index.html (accessed 10 September 2017).

Adebanwi, Wale (2002) '"Sharia" or "pariah" citizens? Muslim legal code and the negotiation of citizenship in Nigeria'. Paper presented at the Fifth International Society for Third Sector Research (ISTR) conference, Cape Town, 7–11 July.

— (2010) 'The clergy, culture, and political conflicts in Nigeria', *African Studies Review* 53 (3): 121–42.

— (2013) 'What are friends for? The fatality of affinity in the postcolony'. Oxford African Studies Annual Lecture, Oxford University, 14 May.

— (2014) *Yoruba Elites and Ethnic Politics in Nigeria: Obafemi Awolowo and corporate agency.* Cambridge: Cambridge University Press.

Adedayo, Wale (2010) *Micro-Seconds Away from Death.* Ijebu-Ife: Journal Communications Limited.

Adeeko, Adeleke (2013) 'Give them a dose of pain!', Sahara Reporters, 16 September, http://saharareporters.com/2013/09/16/give-them-dose-pain-adeleke-adeeko (accessed 3 October 2017).

Adegbamigbe, Ademola (2006) 'Obasanjo's 3rd term agenda and those behind it', Sahara Reporters, 16 February, http://saharareporters.com/2006/02/16/obasanjos-3rd-term-agenda-and-those-behind-it-thenewssaharareporters (accessed 25 June 2017).

Adelakun, Abimbola (2016) 'Aso Rock demons: does Abati need help?', *The Punch* (Lagos), 20 October.

Adeniyi, Olusegun (2011) *Power, Politics and Death.* Lagos: Prestige Books.

— (2016) 'Of Aso Rock demons and "the other room"', *This Day* (Lagos), 20 October.

— (2017) *Against the Run of Play: how an incumbent president was defeated in Nigeria.* Lagos: Kachifo Limited.

Adesina, Femi (2016) 'The unspiritual side of Aso Villa', *Premium Times* (Lagos), 23 October.

Adetayo, Olalekan (2017) 'Politicians hire marabouts, pastors to pray for Buhari's death – aide', *The Punch* (Lagos), 22 May, http://punchng.com/politicians-hire-marabouts-pastors-to-pray-for-buharis-death-aide/ (accessed 10 June 2017).

Adewunmi, Bim, Monica Mark and Jason Burke (2014) 'Nigeria's mass kidnapping: the vital questions answered', *The Guardian* (London), 7 May, https://www.theguardian.com/world/2014/may/07/nigeria-boko-haram-mass-kidnapping-vital-questions (accessed 10 September 2017).

Adogame, Afe (2005) 'Dealing with local satanic technology: deliverance rhetoric in the Mountain of Fire and Miracle Ministries'. Paper presented at the CESNUR International Conference, Palermo, Sicily, 2–5 June.

— (2006) 'Politicization of religion and religionization of politics in Nigeria' in Chima J. Korieh and G. Ugo Nwokeji (eds), *Religion, History, and Politics in Nigeria.* Oxford: University Press of America.

— (ed.) (2011) *Who is Afraid of the Holy Ghost? Pentecostalism and globalization in Africa and beyond.* Trenton NJ: Africa World Press.

Adunbi, Omolade (2017) 'The Facebook president: oil, citizenship, and the social mediation of politics in Nigeria', *Political and Legal Anthropology Review (POLAR)* 40 (2): 226–44.

Agande, Ben (2016) '… Aso Rock: beyond the glitz and the glamour', *Vanguard* (Lagos), 22 October.

Agbaje, Adigun, Rasidi Okunola and Wale Adebanwi (2005) 'Religious pluralism and democratic governance in South-Western Nigeria'. Research report. Kano: Centre for Research and Development (CRD).

Agbese, Andrew (2017) 'Nigeria: I built church, mosque in library to encourage unity – Obasanjo', *Daily Trust* (Abuja), 6 March.

Agbo, Dennis (2007) 'How Yar'Adua died in Abakaliki prison', *Vanguard* (Lagos), 7 December.

Agrama, Hussein Ali (2012) *Questioning Secularism: Islam, sovereignty, and the rule of law in modern Egypt.* Chicago IL: University of Chicago Press.

Ajakaye, Rafiu, Francis Iwuchukwu, Francis Famoroti and Wale Igbintade (2010) 'Condemnation trails cleric's visit to Yar'Adua', *Daily Independent* (Lagos), 6 April.

Ajiboye, Segun and Adesina Abiodun (2002) 'Stormy prophecy', *TEMPO* (Lagos), 14 March.

Akinola, Femi (2015) 'Bakare carpets CAN, PFN for alleged endorsement of Jonathan', *Daily Trust* (Abuja), 2 February, https://www.dailytrust.com.

ng/news/general/bakare-carpets-can-pfn-for-alleged-endorsement-of-jonathan/67841.html (accessed 21 September 2017).

Akinola, G. A. (2006) 'Religion and the Obasanjo administration', *The Guardian* (Lagos), 20 March.

Alabelewe, Abdulgafar (2016) 'Alleged N7bn Jonathan largesse: CAN leaders paid me N1m to keep quiet – cleric', *The Nation* (Lagos), 23 October.

AllAfrica (2014) 'Pastor Tunde Bakare on Buhari', AllAfrica, 21 December, http://allafrica.com/stories/201412220511.html (accessed 14 September 2017).

Amnesty International (2015) *'Our Job is to Shoot, Slaughter and Kill': Boko Haram's reign of terror in north east Nigeria*. London: Amnesty International. Available at: https://www.amnesty.org/en/documents/afr44/1360/2015/en / (accessed 10 September 2017).

Anderson, Allan (2004) *An Introduction to Pentecostalism*. Cambridge: Cambridge University Press.

Andrews, Jaiyeola (2009) 'Adeboye wades into Daniel, Tinubu feud', *This Day*, 11 October.

Anjorin, Femi (2015) 'RCCG's 12-million seater auditorium has made me a beggar, says Adeboye', *The News*, 8 August, http://thenewsnigeria.com.ng/2015/08/rccgs-12-million-seater-auditorium-has-made-me-a-beggar-says-adeboye/ (accessed 21 September 2017).

Apter, Andrew (2005) *The Pan-African Nation: oil and the spectacle of culture in Nigeria*. Chicago IL: University of Chicago Press.

Aribisala, Femi (2012) 'The makings of a false prophet', *Vanguard* (Lagos), 22 January, http://www.vanguardngr.com/2012/01/the-makings-of-a-false-prophet/ (accessed 30 May 2017).

Asad, Talal, Wendy Brown, Judith Butler and Saba Mahmood (2009) *Is Critique Secular? Blasphemy, injury, and free speech*. Berkeley CA: University of California Press.

Asamoah-Gyadu, J. Kwabena (2005) '"Christ is the answer": what is the question? A Ghana Airways prayer vigil and its implications for religion, evil and public space', *Journal of Religion in Africa* 35 (1): 93–117.

— (2013) *Contemporary Pentecostal Christianity: interpretations from an African context*. Eugene OR: Wipf and Stock.

Attah, David (2012) 'CAN secretary under fire for Jonathan resignation call', *The Punch*, 14 August.

Avwenagbiku, Patrick (2000) *Obasanjo & His Footprints*. Abuja: Metro Publishers.

Awoyinfa, Samuel (2014) 'Redeemers varsity student kills dad at Redemption Camp', *The Punch*, 7 July.

Ayansina, Caleb (2014) 'Chibok: CAN releases names of abducted girls', *Vanguard*, 4 May, https://www.vanguardngr.com/2014/05/chibok-can-releases-names-abducted-girls / (accessed 10 September 2017).

Ayimpam, Sylvie (2014) 'The cyclical exchange of violence in Congolese kinship relations' in Jacky Bouju and Mirjam de Bruijn (eds), *Ordinary Violence and Social Change in Africa*. Leiden: Brill.

Aziken, Emmanuel (2016) 'The frustrations of Buhari from 2003 to 2011', *Vanguard*, 12 December, https://www.vanguardngr.com/2016/12/the-frustrations-of-buhari-from-2003-to-2011/ (accessed 13 September 2017).

Bah, Abu Bakarr (2005) *Breakdown and Reconstitution: democracy, the nation-state, and ethnicity in Nigeria*. Lanham MD: Lexington Books.

Bakare, Babatunde (2010) 'State of the nation broadcast by Pastor Tunde Bakare'. Available at: http://savenigeriagroup.com/2010/03/01/state-of-the-nation-broadcast-by-pastor-tunde-bakare/ (accessed 23 June 2017).

— (2014) 'God's judgment will begin from the church', *The News*, 27 October.

Bashorun, Debo (2013) *Honour for Sale: an insider's account of the murder of Dele Giwa*. Ibadan: Bookcraft.

Bayart, Jean-François (2003) 'The state' in Tom Young (ed.), *Readings in African Politics*. Bloomington IN: Indiana University Press.

BBC News (2007) 'Nigerian leaders row over occult', BBC News, 21 May, http://news.bbc.co.uk/2/hi/africa/6678327.stm (accessed 10 June 2017).

— (2010a) 'Nigeria: Goodluck Jonathan becomes acting president', BBC News, 10 February, http://news.bbc.co.uk/2/hi/africa/8507289.stm (accessed 23 June 2017).

— (2010b) 'Nigeria clerics meet ailing President Umaru Yar'Adua', BBC News, 2 April, http://news.bbc.co.uk/2/hi/africa/8600639.stm (accessed 23 June 2017).

— (2014a) 'Goodluck Jonathan: Nigerian girls' abduction a turning point', BBC News, 8 May, https://www.bbc.co.uk/news/world-africa-27328003 (accessed 10 September 2017).

— (2014b) 'Malala meets Nigeria's leader Goodluck Jonathan over abducted girls', BBC News, 14 July, http://www.bbc.com/news/world-africa-28292480 (accessed 10 September 2017).

Bennett, Brian (2014) 'US officials frustrated by Nigeria's response to girls' kidnapping', *Los Angeles Times*, 15 May, http://www.latimes.com/world/africa/la-fg-us-nigeria-schoolgirls-20140515-story.html (accessed 10 September 2017).

Berger, Peter L. (2012) 'A friendly dissent from Pentecostalism', *First Things*, November, https://www.firstthings.com/article/2012/11/a-friendly-dissent-from-pentecostalism.

Bienen, Henry (1986) 'Religion, legitimacy, and conflict in Nigeria', *Annals of the American Academy of Political and Social Science* 483 (1): 50–60.

Binniyat, Luka, Emman Ovuakporie, Levinus Nwabughiogu and Laide Akinboade (2014) '$9.3m arms deal: Oritsejafor opens up', *Vanguard* (Lagos), 30 September.

Birai, Umar M. (1993) 'Islamic Tajdid and the political process in Nigeria' in Martin E. Marty and R. Scott Appleby (eds), *Fundamentalisms and the State: remaking politics, economies and militance*. Chicago IL: University of Chicago Press.

Bouju, Jacky and Mirjam de Bruijn (2014) 'Introduction: ordinary violence in Africa' in Jacky Bouju and Mirjam de Bruijn (eds), *Ordinary Violence and Social Change in Africa*. Leiden: Brill.

Boyd, Lydia (2015) *Preaching Prevention: born-again Christianity and the moral panics of AIDS in Uganda*. Athens OH: Ohio University Press.

Burgess, Richard (2015) 'Pentecostalism and democracy in Nigeria: electoral politics, prophetic practices, and cultural reformation', *Nova Religio* 18 (3): 38–62.

Comaroff, Jean (2010) 'The politics of conviction: faith on the neo-liberal frontier' in Bruce Kapferer, Kari Telle and Annelin Eriksen (eds), *Contemporary Religiosities: emergent socialities and the post-nation-state*. New York NY: Berghahn Books.

Comaroff, John L. and Jean Comaroff (2006) 'Law and disorder in the postcolony: an introduction' in Jean Comaroff and John L. Comaroff (eds), *Law and Disorder in the Postcolony*. Chicago IL: University of Chicago Press.

Comolli, Virginia (2015) *Boko Haram: Nigeria's Islamist insurgency*. London: C. Hurst & Co.

Cooper, Helene (2017) 'In Liberia, an executive mansion fit for a president – and ghosts, too', *New York Times*, 29 October.

Currier, Ashley (2010) 'Political homophobia in postcolonial Namibia', *Gender and Society* 24 (1): 110–29.

David, Ojochenemi J., Lucky E. Asuelime and Hakeem Onapajo (2015) *Boko Haram: the socio-economic drivers*. New York NY: Springer.

Deneen, Patrick J. (2018) *Why Liberalism Failed*. New Haven CT and London: Yale University Press.

Diouf, Mamadou and Rosalind Fredericks (eds) (2014) *The Arts of Citizenship in African Cities: infrastructures and spaces of belonging*. New York NY: Palgrave Macmillan.

Ebimomi, Victor, Aramide Oikelome and Baba Negedu (2010) 'Christian leaders divided over visit to Yar'Adua', *Daily Independent* (Lagos), 9 April.

Edozie, Rita Kiki (2002) *People Power and Democracy: the popular movement against military despotism in Nigeria, 1989–1999*. Trenton NJ: Africa World Press.

Egbeyemi, Olaseni O. (1996) *S. T. Ola Akande: agent of change*. Ibadan: GLJ General Services Ltd.

Elleh, Nnamdi (2017) *Architecture and Politics in Nigeria: the study of a late-twentieth century enlightenment-inspired modernism at Abuja, 1900–2016*. London and New York NY: Routledge.

Ellis, Stephen (2008) 'The Okija shrine: death and life in Nigerian politics', *Journal of African History* 49: 445–66.

Ellis, Stephen and Gerrie ter Haar (1998) 'Religion and politics in sub-Saharan Africa', *Journal of Modern African Studies* 36 (2): 175–201.

— (2004) *Worlds of Power: religious thought and political practice in Africa.* London: C. Hurst & Co.

El-Rufai, Nasir Ahmad (2013) *The Accidental Public Servant.* Ibadan: Safari Books Ltd.

Enwerem, Iheanyi M. (1995) *A Dangerous Awakening: the politicization of religion in Nigeria.* Ibadan: IFRA.

Eyoboka, Sam (2014) 'Don't negotiate with Boko Haram – Pastor Oritsejafor', *Vanguard*, 16 November, https://www.vanguardngr.com/2014/11/dont-negotiate -boko-haram-pastor-oritsejafor/ (accessed 17 June 2017).

Ezeamalu, Ben (2015) '#Nigeria2015: Catholic priest, Ejike Mbaka, attacks Jonathan; wants president out, Buhari in', *Premium Times*, 3 January, https://www.premiumtimesng.com/news/headlines/174187-nigeria2015-catholic-priest-ejike-mbaka-attacks-jonathan-wants president-buhari.html (accessed 21 September 2017).

Falola, Toyin (1998) *Violence in Nigeria: the crisis of religious politics and secular ideologies.* Rochester NY: University of Rochester Press.

Fani-Kayode, Femi (2016) 'Buhari's kitchen wife: the curse and pain of power', *Vanguard* (Lagos), 15 October.

Fatade, Wale (2010) 'Panic in Yar'Adua's camp', *NEXT*, 31 January.

First Weekly (2015) 'Jonathan gave CAN N7bn not N6bn, Pastor Dikwa alleges', *First Weekly*, 20 February, http://www.firstweeklymagazine.com/jonathan-gave-can-n7bn-not-n6bn-pastor-dikwa-alleges/ (accessed 14 November 2015).

Fitzgerald, Frances (2017) *The Evangelicals: the struggle to shape America.* New York NY: Simon & Schuster.

Freeman, Dena (ed.) (2012) *Pentecostalism and Development: churches, NGOs and social change in Africa.* New York NY: Palgrave Macmillan.

Freston, Paul (2008) *Evangelicals and Politics in Asia, Africa, and Latin America.* Oxford: Oxford University Press.

Funke, Joseph (2015) 'Buhari hails Father Mbaka for courage in faulting Jonathan's govt.', *Vanguard*, 19 December, https://www.vanguardngr.com/2015/12/buhari-hails-father-mbaka-for-courage-in-faulting-jonathans-govt/ (accessed 21 September 2017).

Gaiya, Musa A. B. (2002) 'The Pentecostal revolution in Nigeria'. Copenhagen: Centre of African Studies, University of Copenhagen.

Gaudio, Rudolf Pell (1998) 'Male lesbians and other queer notions in Hausa' in S. O. Murray and W. Roscoe (eds), *Boy-Wives and Female Husbands: studies of African homosexualities.* New York NY: Palgrave Macmillan).

Gifford, Paul (2001) 'The complex provenance of some elements of African Pentecostal theology' in Andre Corten and Ruth Marshall-Fratani (eds),

Between Babel and Pentecost: transnational Pentecostalism in Africa and Latin America. Bloomington IN: Indiana University Press.

— (2004) *Ghana's New Christianity: Pentecostalism in a globalising African economy.* London: C. Hurst & Co.

— (2014) 'Evil, witchcraft, and deliverance in the African Pentecostal worldview' in Clifton R. Clarke (ed.), *Pentecostal Theology in Africa.* Eugene OR: Pickwick Publications.

— (2016) *Christianity, Development and Modernity in Africa.* Oxford: Oxford University Press.

Hackett, Rosalind (2003) 'Discourses of demonization in Africa and beyond', *Diogenes* 50 (3): 61–75.

Hall, Donald E. (2006) *Muscular Christianity: embodying the Victorian age.* Cambridge: Cambridge University Press.

Haynes, Jeff (1995) 'Popular religion and politics in sub-Saharan Africa', *Third World Quarterly* 16 (1): 89–108.

— (2016) *Nollywood: the creation of Nigerian film genres.* Chicago IL: University of Chicago Press.

Ibeh, Nnenna (2014) 'Again, Obasanjo goes back to school', *Premium Times* (Lagos), 29 September, http://www.premiumtimesng.com/news/headlines/168820-again-obasanjo-goes-back-to-school.html (accessed 18 May 2017).

Ibekwe, Nicholas (2014) 'Exclusive: revealed: the Nigerians aboard jet that smuggled $9.3 million arms money to South Africa', *Premium Times*, 23 November, http://www.premiumtimesng.com/news/headlines/171732-exclusive-revealed-the-nigerians-aboard-jet-that-smuggled-9-3-million-arms-money-to-south-africa.html (accessed 29 August 2017).

— (2015) 'Moroccan King snubs President Jonathan, rejects telephone conversation over election', *Premium Times*, 7 March, https://www.premiumtimesng.com/news/headlines/178106-moroccan-king-snubs-president-jonathan-rejects-telephone-conversation-over-election.html (accessed 21 September 2017).

Ibrahim, Murtala (2017) 'Sensational piety: practices of mediation in Christ Embassy and NASFAT'. PhD thesis, University of Utrecht.

Ibrahim, Omar Farouk (1997) 'Religion and politics: a view from the north' in Larry Diamond, A. Kirk-Greene and Oyeleye Oyediran (eds), *Transition Without End: Nigerian politics and civil society under Babangida.* Ibadan: Vantage Publishers.

Ikeke, Nkem (2017) 'Nigeria's problems: Pastor Tunde Bakare accuses Obasanjo', Naij.com, https://www.naij.com/325399-nigerias-problems-pastor-tunde-bakare-accuses-obasanjo.html (accessed 22 June 2017).

Ikuomola, Vincent (2012) 'Jonathan: I alone can't solve Nigeria's problems', *The Nation* (Lagos), 1 October, http://thenationonlineng.net/jonathan-i-alone-cant-solve-nigerias-problems/ (accessed 7 September 2017).

Ikuomola, Vincent and Tony Akowe (2013) 'Jonathan fights back as calls for resignation rise', Naij.com, https://www.naij.com/5536.html (accessed 7 September 2017).

Ilesanmi, Simeon O. (1997) *Religious Pluralism and the Nigerian State.* Athens OH: Ohio University Press.

— (2011) 'Sharia reasoning, political legitimacy, and democratic visions', *Journal of Church and State* 53 (1): 27–36.

Iliffe, John (2011) *Obasanjo, Nigeria and the World.* Rochester NY: James Currey.

Imokhai, Charles A. (2015) *The People's Choice.* Bloomington IN: Indiana University Press.

Information Nigeria (2013) 'OBJ is a demon ... GEJ dares not visit my church because ...', Information Nigeria, 19 January, http://www.informationng. com/2013/01/bakare-classic-obj-is-a-demon-gej-dares-not-visit-my-church-because.html (accessed 20 June 2017).

Isike, Christopher and Sakiemi Idoniboye-Obu (2011) 'Throwing out the baby with the bath water: the third-term agenda and democratic consolidation in Nigeria's Fourth Republic', *Journal of African Elections* 10 (1): 143–70.

Isine, Ibanga (2015) 'Before attacking Jonathan, Priest Ejike Mbaka praised president, endorsed his re-election', *Premium Times*, 3 January, https://www. premiumtimesng.com/news/headlines/174210-before-attacking-jonathan-priest-ejike-mbaka-praised-president-endorsed-his-re-election.html (accessed 21 September 2017).

Iwilade, Akin (2014) 'Networks of violence and becoming: youth and the politics of patronage in Nigeria's oil-rich Delta', *Journal of Modern African Studies* 52 (4): 571–95.

Kalu, Ogbu (2004) 'Sharia and Islam in Nigerian Pentecostal rhetoric, 1970–2003', *PNEUMA* 26 (2): 242–61.

— (2007) (ed.) *African Christianity: an African story.* Trenton NJ: Africa World Press.

Kalu, Orji Uzor (2013a) 'President Jonathan: interplay of destiny and providence', *Saturday Sun* (Lagos), 18 May.

— (2013b) 'State of emergency: the real issues', *Leadership*, 25 May.

Kane, Ousmane (1994) 'Izala: the rise of Muslim reformism in Northern Nigeria' in Martin E. Marty and R. Scott Appleby (eds), *Accounting for Fundamentalisms: the dynamic character of movements.* Chicago IL: University of Chicago Press.

— (2003) *Muslim Modernity in Postcolonial Nigeria: a study of the Society for the Removal of Innovation and Reinstatement of Tradition.* Leiden: Brill.

Katongole, Emmanuel (2005) 'Violence and social imagination: rethinking theology and politics in Africa', *Religion and Theology* 12 (2): 145–71.

Kawonise, Sina (2016) 'Still on the spiritual side of Aso Villa', *Premium Times* (Lagos), 25 October.

Keane, John (2015) 'Gods, power, democracy' (in conversation with Irfan Ahmad)', *Journal of Religious and Political Practice* 1 (1): 73–91.

Kellerman, Barbara (2016) 'Leadership – it's a *system*, not a person!', *Daedalus* 145 (3): 83–94.

Kendhammer, Brandon (2016) *Muslims Talking Politics: framing Islam, democracy, and law in Northern Nigeria*. Chicago IL: University of Chicago Press.

Kokori, Frank (2014) *The Struggle for June 12*. Ibadan: Safari Books.

Kolapo, Femi J. (2016) 'Appraising the limits of Pentecostal political power in Nigeria', *Journal of Religion in Africa* 46: 369–89.

Korieh, Chima and Ugo Nwokeji (eds) (2005) *Religion, History, and Politics in Nigeria: essays in honor of Ogbu U. Kalu*. Lanham MD: University Press of America.

Kukah, Matthew Hassan (1993) *Religion, Politics and Power in Northern Nigeria*. Ibadan: Spectrum.

— (2010) 'The Patience of Jonathan', *The Guardian*, 13 May.

— (2012) 'Bishop Kukah's speech at Governor Patrick Yakowa's funeral in Kaduna', Sahara Reporters, 24 December, http://saharareporters.com/2012/12/24/bishop-kukahs-speech-governor-patrick-yakowas-funeral-kaduna (accessed 6 October 2017).

Kulish, Nicholas (2014) 'Writer tells Africa what he couldn't tell "mum"', *New York Times*, 24 January, https://www.nytimes.com/2014/01/25/world/africa/as-africa-debates-gay-rights-writer-comes-out.html (accessed 24 June 2018).

Larkin, Brian and Birgit Meyer (2006) 'Pentecostalism, Islam and culture: new religious movements in West Africa' in Emmanuel Kwaku Akyeampong (ed.), *Themes in West Africa's History*. Oxford: James Currey.

Last, Murray (2014) 'From dissent to dissidence: the genesis and development of reformist Islamic groups in northern Nigeria' in Abdul Raufu Mustapha (ed.), *Sects and Social Disorder: Muslim identities and conflict in Northern Nigeria*. Rochester NY: James Currey.

Lewis, Peter and Michael Watts (2015) 'Nigeria: the political economy of governance'. Paper presented at Doing Development Differently (DDD) programme, World Bank, Washington DC.

Lilla, Mark (2017) *The Once and Future Liberal: after identity politics*. New York NY: HarperCollins.

Liman, Isa (2014) 'Why Jonathan should resign – Sheikh Gumi', *Daily Trust*, 17 May, https://www.dailytrust.com.ng/weekly/index.php/top-stories/16548-why-jonathan-should-resign-sheikh-gumi (accessed 7 September 2017).

Lubeck, Paul M. (2014) 'Explaining the revolt of Boko Haram: demography, governance and crisis in Northern Nigeria'. Presentation at African Studies Program-SAIS, Johns Hopkins University, Baltimore, October.

Luce, Edward (2017) *The Retreat of Western Liberalism*. New York NY: Atlantic Monthly Press.

MacEachern, Scott (2018) *Searching for Boko Haram: a history of violence in Central Africa*. Oxford: Oxford University Press.

Mamah, Emeka (2008) 'ACF declares Yar'Adua fit to rule', *Vanguard*, 10 October.

— (2010) 'ACF blames nation's crisis on Yar'Adua's handlers', *Vanguard*, 5 March.

Manaugh, Geoff (2006) 'Planet of slums: an interview with Mike Davis (pt. 2)', Bldgblog, 24 May, http://www.bldgblog.com/2006/05/interview-with-mike-davis-part-2/ (accessed 2017).

Marshall, Ruth (2009) *Political Spiritualities: the Pentecostal revolution in Nigeria.* Chicago IL: University of Chicago Press.

Maxwell, David (2007) *African Gifts of the Spirit: Pentecostalism and the rise of Zimbabwean transnational religious movement.* Oxford and Athens OH: James Currey and Ohio University Press.

Mbembe, Achille (1992) 'The banality of power and the aesthetics of vulgarity in the postcolony', *Public Culture* (4) 2: 1–30.

Meyer, Birgit (1998) '"Make a complete break with the past": memory and postcolonial modernity in Ghanaian Pentecostal discourse', *Journal of Religion in Africa* 28 (3): 316–49.

— (2015) *Sensational Movies: video, vision, and Christianity in Ghana.* Oakland CA: University of California Press.

Michael, Matthew (2009) 'Divine providence or good luck? A biblical theology of providence compared with "chance" and "good luck" in Greco-Roman and African traditions', *African Journal of Evangelical Theology* 28 (1): 23–41

Momodu, Shaka (2014) 'Buhari is an ethno-fundamentalist', *The Herald,* 20 December, http://www.herald.ng/buhari-ethno-religous-fundamentalist/ (accessed 13 September 2017).

Muhammed, Abdulsalam (2010) 'Yakasai quits Arewa consultative forum over Yar'Adua', *Vanguard,* 6 February.

Murphy, Brian (2006) 'Christianity's second wave?', *Seattle Times,* 26 March.

Mustapha, Abdul Raufu (ed.) (2014) *Sects and Social Disorder: Muslim identities and conflict in Northern Nigeria.* Rochester NY: James Currey.

Mustapha, Abdul Raufu and David Ehrhardt (eds) (2018) *Greed and Grievance: Muslim–Christian relations and conflict resolution in Northern Nigeria.* Rochester NY: James Currey.

Naij.com (n.d.) 'Boko Haram insurgents are advocating for a jihad in Nigeria – CAN President Oritsejafor', Naij.com, https://www.naij.com/69448.html (accessed 17 June 2017).

Nairaland Forum (2010a) 'Yar'Adua: family prays for miracle, marabout summoned to Jeddah', Nairaland Forum, 15 February, http://www.nairaland.com/398715/yaradua-family-prays-miracle-marabout#5518698 (accessed 24 June 2017).

— (2010b) 'Soyinka wants Orisa worshippers to visit Yar'adua!', Nairaland Forum, 7 April, http://www.nairaland.com/426260/soyinka-wants-orisa-worshippers-visit (accessed 10 June 2017).

Newell, Sasha (2007) 'Pentecostal witchcraft: neoliberal possession and demonic discourse in Ivorian Pentecostal churches', *Journal of Religion in Africa* 37 (4): 461–90.

Newman, Paul (2013) 'The etymology of Hausa *boko*'. Nanterre: Mega-Chad Research Network.

Nigerian Times (2011) 'Former President Olusegun Obasanjo has built a mosque', *Nigerian Times*, 18 March, http://nigerian-times.blogspot.com/2011/03/former- president- olusegun-obasanjo-has.html (accessed 2017).

Nsehe, Mfonobong (2011) 'The five richest pastors in Nigeria', *Forbes*, 7 June, https://www.forbes.com/sites/mfonobongnsehe/2011/06/07/the-five-richest-pastors-in-nigeria/#36271b0f6031 (accessed 21 September 2017).

Nwanaju, Isidore (2005) *Christian–Muslim Relations in Nigeria.* Ikeja: Free Enterprise.

Nwodo, Anike (2015) 'South-west obas become richer after Jonathan's visits', Naij. com, https://www.naij.com/402674-south-west-obas-become-richer-after-jonathans-visits.html (accessed 13 September 2017).

Nwokeforo, Ukeje Jonah (2006) *Obasanjo's Presidency and King David's Rule: overwhelming similarities: agenda for national rebirth and development.* Ibadan: Wisdom Publishers Ltd.

Nwolise, O. B. C. (2014) 'Is physical security alone enough for the survival, progress and happiness of man?' Ibadan: Ibadan University Press.

Nzemeke, Vincent (2014) 'President Jonathan's church tourism', *Realnews Magazine*, 7 March, http://realnewsmagazine.net/politics/president-jonathans-church-tourism/ (accessed 19 September 2017).

Obadare, Ebenezer (2004) 'In search of a public sphere: the fundamentalist challenge to civil society in Nigeria', *Patterns of Prejudice* 38 (2): 177–98.

— (2013a) 'Sexual struggles and democracy dividends' in Mojubaolu Olufunke Okome (ed.), *Contesting the Nigerian State: civil society and the contradictions of self-organization.* New York NY: Palgrave Macmillan.

— (2013b) 'A sacred duty to resist tyranny? Rethinking the role of the Catholic Church in Nigeria's struggle for democracy', *Journal of Church and State* 55 (1): 92–112.

— (2013c) 'Rethinking Adedibu: politics, patronage, and the "big man"', *West Africa Review* 22: 26–46.

— (2013d) 'What's luck got to do with it?', *Premium Times*, 1 August, http://www. premiumtimesng.com/opinion/142059-whats-luck-got-to-do-with-it-by-ebenezer-obadare.html (accessed 5 September 2017).

— (2014) 'Blasphemy and secular criticism in the Nigerian public sphere: between Isioma Daniel and Nasir el-Rufai' in Wale Adebanwi (ed.), *Public Intellectuals, the Public Sphere and the Public Spirit: essays in honour of Olatunji Dare.* Ibadan: University of Ibadan Press.

— (2015) 'Sex, citizenship and the state in Nigeria: Islam, Christianity and emergent struggles over intimacy', *Review of African Political Economy* 42 (143): 62–76.

— (2016a) 'The Muslim response to the Pentecostal surge in Nigeria: prayer and the rise of Charismatic Islam', *Journal of Religious and Political Practice* 2 (1): 75–91.

— (2016b) *Humor, Silence, and Civil Society in Nigeria.* Rochester NY: University of Rochester Press.

— (2016c) '"Raising righteous billionaires": the prosperity gospel reconsidered', *HTS Teologiese Studies/Theological Studies* 72 (4): 1–8.

Obasanjo, Olusegun (1998a) *Guide to Effective Prayer*. Ota: ALF Publications

— (1998b) *This Animal Called Man*. Abeokuta: ALF.

— (2000a) *Sermons from the Prison*. Ota: ALF Publications.

— (2000b) *Women of Virtue* Ota: ALF Publications.

— (2001) *Exemplary Youth in a Difficult World*. Ota: ALF Publications.

— (2004) 'From OBJ to Bishop Oyedepo', *Nigerian Tribune*, 23 October.

— (2006a) 'I leave third term to God – Obasanjo', *The Punch* (Lagos), 4 April.

— (2006b) 'Inauguration speech', *The Sun* (Lagos), 10 April.

— (2012) *The Story of Baba Ali Pastor Sunday Gula Theman: juvenile delinquency and criminality: who is to blame?* Abeokuta: OOPL Publications Ltd.

— (2014) *My Watch: early life and military*. 2 volumes. Lagos: Kachifo Limited.

— (2016) 'How I converted squash court into Aso Rock church – Obasanjo', *Nigerian Tribune*, 10 October.

Ochonu, Moses E. (2015) 'Of forbidden handshakes and Buhari's religious claimants', Sahara Reporters, 19 May, http://saharareporters.com/2015/05/19/forbidden-handshakes-and-buhari%E2%80%99s-religious-claimants-moses-e-ochonu (accessed 13 September 2017).

Odebode, Niyi, Adelani Adepegba, Ifeanyi Onuba and Afis Hanafi (2017) 'Saraki, El-Rufai instigated Buhari not to pick me as VP – Tinubu', *The Punch*, 27 April.

Odebode, Niyi, John Alechenu, Friday Olokor, Ade Adesomoju, Simon Utebor and Maureen Azuh (2012a) 'Jonathan opens up on Boko Haram, Azazi, others', *The Punch*, 25 June.

Odebode, Niyi, Olusola Fabiyi, John Alechenu and Ihuoma Chiedozie (2012b) 'Outrage over Jonathan's trip to Brazil', *The Punch*, 20 June.

Odey, David (2013) 'Bakare blasts presidency over cow gift', *PM News* (Lagos), 29 December, https://www.pmnewsnigeria.com/2013/12/29/bakare-blasts-jonathan-presidency-over-cow-gift/ (accessed 6 October 2017).

Odunayo, Adams (2016) 'President Jonathan wants a refund of his election campaign money', Naij.com, https://www.naij.com/424296-president-jonathan-wants-a-refund-of-his-election-campaign-money.html#424296 (accessed 9 October 2017).

Odunsi, Wale (2012) 'The northernality of FCT leadership', *The Nigerian Voice*, 10 September, https://www.thenigerianvoice.com/movie/97960/the-northernality-of-fct-leadership.html (accessed 31 May 2017).

Odunuga, Yomi (2013) 'Jonathan signed one-term agreement – Junaid Mohammed', *The Nation*, 4 March, http://thenationonlineng.net/jonathan-signed-agreement-on-serving-one-term-junaid-mohammed/ (accessed 31 August 2017).

Ogala Emmanuel and Elizabeth Archibong (2010) 'Senate tells Yar'Adua to go', *NEXT* (Lagos), 28 January.

Ogundele, Kamarudeen (2016) 'Chibok girls not missing', *The Punch*, 31 March, http://punchng.com/chibok-girls-not-missing-fayose/ (accessed 10 September 2017).

Ogunranti, John Oluwole (2011) 'Obasanjo's theology' in Terhemba Wuam, Stephen T. Olali and James Obilikwu (eds), *Obasanjo Second Era: 1999–2007*. Abuja: Aboki Publishers.

Oha, Obododimma (2000) 'The rhetoric of Nigerian Christian videos: the war paradigm of *The Great Mistake*' in Jonathan Haynes (ed.), *Nigerian Video Films*. Athens OH: Ohio University Center for International Studies.

— (2005) 'Nation, nationalism, and the rhetoric of praying for Nigeria in distress', *Interventions* 7 (1): 21–42.

Ojo, Matthews (2004) 'Pentecostalism, public accountability and governance in Nigeria', Paper presented at 'Pentecostal–Civil Society Dialogue on Public Accountability and Governance', Agip Rental Hall, MUSON Center, Lagos, 18 October.

— (2006) *The End-Time Army: charismatic movements in modern Nigeria*. Trenton NJ: Africa World Press.

Olaniyan, Azeez Olusola (2010) 'Vocalizing rage: deconstructing the language of antistate forces' in Wale Adebanwi and Ebenezer Obadare (eds), *Encountering the Nigerian State*. New York NY: Palgrave Macmillan.

Olsen, William C. and Walter E. A. Van Beek (eds) (2015) *Evil in Africa: encounters with the everyday*. Bloomington IN: Indiana University Press.

Olukoya, D. K. (1999) *Violent Prayers to Disgrace Stubborn Problems*. Lagos: The Battle Cry Ministries.

— (2003) *Prayer Warfare Against 70 Mad Spirits*. Lagos: The Battle Cry Ministries.

— (2005) *Open Heavens Through Holy Disturbance*. Lagos: The Battle Cry Ministries.

— (2013) *Spiritual Warfare to Tackle the Enemy*. Lagos: MFM.

— (2014a) *Spiritual Warfare to Tackle the Enemy*. Lagos: MFM.

— (2014b) *The Mystery of Water Cure*. Lagos: MFM.

— (2014c) *The Tragedy of Stealing*. Lagos: The Battle Cry Ministries.

— (2014d) *The Hour of Freedom*. Lagos: The Battle Cry Ministries.

— (2014e) *Watching the Serpents of the Magicians*. Lagos: The Battle Cry Ministries.

— (2014f) *What to do When Trouble Comes*. Lagos: The Battle Cry Ministries.

— (2014g) *Battle Cry Compendium*. Lagos: The Battle Cry Ministries.

Olupona, Jacob (2011) *City of 201 Gods: Ile-Ife in time, space, and the imagination*. Berkeley CA: University of California Press.

Omipidan, Ismail and Jibril Musa (2017) '2015: why I backed out on one term agreement – Jonathan', *The Sun* (Lagos), 29 April, http://sunnewsonline.com/2015-why-i-backed-out-on-one-term-agreement-jonathan/ (accessed 31 August 2017).

Omonobi, Kingsley (2011) 'Presidential election: Save Nigeria Group disowns Bakare', *Vanguard*, 14 April, https://www.vanguardngr.com/2011/04/presidential-polls-save-nigeria-group-disowns-bakare/ (accessed 14 September 2017).

Oni, Ademola (2018) 'God has asked me to run for presidency – Bakare', *Punch*, 2 January, http://punchng.com/god-has-asked-me-to-run-for-presidency-bakare/ (accessed 7 April 2018).

Opara, Enyioha (2013) 'Jonathan signed single term pact, Aliyu insists', *The Punch*, 15 March.

Oppenheimer, Mark (2010) 'On a visit to the US, a Nigerian witch-hunter explains herself', *New York Times*, 21 May.

Oritsejafor, Ayo (2012) 'Boko Haram: Christian Association of Nigeria writes Hillary Clinton', Sahara Reporters, 9 August,. http://saharareporters.com/2012/08/09/boko-haram-christian-association-nigeria-writes-hillary-clinton (accessed 17 June 2017).

Osun Defender (2015) 'Recorded audio: CAN collected N7bn bribe from Jonathan to campaign against Buhari on January 26, 2015', *Osun Defender*, 24 February, http://www.osundefender.org/?p=218128 (accessed 14 November 2015).

Owete, Festus (2010) 'Arewa backs power transfer to Jonathan', *NEXT*, 1 February.

Oyeniyi, Bukola Adeyemi (2009) 'Nigeria and the Organization of the Islamic Conference' in Julius O. Adekunle (ed.), *Religion in Politics: secularism and national integration in modern Nigeria*. Trenton NJ: Africa World Press.

Oyetime, Kehinde and Rita Okonoboh (2016) 'What I did to OBJ in 1999 before he became president – Bishop Wale Ok', *Nigerian Tribune*, 29 August, http://www.tribuneonlineng.com/i-obj-1999-became-president-bishop-wale-oke/ (accessed 29 May 2017).

Ozor, Chinenyeh (2014) 'My bone of contention with Obasanjo is my N500m – Orji Uzor Kalu', *Vanguard*, 11 March, https://www.vanguardngr.com/2014/03/bone-contention-obasanjo-n500m-orji-uzor-kalu/ (accessed 2 September 2017).

Paden, John N. (2002) 'Islam and democratic federalism in Nigeria'. Africa Notes 8. Washington DC: Center for Strategic and International Studies.

— (2008) *Faith and Politics in Nigeria: Nigeria as a pivotal state in the Muslim world*. Washington DC: United States Institute of Peace Press.

Peel, J. D. Y. (1983) *Ijesas and Nigerians: the incorporation of a Yoruba kingdom, 1890s–1970s*. Cambridge: Cambridge University Press.

— (2001) *Religious Encounter and the Making of the Yoruba*. Bloomington IN: Indiana University Press.

— (2016) *Christianity, Islam, and Orisa Religion: three traditions in comparison and interaction*. Oakland CA: University of California Press.

Pérouse de Montclos, Marc-Antoine (ed.) (2015) *Boko Haram: Islamism, politics, security, and the state in Nigeria*. Los Angeles CA: Tsehai Publishers.

Phiri, Isabel Apawo (2003) 'President J. T. Chiluba of Zambia: the Christian nation and democracy', *Journal of Religion in Africa* 33 (4): 401–28.

PM News (2011) 'Bakare: God told me to run with Buhari', *PM News*, 1 February, http://www.pmnewsnigeria.com/2011/02/01/bakare-god-told-me-to-run-with-buhari/ (accessed 14 September 2017).

Post, Kenneth and Michael Vickers (1975) *Structure and Conflict in Nigeria: 1960–65*. Madison WI: University of Wisconsin Press.

Premium Times (2015a) 'Jonathan in secret meeting with pastors; says "Osinbajo is my problem"', *Premium Times*, 19 January.

— (2015b) 'Jonathan denies spending N2 trillion on election campaign', *Premium Times*, 19 April, https://www.premiumtimesng.com/news/headlines/181722-jonathan-denies-spending-n2-trillion-on-election-campaign.html (accessed 9 October 2017).

— (2017) 'Bakare speaks on Adeboye's exit, Southern Kaduna crisis', *Premium Times*, 9 January, https://www.premiumtimesng.com/news/top-news/220005-bakare-speaks-adeboyes-exit-southern-kaduna-crisis.html (accessed 7 October 2017).

Quayson, Ato (2001) 'Breaches in the commonplace', *African Studies Review* 44 (2): 151–65.

Ranger, Terence O. (2008) 'Afterword' in Terence O. Ranger (ed.), *Evangelical Christianity and Democracy in Africa*. Oxford: Oxford University Press.

Robertson, Roland (1989) 'Globalization, politics and religion' in James Beckford and Thomas Luckmann (eds), *The Changing Face of Religion*. London: Sage.

Sahara Reporters (2007) 'Orji Kalu and Saminu Turaki arrested by the EFCC', Sahara Reporters, 11 July, http://saharareporters.com/2007/07/11/orji-kalu-and-saminu-turaki-arrested-efcc (accessed 2 September 2017).

— (2010) 'SGF Ahmed Yayale attends anti-Yar'adua Save Nigeria Group rally', *SaharaTV*, 9 March, http://saharareporters.com/2010/03/09/photos-sgf-ahmed-yayale-attends-anti- yaradua-save- nigeria-group-rally/ (accessed 21 June 2017).

— (2015) 'Tinubu confesses he helped make Jonathan president in 2011', Sahara Reporters, 16 March, http://saharareporters.com/2015/03/16/tinubu-confesses-he-helped-make-jonathan-president-2011 (accessed 14 September 2017).

Sampson, Isaac Terwase (2014) 'Religion and the Nigerian state: situating the de facto and de jure frontiers of state-religion relations and its implications for national security', *Oxford Journal of Law and Religion* 3 (2): 311–39.

Samuel, Ayodele (2014) '2015: Nigeria does not need elections now, says Tunde Bakare', *Peoples Daily*, 17 November, http://www.peoplesdailyng.com/2015-nigeria-does-not-need-elections-now-says-tunde-bakare/ (accessed 24 June 2018).

Sanneh, Lamin (2003) 'Shariah sanctions as secular grace? A Nigerian Islamic debate and an intellectual response', *Transformation* 20 (4): 232–44.

Shaw, Rosalind (2007) 'Displacing violence: making Pentecostal memory in postwar Sierra Leone', *Cultural Anthropology* 22 (1): 66–93.

Shiklam, John (2016) 'Kaduna: El-Rufai's controversial religious bill', *This Day*, 3 April, https://www.thisdaylive.com/index.php/2016/04/03/kaduna-el-rufais-controversial-religious-bill/ (accessed 7 October 2017).

Smith, Mike (2016) *Boko Haram: Inside Nigeria's unholy war*. London: I. B. Tauris.

Soniyi, Tobi (2017) 'Tinubu: Osinbajo was hesitant when he was chosen as Buhari's running mate', *This Day*, 27 April.

Southall, Roger (2016) *The New Black Middle Class in South Africa*. Auckland Park, South Africa: Jacana Media.

Stonawski, Marcin, Michaela Potancokova, Matthew Cantele and Vegard Skirbekk (2016) 'The changing religious composition of Nigeria: causes and implications for demographic divergence', *Journal of Modern African Studies* 54 (3): 361–87.

Suberu, Rotimi (1997) 'Religion and politics: a view from the south' in Larry Diamond, A. Kirk-Greene and Oyeleye Oyediran (eds), *Transition Without End: Nigerian politics and civil society under Babangida*. Ibadan: Vantage Publishers.

— (2007) 'Nigeria's muddled elections', *Journal of Democracy* 18 (4): 97–8.

— (2010) 'The sharia challenge: revisiting the travails of the secular state' in Wale Adebanwi and Ebenezer Obadare (eds), *Encountering the Nigerian State*. New York NY: Palgrave Macmillan.

Taylor, Charles (2003) *Modern Social Imaginaries*. Durham NC: Duke University Press.

— (2007) *A Secular Age*. Cambridge MA: Harvard University Press.

The Cable (2017) 'Why we annulled June 12, by IBB', *The Cable* (Abuja), 12 June, https://www.thecable.ng/flashback-annuled-june-12-ibb (accessed 19 May 2017).

The Economist (2016) 'Crude tactics', *The Economist*, 30 January, https://www.economist.com/news/middle-east-and-africa/21689584-cheap-oil-causing-currency-crisis-nigeria-banning-imports-no (accessed 7 October 2017).

The Guardian on Sunday (2006) 'A daughter of Zion: Oby Ezekwezili speaks on what it takes to be a Christian in public office', *The Guardian on Sunday* (Lagos), 1 January.

The News (2014) 'Jonathan visits TB Joshua over building tragedy', *The News*, 20 September, http://thenewsnigeria.com.ng/2014/09/jonathan-visits-tb-joshua-over-building-tragedy/ (accessed 19 September 2017).

Thurston, Alexander (2016) '"The disease is unbelief": Boko Haram's religious and political worldview'. Analysis Paper 22. Washington DC: Brookings Project on US Relations with the Islamic World.

Timberg, Craig (2006) 'Nigerian Senate blocks bid for 3rd presidential term', *Washington Post*, 17 May.

Tran, Mark (2012) 'Former Nigeria state governor James Ibori receives 13-year sentence', *Guardian* (London), 17 April.

Tukur, Sani (2014a) 'Chibok schoolgirls: Patience Jonathan's intervention distracting, counter-productive, APC says', *Premium Times*, 6 May, http://www. premiumtimesng.com/news/160263-chibok-schoolgirls-patience-jonathans-intervention-distracting-counter-productive-apc-says.html (accessed 10 September 2017).

— (2014b) 'APC narrows search for Buhari's running mate to South West', *Premium Times*, 12 December.

Ugbodaga, Kazeem (2011) 'Bakare: God told me to run with Buhari', *PM News* (Lagos), 1 February, https://www.pmnewsnigeria.com/2011/02/01/bakare-god-told-me-to-run-with-buhari (accessed 2017).

— (2015) 'Bakare blasts CAN, PFN for endorsing Jonathan', *PM News* (Lagos), 2 February.

Uhrnacher, Kevin and Mary Beth Sheridan (2016) 'The brutal toll of Boko Haram's attacks on civilians', *Washington Post*, 3 April, https://www.washingtonpost. com/graphics/world/nigeria-boko-haram/ (accessed 6 September 2017).

Ukah, Asonzeh (2007) 'African Christianities: features, promises and problems'. Working Papers 79. Mainz: Department of Anthropology and African Studies, Johannes Gutenberg University.

— (2008) *A New Paradigm of Pentecostal Power: a study of the Redeemed Christian Church of God*. Trenton NJ: Africa World Press.

Ukiwo, Ukoha (2003) 'Politics, ethno-religious conflicts and democratic consolidation in Nigeria', *Journal of Modern African Studies* 41 (1): 115–38.

Ukpong, Cletus and Nicholas Ibekwe (2016) 'Chibok schoolgirls not missing; it's all a sham', *Premium Times*, 31 March, https://www.premiumtimesng.com/news/top-news/201075-chibok-schoolgirls-not-missing-sham-fayose.html (accessed 10 September 2017).

Uzodinma, Emmanuel (2016) 'God rejected Jonathan's dollar gift to me – Fr. Mbaka', *Daily Post*, 2 February, http://dailypost.ng/2016/02/02/god-rejected-jonathans-dollar-gift-to-me-fr-mbaka/ (accessed 21 September 2017).

van der Veer, Peter (2001) *Imperial Encounters: religion and modernity in India and Britain*. Princeton NJ: Princeton University Press.

Vanguard (2014) 'Jonathan's speech at the inauguration of national conference', *Vanguard*, 17 March.

— (2015a) 'Jonathan, Obasanjo, Adeboye, Oyedepo meet in Abeokuta', *Vanguard*, 12 January, https://www.vanguardngr.com/2015/01/jonathan-obasanjo-adeboye-oyedepo-meet-abeokuta/ (accessed 19 September 2017).

— (2015b) 'APC attacks Bishop Oyedepo over 'Gate of Hell' controversy', *Vanguard*, 26 January, https://www.vanguardngr.com/2015/01/apc-attacks-bishop-oyedepo-gate-hell-controversy/ (accessed 19 September 2017).

— (2017) 'George Weah meets TB Joshua, seeks God's face at Synagogue church', *Vanguard*, 22 October, https://www.vanguardngr.com/2017/10/george-weah-meets-tb-joshua-seeks-gods-face-synagogue-church/ (accessed 30 March 2018).

Varin, Caroline (2016) *Boko Haram and the War on Terror*. Santa Barbara CA: Praeger.

Vaughan, Olufemi (2016) *Religion and the Making of Nigeria*. Durham NC: Duke University Press.

Vigh, Henrik E. (2006) *Navigating the Terrains of War: youth and soldiering in Guinea-Bissau*. New York NY: Berghahn Books.

Vogler, Candace and Patchen Markell (2003) 'Introduction: violence, redemption, and the liberal imagination', *Public Culture* 15 (1): 1–10.

Walker, Andrew (2016) '*Eat the Heart of the Infidel': the harrowing of Nigeria and the rise of Boko Haram*. London: C. Hurst & Co.

Wariboko, Nimi (2008) *The Depth and Destiny of Work: an African theological interpretation*. Trenton NJ: Africa World Press.

— (2012) *The Pentecostal Principle: ethical methodology in new spirit*. Grand Rapids MI: William B. Eerdmans Publishing Company.

— (2014) *Nigerian Pentecostalism*. Rochester NY: University of Rochester Press.

— (2018) *The Split God: Pentecostalism and critical theory*. Albany NY: SUNY Press.

Warner, Michael, Jonathan van Antwerpen and Craig Calhoun (eds) (2010) *Varieties of Secularism in a Secular Age*. Cambridge MA: Harvard University Press.

Wickramasinghe, Nira (2001) 'A comment on African modes of self-writing', *Identity, Culture and Politics* 2 (1): 40–5.

World Bank (2016) *Poverty Reduction in Nigeria in the Last Decade*. Washington DC: World Bank. Available at: https://openknowledge.worldbank.org/handle/10986/25825.

Yong, Amos (2010) *In the Days of Caesar: Pentecostalism and political theology*. Grand Rapids MI: William B. Eerdmans Publishing Company.

Zink, Jesse (2012) '"Anglocostalism" in Nigeria: Neo-Pentecostalism and obstacles to Anglican unity', *Journal of Anglican Studies* 10 (2): 231–50.

INDEX

www.ingramcontent.com/pod-product-compliance
Ingram Content Group UK Ltd.
Pitfield, Milton Keynes, MK11 3LW, UK
UKHW020733280225
455688UK00012B/638

Also available in the *Classmates* series: